# THE FRAGMENTATION OF YUGOSLAVIA

*Also by Aleksandar Pavković*

CONTEMPORARY YUGOSLAV PHILOSOPHY: An Analytic Approach (*editor*)

NATIONALISM AND POSTCOMMUNISM:  A Collection of Essays (*co-editor*)

SLOBODAN JOVANOVIC: An Unsentimental Approach to Politics

# The Fragmentation of Yugoslavia

## Nationalism in a Multinational State

Aleksandar Pavkovic
*School of Modern Languages*
*Macquarie University*
*Sydney*

First published 1997 by
**MACMILLAN PRESS LTD**
Houndmills, Basingstoke, Hampshire RG21 6XS
and London
Companies and representatives
throughout the world

ISBN 0–333–64229–5

A catalogue record for this book is available
from the British Library.

This book is printed on paper suitable for recycling and
made from fully managed and sustained forest sources.

| 10 | 9  | 8  | 7  | 6  | 5  | 4  | 3  | 2  | 1  |
|----|----|----|----|----|----|----|----|----|----|
| 06 | 05 | 04 | 03 | 02 | 01 | 00 | 99 | 98 | 97 |

Printed in Great Britain by
The Ipswich Book Company Ltd
Ipswich, Suffolk

Published in the United States of America by
ST. MARTIN'S PRESS, INC.,
Scholarly and Reference Division
175 Fifth Avenue, New York, N.Y. 10010

ISBN 0–312–16342–8

# Contents

# List of Maps

# Preface

The conflict in the former Yugoslavia which erupted in 1991, I shall argue in this book, was essentially a result of competing national ideologies laying claim to one and the same territory for their respective national groups. There are generally two ways of resolving such a conflict: either the territory in dispute is incorporated in a state in which competing national groups cohabit peacefully, or the territory is divided among them and their separate national states. The state of Yugoslavia was an attempt to solve competing national claims by the first method: it was a single state in which different national groups cohabited. By the end of the 1980s this approach appeared no longer successful and the second method of creating separate national states has been attempted. But since various national groups in the former Yugoslavia lived intermixed on large stretches of territory, their national political elites have been unable to reach agreement on the peaceful division of such territory. As a result, a series of successive wars broke out in which each side endeavoured to establish its own national state on territory it claimed by force of arms, and, in the process, expelled, imprisoned or killed members of the opposing national group(s). Various international organisations such as the EC and the UN have tried to stop the armed conflict once it broke out or, failing that, to protect civilians (primarily of one national group, the Bosnian Muslims) from violence and to provide humanitarian aid to all. These organisations have, in the process, attempted to work out a peaceful overall settlement to the territorial disputes among the competing national elites, which would involve a partition of territories with nationally mixed populations. This is an unenviable task which, in this region of Europe, has not been successfully performed before: these territories have never been partitioned in a peaceful way to the satisfaction of all national elites involved. Even the settlement in Bosnia–Hercegovina which the US administration negotiated in November 1995 in Dayton, Ohio – ending, at least for the time being, the war in this former republic of Yugoslavia – failed to satisfy the territorial claims either of the Bosnian Muslim or of the Bosnian Serb elites.

This book attempts to trace the political processes which led to the fragmentation of Yugoslavia and the ensuing armed conflict as well as the search for its peaceful settlement ending with the Dayton peace agreements and their immediate aftermath in January 1996. The key factors in these processes, I shall argue, were the national political elites which have engaged in mass mobilisation of their target national groups by using national ideologies constructed by nationally-minded intellectuals. Judging by the results of the 1990 multi-party elections, political platforms based on such ideologies attracted large segments of the electorate in all national groups in Yugoslavia. The book offers no systematic explanation of why the national ideologies – which ultimately led to the conflict – had so widespread an appeal. This topic, I think, would require a separate book. But since these ideologies appeared to shape the policy-making of the national elites, I examine in some detail the main themes and arguments found in the most influential ideological writings published prior to the outbreak of the conflict, indicating how they could have influenced the policies of their advocates. Endorsing the arguments and the attendant myths and stereotypes of any one of the ideologies could, however, hardly be of help in understanding the process of the country's fragmentation; no attempt is, therefore, made in the book to evaluate these arguments. In any case, I find nothing appealing in any national ideology, however romantic some of them may appear to intellectuals in search of a good cause.

My approach – as well as the limitations of space – does not allow for the 'voices from below' to be heard – the opinions and sentiments of non-elite, ordinary men and women, who have suffered most from the fragmentation of, and civil wars, in Yugoslavia. The book does not tell their story and offers little if any insight into their attitudes and views. As a result, to most people who have lived through – and to those who are still living through – the horrors of war in former Yugoslavia, the story told in the book must appear somewhat unreal. Moreover, I have made no attempt to describe the impact of war on civilians and soldiers or to detail the atrocities and crimes committed against them. The widespread torture and sexual abuse of persons of all nationalities in these successive wars appear to me so pathological as to preclude an attempt to comprehend these phenomena within the realm of study of politics and ideologies alone. Having restricted my inquiry to the latter, I have tried to avoid a discourse of moral indignation and condemnation. I do, however, condemn such crimes and atrocities as well as their perpetrators. It is to the victims of the wars that the book is dedicated.

Peter Radan of the University of Western Sydney, Macarthur, put his library, with its most comprehensive holdings on former Yugoslavia, at my disposal and shared with me his vast erudition of sources on this topic. Steven Kosovich read successive drafts of the manuscript with extreme care and suggested a great many improvements. Derek Verall gave me the idea of writing this book and suggested its title when, in 1993, he commissioned me to write a short booklet under that title for the students of Deakin University. In 1994 Macquarie University supplied a research grant to aid the writing of the book. To all, my heartfelt thanks.

ALEKSANDAR PAVKOVIĆ

# Guide to Pronunciation

Č, č and Ć, ć are pronounced as 'ch' in *che*que or *che*w.

Dž, dž and Dj, dj or Đ, đ are pronounced as 'dz' in *jazz* or *joy* (dj and đ are alternative transcriptions of the same letter; thus 'Tudjman' is often spelled as 'Tuđman').

Lj, lj is pronounced as 'lj' in mi*lli*on.

Nj, nj is pronounced as nj in o*ni*on.

Š, š is pronounced as 'sh' in *she*.

Ž, ž is pronounced as 'zh' in lei*s*ure or trea*s*ure.

# Part I
# A Common Homeland of the South Slavs

# 1 Yugoslavia at the Crossroads of Competing National Myths

## THE CREATION OF A UNITED KINGDOM

In the evening of 1 December 1918, in a small villa in the centre of Belgrade, the regent of the Kingdom of Serbia, Prince Aleksandar Karadorđević flanked by ministers of the Serbian government and members of its general staff received the Delegation of the National Council of Slovenes, Croats and Serbs from Zagreb. The National Council was the legislative body of the State of Slovenes, Croats and Serbs, formed on 6 October 1918 out of the South Slav lands of the defeated and disintegrating Austria–Hungary. The vice-president of the Council and leader of the Delegation, the Croat deputy Dr Ante Pavelić,[1] read the Address of the Delegation to the Throne which informed the regent of the National Council's decision to pursue a union of the State of Slovenes, Croats and Serbs with Serbia and Montenegro. The unified state, the Address stated, should be based on democratic constitutional and parliamentary principles. The Address went on to note that 'large and precious parts' of the South Slav lands were now under Italian occupation and expressed the hope that the prince regent would endeavour to secure the final borders of the unified South Slav state in accordance with the principle of national self-determination proclaimed by president Wilson and the Entente Powers. In response, Prince Aleksandar declared:

> In accepting this announcement, I am convinced that by this act I am fulfilling my duty as a ruler, for I am thereby only at last carrying out that for which the best sons of our blood, of all three religions, all three names, on both sides of the Danube, Sava and Drina, began to work even during the reign of my grandfather of blessed memory Prince Alexander I and of Prince Michael, that which corresponds to the desires and views of my people, and so in the name of His Majesty King Peter I, I proclaim the unification of

Serbia with lands of the independent State of Slovenes, Croats, and Serbs in a single Kingdom of the Serbs, Croats and Slovenes.[2]

The first Yugoslav state was thus created by a royal proclamation in response to an address of Croat, Serb and Slovene politicians from the former lands of Austria–Hungary. The difference in the content of the two statements exhibits the differences in the conception of the new state which were to plague it from its inception. The regent spoke of the sons of 'our blood, of all three religions and all three names'; by this he (and many Serb politicians) meant the single nation whose members belong to the Eastern Orthodox and Roman Catholic (as well as Islamic) faiths and call themselves Serbs, Croats, and Slovenes. The Delegation from Zagreb spoke not of a single nation but only of the idea of the national unity of the Slovenes, Croats and Serbs which led them to seek union with Serbia and Montenegro. The former is the conception of unitary Yugoslavs which seeks to dissolve all national differences into one unified nation and to create, correspondingly, a unitary state. The latter is a conception of a South Slav kinship which preserves the national differences among the South Slavs and demands, accordingly, a federal state structure. The struggle between these two general conceptions of the Yugoslav state dominated the politics of the first Yugoslavia from 1918 to 1941. It reappeared in a different guise in the second, communist Yugoslavia and culminated in the late 1960s with the victory of the federalist conception advocated by the communist elites of the five (later, six) officially recognised constituent nations of Yugoslavia.

While the regent saw in the union the fulfilment of the struggle of several generations of Yugoslavs, the single issue which appeared to dominate the Zagreb Delegation's Address was the Italian occupation of the South Slav lands and the urgent need to secure the ethnic borders of the new state. This brings to light the difference in the conception of the primary goal of the unified state: the regent and many Serb politicians regarded, as the principal achievement of the new state, the unification of all Serbs and other South Slavs in one state and under the Serbian crown, the goal for which several generations of Serbs had fought. Many Croat and Slovene politicians saw the primary role of the new state in the recovery and defence of Croat- and Slovene-populated territories from the domination of neighbouring states.

In 1990 the new Slovene and Croat political elites, which came to power through multiparty elections, saw in the common Yugoslav state not a protector from outside domination but a threat to their own newly won power. The only organ of the Yugoslav state which effectively restricted their control over their republics was the federal armed force, the Yugoslav People's Army. This army, most of whose officers still stood for a common state of Yugoslavia, was the only Yugoslav force which could topple the new Slovene and Croat elites from power. To secure their power, the new Slovene and Croat regimes had to remove this last vestige of the Yugoslav state from their territory. In 1918 the Slovene and Croat politicians sought protection from outside powers in the creation of a common Yugoslav state. In 1991, when no such protection was needed, the Yugoslav state and its army became the last obstacle to the unfettered rule of the newly established Slovene and Croat political elites.

The new regimes of Slovenia and Croatia – as well as Serbia – sought justification in the national myths and ideologies of their separate nations which preceded the formation of Yugoslavia. Yugoslavia, as we have seen, arose from the differing versions of the Yugoslav national ideology. Before its creation and for the duration of its existence, this national ideology was competing with national ideologies of the separate South Slav nations – at first, of Croats, Serbs and Slovenes and, later, of Macedonians and Muslims. To understand how the state of Yugoslavia was destroyed in 1991 it would be useful to review the history of these competing national myths and ideologies.

THE COMPETING NATIONAL MYTHS

In the early nineteenth century, Serb and Croat historical myths, like numerous other East European national myths, formed the core around which their national liberation ideologies were constructed. East European national myths often originated as a response to attempts to justify the domination of the aristocracies in East European countries by an appeal to the latter's alleged historical rights. The right of the ruling aristocracies to lord over their populations, often of different ethnic and national background, both before and after the French revolution, was justified in terms of their alleged historic experience of rule and administration. The long history of their rule, it was thus argued, gave the lords both the necessary skill and the right to rule over others. This argument, somewhat generalised and modernised, introduced the right of 'historic nations' to rule over the 'non-historic' ones. The dominance of the German and, later Hungarian, nations over other East European nations was, accordingly, explained as the right of the nations with a history – a history of being a sovereign state – to rule over others who have, allegedly, had no history of this kind. To counter this argument and to justify their striving for national independence, patriotic historians and intellectuals of the emerging smaller nations of Eastern Europe started, in the eighteenth century, to search the history of their nations for suitable independent and sovereign states which could be used to prove that they too have a history on a par with those of the dominant nations. In the process, these intellectuals came to interpret the history of their emerging nations as a mission of recovery of the freedom and independence which these nations possessed in the past.

While the Croat and Serb historical myths were of crucial importance in shaping Croat and Serb national identities and ideologies, the initial differentiation between these two national groups originated neither in these historical myths nor in the variety of dialects which the inhabitants of the South Slav lands speak. The Roman Catholic inhabitants of Croatia speak South Slav dialects which widely differ from each other or – such as kajkavian and štokavian – are barely mutually comprehensible. Yet the štokavian dialects which some of them speak are similar to the dialects of the Eastern Orthodox inhabitants of Croatia, of Bosnia-Hercegovina, and Serbia and Montenengro. In view of the similarity of these štokavian dialects, the difference in their religion provided a much better or more effective marker of national or ethnic identity than their vernacular language. In fact, each of the two churches, the Roman Catholic and the Serbian Eastern Orthodox, created distinctive customs, rituals and beliefs which shaped the everyday life of their followers. The separate calendars – Julian for the Eastern Orthodox, Gregorian for the Roman Catholic – prescribed a separate set of feast days even for the common Christian celebrations. In particular, Serb Eastern Orthodoxy developed two distinct cults: that of the medieval founder of the Serb Orthodox Church, St Sava, and that of the Kosovo martyrs. In addition, one of its central family rituals is the celebration of the family patron saint day (*slava*). The celebration of *slava* and of these two cults clearly mark off the Serb Orthodox from other Eastern Orthodox as well as Roman Catholic believers. In the areas of Croatia, southern Hungary and Bosnia-Hercegovina where Roman Catholics and Eastern Orthodox, speaking the same or similar dialects, lived side by side, Roman Catholicism thus became the defining mark of the Croats and Eastern Orthodoxy of the Serbs.

But the differences of religion and/or of language are not, among the South Slavs, necessary for the development of separate national identities. Montenegrins share with the Serbs both Serb Eastern Orthodoxy and the štokavian dialect. It was the distinctive way of life of the Montenegrins, based on the still surviving clan relations, and Montenegro's history of a separate struggle for independence and statehood, that provided the differentiating markers of a separate Montenegrin national identity. Of course, not all Montenegrins would feel that they belong to a nation different from the Serbs. But even those who regard themselves as Serbs, would still cite their history along with their customs and attitudes to show how different Montenegrins, as a branch of the Serb nation, are from other Serbs. In the Balkans, the markers which, according to some, distinguish simply two branches of the same nation are, according to others, the very markers which separate two nations. The indeterminacy of the nation-separating markers forces national ideologues to keep searching everywhere they can – in history, folklore, religion, legend and language – for further markers of national differences.

The differences in the way of life and religion, although sufficient to differentiate individuals and their communities one from another, are usually not sufficient to shape a fully-fledged national ideology which purports to explain what a nation is and what historical goal it has. By shaping the way of life, beliefs and attitudes of South Slavs, the three religions – Roman Catholicism, Eastern Orthodoxy and Islam – have provided only necessary but not sufficient conditions for the development of three distinct national identities – Croat, Serb (including Montenegrin) and Bosnian Muslim (or Bosniac).[3] The development of these and other national identities among the South Slavs was closely linked with the historical myths which were often quite unrelated to the respective religious dogmas.

The Croat historical myth is based on the medieval kingdom of kings Tomislav (tenth century) and Krešimir (eleventh century). The Croatian kingdom lost its independence in 1097 after the battle of Gvozd in which the Croatian forces were defeated by those of the King of Hungary. From 1102 the crown of Croatia passed to the kings of Hungary so that in assuming the Hungarian crown in the sixteenth century, the Austrian Habsburgs also gained the Croatian crown. Within the historical myth, the medieval Croat Diet (*Sabor*) is held to have continued the tradition of Croat state independence by freely electing (thrice in the span of almost a thousand years) kings other than the rulers of Hungary. In fact, the thousand-year-long history of the Croatian Diet is, within this myth, portrayed as a protracted political struggle for the preservation of old historic rights of the Croatian state against the encroachments of the Austrian Habsburgs and, later, the Hungarian parliament – both of which were aimed at assimilating Croats and Croatian lands. This protracted struggle, according to this myth, continued in the Yugoslav state in which the Serbs, like the Austrians and Hungarians before them, denied the Croats their distinct national identity as well as sovereignty and political independence. The ultimate goal of this mythical struggle is clearly a sovereign and independent Croatian state, the very state which was created in 1991 by Croatia's 'disassociation' from the Yugoslav federation. The present day Croatia, like many other East European states, is a creation of an old historical myth.

The Serb historical myth harks back to the royal house of Nemanjići and their medieval state which flourished in the twelfth and thirteenth centuries on the territory of the present day Serbia, Hercegovina and Macedonia. Within the myth, the history of this medieval Serb state was viewed primarily as a liberation of Serb territories from foreign – in this case Byzantine – rule. Under Dušan the Mighty, crowned Tsar (Emperor) of the Serbs and Romans (Greeks) in 1346, the state reached its peak, extending over the areas of present-day Greece, Bulgaria and Albania. From this tale of a short-lived empire arose the myth of the historic mission of the Serbs to recover the glory of Dušan's and the Nemanjići state by freeing themselves from foreign rule. Soon after Dušan's death, his empire disintegrated into smaller principalities which were in turn conquered by the armies of the Islamic Ottoman empire. The battle on the field of Kosovo in 1389 against the Ottomans became the focus of another historical myth. In this battle, according to the legend, the cream of the Serb nobility sacrificed their lives for their faith and liberty: 'for the golden cross and an honourable freedom'. According to the legend, a Serb nobleman, Miloš Obilić, sacrificed his life by assassinating the Ottoman sultan. The Serb leader Prince Lazar Hrebljanović, who lost his life in the battle, was canonised as a saint in the Serbian Orthodox Church and the day of the battle, 28 June, St Vitius's day (*Vidovdan* in Serbo-Croatian) became one of the central feast days, the day of the Kosovo martyrs. A cycle of magnificent folk epics extolled their sacrifice and exhorted every self-respecting Serb to avenge the defeat at Kosovo. Serb children were thus able to learn by heart the stirring call of Prince Lazar – Prince Lazar's curse – to fight at Kosovo:

> Whoever is a Serb and of Serb blood,
> And he comes not to fight at Kosovo,
> May he never have any progeny
> His heart desires, neither son nor daughter;
> Beneath his hand let nothing decent grow
> Neither purple grapes nor wholesome wheat;
> Let him rust away like dripping iron
> Until his name shall be extinguished.[4]

During the nineteenth century Prince Lazar's legendary call for personal sacrifice on the field of Kosovo became transformed into an exhortation for the liberation of the Serbs from foreign rule.

In the nineteenth century the historical myths formed a basis for the development of political ideologies, ideologies whose projected national goals were to be achieved, not by the blind march of history, but by planned political action. Although articulated by intellectuals, the primary role of these political ideologies was to mobilise popular support for the emerging political parties or movements. The core of Croat historical myth – the unbroken line of Croat statehood from the early medieval Croatian kingdoms onwards – was articulated by a Croat nobleman[5] at the beginning of the eighteenth century in a polemic against Venetian claims on Dalmatia and in the hope of gaining Habsburg support. In addition to this historical myth, this nobleman propounded the territorial myth of Greater Croatia which, in his version extended from the region north of the Danube to Thrace in Greece.[6] While the myth of the historical continuity of the Croat state became the focus of Croat national ideologies in the nineteenth century, the myth of Greater Croatia came to characterise a particularly anti-Serb form of Croatian nationalism. This was the ideology of Ante Starčević for whom Croatia extended from the Julian Alps to the river Timok on the border of Serbia and Bulgaria. According to Starčević, this territory was populated only by Croats. Slovenes were highland Croats while Serbs were decatholicised Croats of lower classes (hence the name 'Serbs', he argued, from Latin *servus* for servant). For Starčević Serbs and Slovenes, as separate nations, simply did not exist.[7] In 1861 he helped found the Party of (Croat State) Right which stood for the full assertion of Croatian state rights, that is, for the independence of Croatia from Hungarian and Habsburg domination and for the unification of Croatia–Slavonia with Dalmatia (then a separate province).

The Serbian uprisings against Ottoman rule in 1804 and 1815, which brought autonomy to Serbia within the Ottoman empire, were, in the view of some of its educated participants and outside observers, attempts at national liberation from arbitrary and oppressive as well as foreign, Islamic rule. Accordingly, the Kosovo tradition of personal sacrifice in the struggle against foreign domination provided the Serb insurgents with the motivational framework for the uprising. Only in 1844 was the recovery of emperor Dušan's lands used as a legitimist justification in the first fully articulated Serb national liberation programme, the *Načertanije* of Ilija Garašanin. This secret government memorandum, presented to the prince of the then semi-independent

Principality of Serbia, laid out plans for the recovery of Serb-populated territories of the Ottoman empire, the present-day southern Serbia, Kosovo and Metohija, Macedonia and Bosnia-Hercegovina. The choice of Ottoman-held territories appears to have been made on pragmatic grounds: the Ottoman empire, torn as it was by persistent provincial revolts both of its disadvantaged Christian population and its privileged Muslims, was regarded to be on the decline.[8] Only with the Austro-Hungarian occupation of the previously Ottoman-ruled province of Bosnia-Hercegovina in 1878 and the incorporation of the Austrian Military Frontier into Croatia-Slavonia in 1881, did the Serb-populated areas of the Habsburg empire come to be included in the plans of Serb national liberation. The Military Frontier, administered by the Austrian Imperial War Ministry, appeared to Serb political leaders in Austria-Hungary as the best protection of the special status which the Serbs enjoyed since the late seventeenth century. In 1690, following the largest migratory wave of Eastern Orthodox Serbs (the Great Migration of the Serbs)[9] from the Ottoman lands, the Habsburg emperor Leopold I granted these Serb refugees church self-government on condition that they enter imperial service as farmer-soldiers on the Military Frontier. This special status, their leaders thought, prevented the assimilation of the Serbs into the predominant Roman Catholic population of Croatia and Hungary. In contrast, Croat politicians regarded the existence of the Austrian Military Frontier as an infringement of Croatian state rights and sovereignty. The incorporation of the major portion of the Military Frontier (*Vojna Krajina* in Serbo-Croatian) into Croatia-Slavonia in 1881 – which made Serbs one quarter of the latter's population – forced the Serb political leaders in Croatia and in Hungary to look for protection elsewhere. At first their alliance with the Hungarian appointed governor (*ban*) of Croatia against the Croat national parties offered a semblance of continuity of the special status of their nation. But the favours and official patronage of the much hated governor made the Serbs look like traitors to the cause of Croatia's freedom and independence. Under these circumstances, Serb political leaders in Croatia and in Bosnia-Hercegovina turned to the ideology of Serb national liberation promoting the unification of all Serb-populated regions of these two provinces with the (by then) independent Kingdom of Serbia.[10]

Thus in the late nineteenth century the Serb and Croat national liberation ideologies came into conflict over the question of the territory to be liberated from foreign rule. The ideology of Croat state rights claimed, on the basis of the historic rights and the continuity of the Croat medieval state, the whole of Croatia, Slavonia, Dalmatia and

Bosnia–Hercegovina as Croat lands which were to form the future independent Croatia. The Serb national liberation ideologies proclaimed (a rather non-historic) right of the Serbs living in the very same regions to be freed from foreign rule and unified with Serbs in Serbia. Although the boundaries of this latter claim had never been clearly demarcated, substantial portions of Croatia, Slavonia and Dalmatia and the whole of Bosnia–Hercegovina were often included in the territories to be liberated by each side. Even before the national liberation of Serbs and Croats from foreign domination had started in earnest in the late nineteenth century, their two liberation ideologies were in competition over the same territory.

The Yugoslav idea – the idea of unity of the South Slav peoples – would appear to be a way of avoiding the competition over territory: if Serbs and Croats are one nation, it is their common homeland which they need to liberate from foreign rule. The simplicity and ingenuity of this idea, as we shall see, could not hide its own rather mythical origins.

## THE YUGOSLAV IDEA: A BELATED NATIONAL MYTH

The origins of the Yugoslav idea are traditionally sought in the myth of linguistic and cultural unity of the South Slav peoples which first gripped the imagination of a small student circle in Croatia in 1815. Influenced by Herder's view of language and folk customs as the expressions of the soul of each nation, a young law student from Zagreb, Ljudevit Gaj set about to discover the soul of his nation as expressed in its folk poetry and customs. Searching for a name for the newly discovered nation, he settled on the term 'Illyrian' used earlier by Croat writers and the short-lived Napoleonic administration of the South Slav-populated Habsburg provinces. Through his linguistic reforms and his newspaper (the first in a Croat native dialect), Gaj did his best to turn his Romantic myth of an Illyrian nation into reality. He chose the štokavian dialect spoken by both Serbs and Croats as the basis for what was to become the Croat literary standard and modelled the orthography of its Roman script on the orthography of spoken Serbian published in 1814 by the Serb linguistic reformer Vuk Stefanović Karadžić. In this way he hoped to facilitate the creation of a literary standard common to all South Slavs. Partially as a result of his efforts, Serb and Croat linguists and men of letters, including Karadžić, signed in 1850 in Vienna an agreement establishing the štokavian ijekavian dialect as the literary standard for both Serbs and Croats. Thus the leading Serb and Croat men of letters laid the foundations for what promised to be the linguistic unity of their two respective nations. This unity never came about: while the Croat writers came to accept štoka-vian ijekavian as their literary standard, writers from Serbia have never done so.[11] Even after the creation of Yugoslavia, the differences between the Croat and the Serb literary standard were jealously preserved as symbols of the difference between the two nations. In spite of this, for those South Slav intellectuals who wished to see cultural – and, later, political – unity of their nations, the Vienna agreement became a sym-bol of this unity or, even more, its living proof.

At its next stage of evolution, the idea entered the realm of practical politics. Roman Catholic bishop Josip Strossmayer and canon Franjo Rački were co-founders of the National Party in Zagreb which from 1860 propagated the principle of national self-determination in the Habsburg monarchy. In their view, the subject of self-determination in Croatia and Slovenia was the nation of South Slavs or Yugoslavs. The Serbs, Croats, Slovenes and Bulgarians were, in their terminology, the tribes or branches of 'our nation' (*naš narod*). As it happened, apart from the newly created literary standard, the branches of 'our nation' had little in common – least of all a sense of a common national or even cultural identity. However, from the linguistic unity, Rački sug-gested, a cultural unity would be built by the common efforts of the Yugoslav intelligentsia and this, in turn, could lead to a political unity in a common state. In this respect, the successful creation of common German and Italian cultures and, subsequently, of their nation-states offered the models which South Slavs should follow. To foster cultural unity, in 1866 Strossmayer founded the Yugoslav Academy of Arts and Sciences in Zagreb of which Rački was the first president; and then, in 1874, he opened the University of Zagreb. In spite of their efforts to forge alliances with the politicians of the Principality of Serbia, their Yugoslavism remained restricted to a small group of enthusiastic intel-lectuals. At the end of the century the mistrust and distaste of Serbs liv-ing in Croatia increased (partly as a result of Serb collaboration with the much hated Hungarian governor) leading, in 1903, to large anti-Serb riots in Zagreb. As the Serbs and their property came under at-tack in the capital of Croatia, the idea of South Slav or Croato-Serb political unity appeared to be a hollow intellectual dream.

However, in 1905 a coalition of five Serb and Croat parties in Croatia published a manifesto, committing itself to united political action and solidarity of 'both parts of our nation', that is, of Serbs and Croats. Apart from this implicit endorsement of the idea of Yugoslav unity, this was the first document of a Croatian political party or parties in which the principle of national self-determination was presented as a fundamental political credo.[12] In 1906 the Croato-Serb Coalition won the elections for the Croatian Diet and was soon forced to fight the Hungarian government's attempts to impose the use of Hungarian in Croatia. Despite the persistent attempts of the Austrian and Hungarian governments to discredit its Serb and Croat members (through press campaigns and court proceedings), the Coalition retained its dominance in the Diet until 1914.[13] As the Coalition's platform made references to the 'national unity', the support of the electorate was perceived as an electoral mandate to foster the idea of Yugoslav national unity.

Yet this Croato-Serb political cooperation and resulting political union with Serbia in 1918 was clearly not based on the Yugoslav cultural unity which, according to Rački and Strossmayer, was a prerequisite for the political union of the South Slavs. On the contrary, in spite of the Yugoslav idea which they endorsed, the political unity achieved in 1918 was based on relatively short-term practical political interests. The Croat parties (both those which entered into the Croato-Serb Coalition in 1905 and those which joined it in voting for the union with Serbia in 1918) were primarily motivated by the need to defend Croatia from foreign domination. Once they decided that the defence of Croatia could be achieved outside the union with Serbia and without Serb cooperation, they were ready to abandon or renegotiate the union and the terms of cooperation. The Serb parties from Croatia saw in the union with Serbia not only a guarantee of the preservation of Serb cultural identity but a principal source of their political influence in Croatia and in the newly established kingdom. In the newly unified kingdom in 1918, Serb parties, instead of being political parties of a minority in Croatia, became parties of the largest nation in the new kingdom. Unlike the Croat parties, it was not in their interest to renegotiate the terms of the union to their own disadvantage nor were they ready to abandon the union with Serbia. The divergence of the political interests which led Croat and Serb parties in Croatia to cooperate and to vote for the creation of the Yugoslav state created a rather fragile political basis for the new state.

In contrast to Croatian politics, the idea of Yugoslav national unity played no significant role in the politics of Serbia from 1815, when the country was granted a limited de facto autonomy in the Ottoman empire, until 1878 when Austria–Hungary occupied the Ottoman province of Bosnia–Hercegovina. The liberation of the Serbs, living in the Ottoman, and later Austro-Hungarian empire was, by general political consensus, the main foreign policy goal of this small principality which only in 1882 became a kingdom. While agreeing on the general goal, Serbian political parties naturally differed in their conception of the means to be employed in liberating their compatriots. As the Principality of Serbia gained its initial autonomy and expanded its territory within the Ottoman empire by a combination of military uprisings and international diplomacy, most Serbian politicians held that some such combination of military action and diplomacy would ensure a further expansion of the Serbian state into the Serb-populated areas of the Ottoman empire. In contrast to this idea of national liberation, the prominent Serbian socialist, Svetozar Marković argued that Serbs, as well as other oppressed Balkan peoples, could gain their freedom only within the framework of a democratic Balkan federation.[14] This idea of a federation of Balkan peoples – which originated in the writings of Serb liberals active in south Hungary – never spread beyond the confines of liberal and left-wing intellectuals and small social democratic parties. Since prior to 1913 the population of Serbia was nationally homogenous, the federal system had little if any appeal to the political elites or to their peasant constituency. The issue of the relations of Serbs to other South Slavs – Bulgarians, Croats and Muslims – arose, however, at the point at which the way for further expansion of the Serbian state cut through the territory inhabited by non-Serb South Slavs.

The Austro–Hungarian occupation of the Ottoman province of Bosnia–Hercegovina in 1878 appeared to rule out the possibility of expansion of the Serbian state into this multinational region: unlike the declining Ottoman empire, Austria–Hungary was a major European power for which the small, agrarian Principality of Serbia was no match. In Bosnia–Hercegovina the Eastern Orthodox, Roman Catholic and Islamic religions provided a basis for the development of separate national identities. By 1878 the Eastern Orthodox and the Roman Catholics, under the influence of the respective national ideologies, had already formed distinct national groups of Serbs and Croats. In contrast, the native Bosnian Muslims – who spoke the same language as the Christian population – lacked a distinct national ideology on a par with the national liberation ideologies of the Serbs and Croats. Under the Ottoman regime, the Muslims had a legally privileged status which gave their local leaders considerable political and economic control of the whole province. In defending this privileged status and their political power, the native Muslim elites opposed (at times with armed force) the modernisation of the legal and political system promoted by the central Ottoman government in Istanbul. In defending their feudal privileges based on Ottoman rule of the province, the native Muslim

elite failed to develop a modern national ideology and national identity
which would articulate the national goals of the Muslims independent
of Ottoman rule. This only entrenched the view according to which
they were a foreign occupier of the native Christian lands.

The majority Christian population of Bosnia–Hercegovina formed a
class of indentured tenant farmers whose civil rights were restricted
and who had no political rights. Until the middle of the nineteenth century, Christians could not occupy any administrative or judicial posts,
were effectively barred from gaining legal titles to land and their access
to Ottoman Islamic courts was restricted by procedures discounting
their testimony. They had also no right to bear arms and were prohibited from wearing a certain form of dress. In this way they were visibly
segregated from their Muslim rulers as well as ordinary Muslims. For
the Christians, liberation from the rule of the Ottomans and their local
Muslim masters appeared to be the only way to secure civil and political rights which their co-nationals in Austria–Hungary and in Serbia
had already enjoyed for some time. In 1875 the Christian peasants in
several areas of Bosnia–Hercegovina rose in arms against the Ottoman
regime. In Hercegovina the Serbs and Croats joined forces to drive out
Ottoman garrisons and local Muslim troops from several towns. In
northeast Bosnia only the Serb peasantry rose against the Ottomans
while central and east Bosnia, with its large Muslim population, was not
affected by the fighting in other parts of the province.[15] The insurrection,
sparked by increased taxation and tax abuses by the local Muslim landlords, was the largest rebellion in a series of uprisings against the Ottoman administration which both the Christians[16] and the local Muslim
elites staged in Bosnia–Hercegovina during the nineteenth century.

Serbian, Montenegrin and Russian Panslavist public opinion supported the rebels who also attracted numerous volunteers (including
the future king Petar I Karađorđević) from other South Slav lands and
Russia. The Montenegrin government dispatched some of its units to
Hercegovina and the Serbian government supplied arms to the rebels.
In attempting to suppress the uprising, the local Muslim leaders as
well as Ottoman military commanders imposed a reign of terror over
the Christian population which resulted in massacres of Christians,
both Serbs and Croats, and the consequent flight of hundreds of thousands of refugees to neighbouring countries. The reports in the European press of the large-scale pillage and massacres of the Christians
in Bosnia–Hercegovina coincided with the news of similar massacres
in Bulgaria. This was an issue – the so-called 'Bulgarian atrocities' –
which contributed to Gladstone's election victory in Great Britain and

his abandonment of the traditional British policy of unconditional support of the Ottomans in the Balkans. The victory of Russia over the Ottomans in 1877 and the creation of a large Bulgarian state out of the former Ottoman territories forced the European powers, including Britain, to redraw the map of the Balkans at the Congress of Berlin in 1878. This was, one could say, the first instance of map-drawing of the Balkans which the popular media, in part, initiated by reporting wide-scale atrocities against civilians.

The Berlin Congress sanctioned the creation of several independent nation states whose population was predominantly Christian out of the former territory of the Islamic Ottoman empire. In addition to Romania, Serbia and Montenegro were recognised as fully independent states. But Bosnia–Hercegovina, it was decided, was to exchange Ottoman for Austro-Hungarian rule. For the Serb political leaders in both in Serbia and in Bosnia–Hercegovina, the Austro-Hungarian occupation was only a change of one foreign ruler for another, in spite of the fact that Austria–Hungary's laws brought to the Christians, for the first time, legal and political equality with the Muslims.[17] To counter the influence of Croat and Serb nationalisms and to legitimise their rule, the Austro-Hungarian authorities constructed yet another national identity: that of Bosnians encompassing all three faiths. Although this new Bosnian identity failed to take root, the attempt illustrates well the role national identities were (and still are) supposed to play in the politics of this region: their primary political role has been to prepare the ground for mass mobilisation in support of an existing or a prospective regime.

Confronted with the need to deny the Austro-Hungarian authorities the right to govern a province which was not populated only by Serbs, the Serb national ideologues came to adopt the idea of the national unity (*narodno jedinstvo*) of Serbs and Croats. The Muslim population, lacking a national identity tied to a national ideology, was considered to belong to this unity, as the Muslims were (in the eyes of the Serb ideologues) primarily Serbs who centuries ago converted to Islam. This idea of national unity was universally regarded as an instrument – or rather, a weapon – in the struggle for national liberation of these peoples. Its acceptance in this instrumental form spread even to the militant pan-Serbian journals such as *Pijemont*[18] which readily accepted that the unification and liberation of all Serbs needed to be based on the national unity of Serbs and Croats and brotherhood with the Bulgarians and Slovenes.[19] The liberation of all Serbs and their brothers, in the view of this weekly, could be carried out only by the armed force of Serbia and under its leadership.

The Balkan wars in 1912–13 appeared to many enthusiastic South Slav nationalists to be the beginning of the final liberation of their lands from foreign rule. Serbia, by the force of its arms, and in cooperation with its Balkan neighbours, liberated the areas of the present-day Kosovo–Metohija, south Serbia and Macedonia from Ottoman rule. But the Balkan wars also revealed the shortcomings of the ideologies of national liberation by armed force. The second Balkan war in 1913 was fought mainly between Bulgaria and Serbia over the territory – present-day Macedonia – which each state claimed by historic and national right. The Serbian government claimed that the territory was populated by Serbs and was part of Dušan's empire; the Bulgarian government staked its claim on the population's membership of the Bulgarian Orthodox church, its Bulgarian dialects and the borders of the medieval Bulgarian empire. In the process, each state claimed to be liberating the territory from a foreign ruler while neither was prepared to offer the population of the territory any voice in the decision whether it wanted to be thus liberated and by whom. The absence of the need for any democratic consultation of the liberated-to-be displays the first shortcoming of the dominant Serbian as well as other national liberation ideologies in the Balkans: it was not democratic.

Serbia won the second Balkan war and the Bulgarian government was thus forced to cede the territory of Macedonia (formerly held by the Ottomans) which it claimed. The Bulgarian national ideologues have, however, never acquiesced in the loss of this territory. A result of the Serbian expansion was that the Serbian state, for the first time, came to include a large number of Christian Slavs who had not considered themselves Serbs before as well as a large number of Slav and Albanian Muslims who could not have been regarded as Serbs. The ideology of Yugoslav national unity did not mobilise the support of these groups for liberation by the Serbs: the Albanians actively resisted while most Christian and Muslim Slavs in Macedonia failed to support the Serbian military campaign of liberation. After the Balkan wars the Serbian (and after 1918, the Royal Yugoslav) government planned to assimilate the Christian Slav population into the Serb nation while the political significance of the unassimilable Muslim population would be reduced by their emigration to Turkey and by Serb colonisation of the areas. These plans failed: the Christian Slavs of Macedonia resisted assimilation and from 1944 onwards were constituted into a separate nation of Macedonians. In spite of migrations to Turkey, the Muslim population of Serbia grew in number and under the Yugoslav communist regime in 1968 formally gained, along with their

Bosnian brethren, the status of a nation. In the same period, the Albanian population was virtually (but not formally) granted the same national status. This upgrading of the national status of these groups was, at least in part, a result of the Yugoslav communist ideology of national liberation which insisted on the equality of all nations in Yugoslavia.

In contrast, the 'national unity' ideology endorsed by many Serb politicians in 1912, was a 'dominant nation' type of ideology: it assumed the domination of the 'nationally unified' nation (whose core would be constituted by the Serbs) over other nations in a new state. This ideology could not justify Serbian rule to those who considered themselves neither Serbs nor Croats, or to those, such as Albanians, who were not Slavs. A national ideology which assumes the assimilation of one national group by another obviously offers no legitimation of the rule of the dominant nation to the unassimilated or unassimilable. This is the second shortcoming of this type of 'dominant nation' ideology: it offered no effective legitimation to those who were neither Serbs nor Croats (nor Slovenes). Both the undemocratic and the assimilationist aspects of the ideology of Yugoslav national unity as propagated by Serb national ideologues formed part of the general discourse of strident self-assertion which came to characterise European national ideologies in the late nineteenth century. These ideologies were used to legitimise territorial conquest and the use of armed force both within and outside Europe. Within this discourse only the stronger and thus 'naturally' dominant national groups could survive in the competition for the territory and allegiance of the smaller and undeveloped national groups.

The liberation from Ottoman rule in 1913 and from Austro-Hungarian rule in 1918 was a liberation of the national groups whose national identity had formed during the Romantic awakening of nations in the first half of the nineteenth century. The drive for the liberation of so-selected national groups triggered, by imitation, a similar drive for liberation or political autonomy of other ethnic or national groups whose national identity and political organisation was formed only later in the century. Thus the first Albanian political organisation, the League of Prizren, formed in 1878, initially demanded the unification of all Albanians in one state.[20] Similarly, the first political organisation promoting Slav Macedonian national self-determination, the Internal Macedonian Revolutionary Organisation (IMRO), established only in 1893, propagated the liberation and unification of all Macedonians in one autonomous state. The first Bosnian Muslim political organisation – the Muslim National Organisation – was established in 1906 in Sarajevo to promote the autonomy of the Bosnian Muslim population and of Bosnia–Hercegovina within the Austro-Hungarian empire. The political demands and territorial claims of all three of these organisations clashed with the demands of Serb national liberation ideology made in the early nineteenth century and endorsed later by the Serbian government. Prior to 1878 the Serbian national ideology had already claimed, on various grounds, the Ottoman-ruled territories of Kosovo and Metohija (claimed by the League of Prizren), of South Serbia or Macedonia (claimed by the IMRO) and Bosnia-Hercegovina (claimed by Bosnian Muslim political organisations). The Macedonian territorial demands also clashed with those of the Bulgarian and Greek national liberation movements whereas the Bosnian Muslim claims competed with those of the Croat national parties which demanded the whole of Bosnia–Hercegovina for Croatia.

By the beginning of the twentieth century, the Balkans and the South Slav lands of the Austro-Hungarian empire became an area of fierce competition for the same territory among numerous mutually conflicting national ideologies of the 'dominant nation' type. The social democratic vision of equal nations, first propagated in Serbia by Svetozar Marković and his followers, appeared at the time naive and unrealistically pacifist.[21] But its non-pacifist communist variant, which rejected national dominance and assimilation and treated all nations and nationalities of Yugoslavia as ostensibly equal, proved, during and after World War II, to be a much more successful national liberation ideology than the traditional ideologies of the 'dominant nation' type. However, communist national elites in Yugoslavia, in their competition for economic and political power from the 1970s onwards, no longer had any use for this equalising ideology. In the 1980s national ideologies of the 'dominant nation' type were resurrected. By the 1980s, however, the number of such ideologies had increased: in addition to the Serb, Croat and Slovene ideologies, there were now Muslim, Albanian and Macedonian ideologies of the same type. Since each of these ideologies now claimed the dominance of one nation over others on a given territory and several of them competed over the same territory, the stage was set for a renewed conflict.

TOWARDS A YUGOSLAV STATE: WORLD WAR I

The assassination of the Austrian Archduke Franz Ferdinand on 28 June 1914 in the capital of Bosnia–Hercegovina, Sarajevo, precipitated the Austro-Hungarian ultimatum to Serbia, the first in the series of ultimata which started World War I. The Archduke's assassin and his comrades were members of the revolutionary youth organisation 'Young Bosnia' which was committed to the liberation of Bosnia–Herce-govina from Austro-Hungarian rule and its union with Serbia and other South Slav lands. The ideology of the national unity of South Slavs provided the underage assassin and his comrades with a vision of national liberation and unification of their peoples through armed struggle and terrorism while the Serbian secret organisation 'Unity or Death' (the Black Hand) provided them with arms.

The Serbian government (which attempted, rather vaguely, to alert the Austro-Hungarian government of the possibility of the assassina-tion),[22] unprepared for a war with its powerful northern neighbour, accepted all the conditions of the Austro-Hungarian ultimatum claiming, however, the protection of its national sovereignty as provided by international law.[23] The Austro-Hungarian government, intent on halting what it regarded as Serbia's persistent expansionism in the Bal-kans, declared war nonetheless. At the time, the leading Belgrade daily *Politika* argued that just as in 1859 the Austrian ultimatum to Piedmont led to Austrian defeat and the unification of Italy, so in 1914 the Aus-tro-Hungarian ultimatum to Serbia would lead to a similar defeat and the unification of the South Slavs.[24] The Serbian government, initially much more cautious, on 7 December 1914 issued a declaration, (against which voted only the two Social Democratic deputies)[25] stating that its principal war aim was the liberation and unification of 'their captive brethren Serbs, Croats and Slovenes' of Austria–Hungary. This first Ser-bian government programme of the national liberation of South Slavs was issued partly in an attempt to pre-empt any postwar allotment of the South Slav lands of Austria–Hungary to any of the neighbouring states (such as Italy). At the same time the Serbian government encour-aged the creation of a committee of Croat, Slovene and Serb politicians who fled Austria–Hungary – the future Yugoslav Committee – which was to promote in allied capitals the cause of the national liberation of South Slavs from Austria–Hungary. In addition, the most prominent Serb historians, linguists and anthropologists were commissioned to prove that the Serbs, Croats and Slovenes are in fact a single nation with three names. This view not only became the principal plank of Serbian propaganda but provided a justification for the unitary consti-tutional arrangements of the future South Slav state which the ruling Serbian Radical party and its leader Nikola Pašić consistently advo-cated from 1914 onwards.

For almost two years the Serbian army was able to hold in check the superior Austro-Hungarian forces, severely defeating them in several battles on Serbian soil. But the Bulgarian attack on Serbia in 1915 and a joint German–Austro. Hungarian offensive forced the Serbian government, together with its army, to withdraw, with heavy losses, through the rugged mountains of Albania to the Adriatic coast and then to the Greek island of Corfu. Faced with the prospect of an unsatisfactory separate peace with Austria–Hungary and under pressure from the Allies to come to an agreement about their future state, the Serbian government and the Yugoslav Committee, after six weeks of negotiations, issued in July 1917 on Corfu a 14 point declaration concerning the future state of the three peoples. The Corfu declaration stated that the future Kingdom of Serbs, Croats and Slovenes would be 'a constitutional, democratic and parliamentary monarchy headed by the [Serbian] Karađorđević dynasty' in which the two alphabets, three names (Serb, Croat and Slovene) and three major religions (Eastern Orthodox, Roman Catholic and Muslim) would be equal. Its constitution should be passed by 'a numerically qualified majority' in the future constituent assembly which is to be elected by universal and equal, direct and secret suffrage. The principle of free self-determination of the 'three-named people', the declaration stated, guaranteed the territorial indivisibility of the country.[26] This was primarily intended to annul the Allied promise of a large part of Dalmatia and its islands to Italy made in the secret clauses of the Treaty of London in 1915. The Yugoslav Committee, partly because a large number of its members, including its chairman, came from Dalmatia, considered the denial of Italian claims and the inclusion of Dalmatia and its islands in the future South Slav state its first priority. For Pašić and the Serbian government the first priority was the acceptance of the Serbian Karađorđević dynasty, its right to sanction the future constitution and the absence of any territorial or constitutional division along 'ethnic' or 'historic' lines.

However, once the National Council of Slovenes, Croats and Serbs in Zagreb on 29 October 1918 proclaimed the independence of the State of Slovenes, Croats and Serbs from Austria–Hungary and declared its non-belligerence, it also attempted to renegotiate the terms of unification laid down in the Corfu declaration. The new declaration signed by the representatives of the Serbian government and opposition the Yugoslav Committee and the National Council in Geneva on 9 November 1918 envisaged a confederal arrangement, with separate jurisdictions for the Serbian government and the National Council in Zagreb as well as a joint cabinet with an equal number of ministers. As this arrangement went against the Serbian ruling Radical party's insistence on a unitary state, Pašić and his cabinet repudiated it a few days later and resigned. Thus the first, confederal attempt at the unification of the two states failed only a few days after it was made.

As Austria–Hungary started to disintegrate in autumn 1918, peasants in some parts of Croatia and Bosnia–Hercegovina took to plundering their landlords' estates in the expectation of a new social order which would give them the land they tilled. The newly established regional national councils had no effective armed force to stem this unrest. Moreover, an increasing number of national councils in the Serb-populated areas of the former Austria–Hungary had already proclaimed their direct unification with Serbia and Montenegro. The regional assembly of Vojvodina as well a large number of district national councils of Bosnia–Hercegovina had done so before the regent proclaimed the new unified kingdom on 1 December 1918. The Italian army, apart from occupying parts of Dalmatia, started advancing, unopposed, on the capital of Slovenia, Ljubljana. The National Council of the Slovenes, Croats and Serbs in Zagreb was thus confronted with a rapid loss of territory from its newly established state as well as spreading social unrest. Having failed to win recognition for the State of Slovenes, Croats and Serbs from the major Allied powers, its Central Committee in Zagreb had literally no one else but the Serbian government to turn to for help. Well aware of this, in late November 1918 the Central Committee of the National Council elected a delegation to seek an immediate union with Serbia and Montenegro.

As the Council was the only elected body of South Slavs in Austria–Hungary in existence, the great majority of its Committee's members had no doubt that they had a popular mandate to seek this union. Yet both the need for a hasty union and the electoral mandate of the Council was questioned by Stjepan Radić the leader of one of the smaller parties in the Croatian Diet, the Croatian People's Peasant Party. At the very start of the deliberations on the union, he rejected unification under a Serbian royal house, proposing instead a transitional regency and a federation of four autonomous states (Slovenia, Croatia, Serbia and Montenegro) and three provinces (Bosnia–Hercegovina, Dalmatia and Vojvodina). Later, in an impassioned speech he argued that the union would also fail to accomplish the historical goal of the Croat nation, the achievement of independence through self-determination; while the Serbs could regard the united kingdom as a resurrection of Tsar Dušan's Serb empire.[27]

In spite of Radić's fiery but lone opposition, the Council's delegation was issued, in the best traditions of the past Croato-Hungarian parliamentary negotiations, a set of specific instructions concerning the terms of the union. These terms included the requirement of a two-thirds majority in the future Constituent Assembly for passing the constitution of a united state and a considerable legislative autonomy for the existing provincial governments and the Ban of Croatia.[28] As the Serbian ministers in Belgrade, instructed by the regent alone, took exception to some of the terms and imposed a very short timetable for the completion of the agreement on the union, the Zagreb delegation was forced to drop these two conditions. Thus the agreement on the terms of the union contained in their Address to the Throne accorded not with the terms set out by the National Council in Zagreb but with specifications of the 30-year-old Prince Aleksandar Karadorđević.

Although this second attempt at unification was greeted with violent protests in Zagreb,[29] neither the general public nor the negotiating parties wished to see the union only as an uneasy political deal. To many the union appeared to herald the triumph of the idea of Yugoslav national unity over separate national ideologies of Serbs, Croats and Slovenes. Having liberated their common homeland from foreign rule, and uniting in a common state, there was, it seemed, no further role for the separate national ideologies to play. In reality, however, the separate national ideologies quickly resumed their old role in the newly liberated homeland, the role of identifying the inequalities among the nations and, consequently, identifying new national oppressors. It was the largest and most dominant nation in the new kingdom, the Serbs, that, in the view of the Croat national ideology, assumed the role of the oppressor of other nations which was previously assigned to the Hungarians and Germans. In their endeavour to identify national inequalities and to find scapegoats for them, the separate Croat and Serb national ideologies retained their appeal as programmes of national liberation and proved to be a potent tool for political mass mobilisation. In contrast, the ideology of Yugoslav national unity, appeared to have exhausted its role as a national liberation ideology. After 1918 it certainly failed to develop a grassroots appeal comparable, in particular, to the Croat national ideologies. It also failed to provide the mass of Yugoslav citizens with a national identity replacing that of Serb, Croat or Slovene varieties. Moreover, it failed to offer a sense of historic mission which would go beyond that of liberation from foreign rule. Having provided an ideological legitimisation of the struggle for national liberation of the South Slavs, the Yugoslav national ideology failed to provide a comparable legitimisation of the new constitutional and state structure which would be acceptable to the various national political elites. In short, the ideology of Yugoslav national unity failed to transform itself into an effective ideology for the legitimisation of the new state.

# 2  The First Yugoslavia

The devastation of World War I affected the new state unequally: while Serbia endured large-scale destruction of its fledgling industrial plants and railway communications as well as its livestock, the already more developed industries in the Slovenian and Croatian parts of the Kingdom were spared war damage and even expanded during the war. Out of Serbia's 4.5 million inhabitants, 28 per cent died in the war (including 62 per cent of its male population aged from 15 to 55) while the former Austro-Hungarian parts of the Kingdom lost less than 10 per cent

*Map 1*    Yugoslavia at the time of creation, 1918–20
*Source*: *A Short History of Yugoslavia*, ed. S. Clissold, Cambridge University Press, 1996.

of their pre-war population.[1] But even in the areas not affected by military operations, such as large parts of Bosnia–Hercegovina, a cycle of violence and terror had been set in train by the war. At the beginning of the war, the Austro-Hungarian auxiliaries, recruited from the local non-Serb population, mainly Muslims, spread terror among the Serbs by their indiscriminate killing and beatings. At end of the war, Serb irregulars in turn plundered and terrorised Muslim villagers in some parts of Bosnia–Hercegovina.

Apart from the uneven level of industrial development, there were huge differences in the pattern of landholding. In Serbia and Montenegro most agricultural land was held by smallholders, while in the former Austro-Hungarian provinces there were also large landholdings. In Croatia and Slovenia the large landholders were often non-Slavs while in Bosnia–Hercegovina the great majority of large landowners were members of the Bosnian Muslim aristocracy. As in other newly created East European national states, the government's agrarian reform, promulgated after the war, was intended, among other things, to benefit the poor peasantry of the new dominant nations. In accordance with this policy, the land from the large estates of German, Hungarian and Muslim owners was distributed to poor Serb, Croat and Slovene peasants; a considerable number of Serb war veterans were settled on lands of this kind. The break-up of large estates did not alleviate persistent rural overpopulation.[2] Poorer agricultural regions of Dalmatia, Hercegovina, Croatia and Macedonia experienced a high rate of migration to North America and West Europe. In addition, Muslims – Slavs as well as Turks and Albanians – continued to emigrate to Turkey.

As a whole, the new kingdom was an industrially underdeveloped country in which around 80 per cent of the inhabitants derived their income from agriculture. However, its politics from the very start was dominated by the issues deriving from its multinational and multiethnic composition rather than its relative economic underdevelopment. Out of less than 12 million inhabitants in 1918, around 2 million were members of national minorities, the largest of which were the Germans, Hungarians and Albanians (each with a population around half a million). In addition to the three constituent nations – Serbs, Croats and Slovenes – there were ethnic groups whose national status was not recognised. The Muslims of Bosnia–Hercegovina and the Sandžak region of Serbia were considered to be either Serbs or Croats of Islamic faith; the Slav inhabitants of South Serbia – later the federal republic of Macedonia – were regarded as Serbs, in spite of the closeness of the dialects which they spoke to Bulgarian. The Eastern Orthodox inhabitants of Montenegro were generally acknowledged as Serbs.

The politics of the first provisional government and parliament of the Kingdom of Serbs, Croats and Slovenes, formed on 20 December 1918, displayed the pattern which became characteristic for the entire life of this state. Except for the social democratic parties (and the minuscule Republican party), all other parties in the parliament were national or ethnic parties. The Serb parties, although taking the largest number of deputies and cabinet portfolios, could never form an absolute and permanent majority in the parliament which would allow them to govern without the support of other national parties. As no single national group could dominate the parliament, the government had to be formed out of short-lived multinational coalitions, the partners of which frequently had highly divergent, often conflicting, political programmes. Moreover, one of the first acts of Prince (later King) Aleksandar as the regent was to reject the proposal by the newly convened provisional government to appoint the wartime Serbian premier, Nikola Pašić, the first premier of the new kingdom. This was a clear sign that he intended to take an active part in politics, not altogether suitable for a constitutional monarch.

In the November 1920 elections for the Constituent Assembly, 65 per cent of the eligible (only male) voters cast their ballots. From the 16 parties or groups which entered the Assembly (22 contested the election), the largest numbers of votes were cast for the Democratic (92 seats), the Radical (91), the Communist (59), the Croat Peasant (50), the Agrarian (39), the Slovene People's (27) parties and the Yugoslav Moslem Organisation (24 seats). The only party whose support was not limited primarily to one national group was the Communist party. Using its links with the Soviet-controlled Communist International as a pretext, the government banned the Communist party soon after the elections and later cancelled its seats. The bulk of the supporters and deputies of the largest party, the Democratic party, were Serbs, although it also had supporters among non-Serbs. The Radical and Agrarian parties drew their main support from Serbia and Serb-populated regions of Vojvodina and Bosnia–Hercegovina. The main Croat party became Stjepan Radić's Croat Peasant party which, at a rally in Zagreb in December 1920, declared itself for a Neutral Republic of Croatia, inserted 'Republican' in its title and decided to boycott the Constituent Assembly. The other Croat parties, which voted for the union and participated in the provisional parliament were routed in this election.[3]

Among the constitutional drafts presented to the Assembly, the Croat and Slovene drafts urged, as expected, a federalist structure of the state which was justified by reference to history and to national differences. As history had created borders among different provinces, it was argued, these borders should be maintained as borders between federal units. Further, a federal structure of the state would enable the nations of Yugoslavia to preserve and develop their different national cultures and traditions. In contrast, the Radical and Democratic parties proposed unitarist constitutional drafts which allowed for a limited self-government of smaller territorial units whose boundaries were not based on any historical frontiers. The new state, they argued, should overcome all past differences among cultures and traditions. As the historical boundaries were imposed by foreign oppressors and not freely chosen, they should not be allowed to threaten the unity of the new state. The Radical party draft was rejected by the deputies of the Slovene People's party and the remaining Croat deputies; the Croat Peasant Party deputies had boycotted the Assembly from the start and the Communist party deputies left the Assembly before the vote. In consequence, out of 419 deputies, only 258 voted on the Radical constitutional draft. Out of those voting, only 223 voted for, 35 against; 161 had abstained or boycotted the vote. Of those who voted in favour, 184 were Serbs, 18 were Muslims, 11 Slovenes and 10 Croats. The mainly Serb Radical and Democratic parties alone, without the deputies of Muslim and Slovene parties, would not have been able to carry through this constitution by the required qualified majority.[4] But since the constitution was submitted by the predominantly Serb parties, it was regarded as a basis for the Serb hegemony in the new state.

As no grouping of national parties from one nation could form a stable government, the politics of the country up to June 1928 was marked by short-lived coalition governments involving various national parties and frequent elections. Stjepan Radić and his Croat Peasant party at first boycotted the parliament but after his arrest in February 1925 on charges of anti-state activities, he agreed to enter a short-lived government with the Serbian Radical party and its leader Nikola Pašić. After the demise of this coalition and Pašić's death in 1926, Radić formed an opposition block with various Serb opposition parties. From the beginning of 1928 this new Serbo-Croat opposition bloc endeavoured to obstruct the coalition government by inciting disorder in the parliament and street demonstrations outside it. In response, a group of Radical deputies led by Puniša Račić, unsuccessfully proposed that a panel of medical experts examine Radić to determine whether he was mentally fit to be a deputy, and if so, punish him for his persistent breach of parliamentary procedures and orders. At a later session on 20 June 1928, when confronted by the usual jeers and insults from Croat Peasant party deputies, Račić opened fire with his pistol at the opposition deputies, killing two of them and gravely wounding Stjepan Radić among others.[5]

As large demonstrations in Zagreb were suppressed by police with a loss of life, the opposition bloc demanded a reconstitution of the country on a federalist model. To calm the situation the king asked the Slovene politician Anton Korošec to form yet another coalition government which lasted only until December 1928. After its resignation, King Aleksandar, in his consultation with party leaders, mooted the idea of a mutually agreed secession[6] of the Croat and Slovene lands from the rest of the country. As this idea had already been rejected by Stjepan Radić (who died two months after his wounding in the parliament), his successor Vladko Maček as well as other opposition leaders rejected it. The king refused the opposition's demand for a federal reorganisation of the state, and in January 1929 dissolved the parliament – as an unnecessary 'intermediary between the people and the king' – and proclaimed a personal regime. In addition, he abolished all organisations, political or otherwise, based on national or religious foundations, vowing, in the name of Yugoslav national unity to banish all national or 'tribal' differences from the public life of the country which, in October 1929, he renamed the Kingdom of Yugoslavia.

The proclamation of King Aleksandar's personal regime ended the attempt at a unitarist parliamentary system based on the dominance of the Serb parties. The Serb parties were unable to create a stable and effective, let alone fully legitimate government, for two reasons. First, due to their disunity, they could rarely command a parliamentary majority without the support of non-Serb parties; and, second, the Croat Peasant party persistently questioned the legitimacy of the constitution and of parliamentary government based on this constitution. In their attempts to gain as much political independence for the Croats as possible, the Croat Peasant party and its leader Stjepan Radić used any means at their disposal; to many Serb politicians these maximalist tactics appeared treasonable. Many Croat politicians regarded the attempts of the two major Serb parties to secure parliamentary majorities and dominance in government not as a standard parliamentary practice but a policy of imposing political hegemony over non-Serbs. In view of such divergent views of parliamentary politics, it is not surprising that this first – and in effect the last – experiment in multi-party parliamentary politics in Yugoslavia failed as it did.

King Aleksandar's direct rule ended in September 1931 with the proclamation of a new constitution which was rejected by the Croat

Peasant party as well as by Slovene and Serb opposition politicians; to this the king's government responded by jailing opposition politicians from all national groups. Even before the regime embarked on repression of the opposition, the Croat politician Ante Pavelić emigrated to found a separatist Croat organisation – the *Ustashe* (meaning 'insurgents' in Serbo-Croatian) – which embarked on a terrorist campaign against the Yugoslav state. The organisation's aim was the creation of a greater Croatia, including Bosnia–Hercegovina, which would be then 'freed' of all Serbs. As his organisation aimed at the dismemberment of Yugoslavia, it received support from neighbouring governments – those of Hungary, Bulgaria and Italy – which made claims on parts of Yugoslav territory. It also found allies in an older terrorist organisation, the Internal Macedonian Revolutionary Organisation (IMRO) which was by that time based in Sofia and fought for the separation of Macedonia from Yugoslavia and its incorporation into Bulgaria. With the support of the Ustashe, members of IMRO assassinated King Aleksandar during his visit to Marseilles in October 1934 thus ending his attempt to create a single nation of Yugoslavs by government *fiat*.

The regency, which was appointed to rule until the late king's son Petar came of age, had other more urgent tasks than promoting his ideology of unitary Yugoslavism; it faced serious economic problems arising from the rapid impoverishment of the rural population due to the worldwide depression, as well as the Croat Peasant party's rejection of the regime's legitimacy. The coalition cabinet consisting of the Bosnian Muslim party, the Slovene clerical party and a segment of the Serb Radicals, led by a successful banker and Radical politician Milan Stojadinović, appointed by the first regent Prince Pavle Karađorđević in 1935, succeeded in reducing rural indebtedness and improving the country's finances as well as in winning the elections of December 1938. It also changed the traditional Serbian policy of reliance on France by seeking accommodation with Mussolini's Italy and Hitler's Germany. Stojadinović's supporters, his political rivals pointed out, started to ape the style of the two dictators, parading in green uniforms and calling him 'the leader'. Whatever his ideological outlook might have been, his unbroken four years in office, proved that it was possible to govern Yugoslavia, relatively effectively, without the participation of the Croat Peasant party, provided that the government had the support of Bosnian Muslim and Slovene parties and of the major outside powers (in this case Italy and Germany).

It was probably Stojadinović's disinclination to seek a compromise with the Croat Peasant party that led Prince Pavle suddenly to dismiss him in February 1939 and to replace his government with a cabinet of pliant minor politicians whose main task was to find such a compromise. The looming European war and Maček's lobbying of Mussolini's government in support of an independent Croatia made this task quite urgent. In August 1939 the cabinet signed an agreement with Maček which introduced a one-unit federalism into the Kingdom of Yugoslavia. The agreement (*Sporazum*) of 1939 created a large province (*banovina*) of Croatia, incorporating Dalmatia, a large part of Hercegovina and parts of Bosnia. This province was granted legislative and political autonomy on most internal matters while foreign policy, defence, transport, communications and monetary policy was conducted by the central government in Belgrade. In addition to governing this province, the Croat Peasant party was given five out of fifteen cabinet portfolios, including the post of vice-premier which was taken up by Maček. This was an agreement between a government appointed by the crown and the leader of the largest Croat political party; it was never endorsed by the Yugoslav parliament nor put to a referendum. In effect, it created a semisovereign Croat national state incorporating the great majority of Croats living in Yugoslavia as well as almost one million Serbs (out of the province's total population of four and a half million). By incorporating Serb-populated regions of Croatia and Bosnia–Hercegovina into the Croat federal unit, this agreement virtually precluded the formation of a similar unit incorporating most Serbs in Yugoslavia.[7] Not surprisingly, most Serb opposition politicians (including many Radicals) rejected the agreement, regarding it as an undemocratic concession to the Croat demands in return for their acceptance of Yugoslavia. These concessions, they thought, were forced by the threatening developments abroad, such as Hitler's dismemberment of Czechoslovakia and Mussolini's increasing support for the Ustasha policy of an independent Croatia. In order to secure a politically united Yugoslavia, Prince Pavle and his government apparently had little choice but to grant the long-standing demands for Croat autonomy.

The concessions failed to preserve either Yugoslavia or Prince Pavle and his government. Yielding to intense pressure from Hitler and having no hope of any help from Britain, on 25 March 1941 Prince Pavle's government signed Yugoslavia's accession to Hitler's Tripartite Pact. Two days later, a group of Serb officers, supported by British intelligence agencies, staged a bloodless coup abolishing the regency and elevating Petar II Karađorđević, still a minor, to the throne. Mass demonstrations in support of the coup in Belgrade and other Serb cities appeared to confirm the unpopularity of pro-German policies at least among the Serbs. After the coup, in the coalition government formed, for the first time, of all the major parties Maček retained his vice-premiership. On 6 April 1941 Axis forces attacked Yugoslavia and bombed Belgrade. The poorly led and equipped royal Yugoslav military was defeated in twelve days. During this time the young king and government prepared to fly out to Cairo while the vice-premier Maček returned to Zagreb. Even before the Yugoslav High Command capitulated to the Germans, on 10 April 1941 he broadcast a call to the Croats to obey the Ustasha regime which the Germans were installing in power in Croatia; on the same day, small groups of Ustashe, aided by the Croat Peasant party armed guards, took over control of Zagreb whose populace turned out to welcome enthusiastically the German troops.

With the proclamation of the puppet Ustasha Croat state began the Axis carve-up of Yugoslavia. Slovenia was divided between Italy and the Third Reich, large parts of Macedonia and southern Serbia were incorporated into Bulgaria, a large part of Vojvodina into Hungary; much of Dalmatia and all of Montenegro went to Italy while Kosovo and western Macedonia were attached to the Italian-controlled Albania, creating for the first time a greater Albanian state. The whole of Bosnia–Hercegovina and Srem became a part of the Ustashe's Independent State of Croatia. Central Serbia with Belgrade was at first administered directly by the Nazis; later a quisling government led by a Serb general was installed. Thus ended the first Yugoslavia.

During the twenty-three years of its existence, Yugoslavia had experienced three types of constitutional arrangement: a unitarist parliamentary system in which the Serb parties formed an unstable majority; a centralist system based on the dominance of the crown and on the suppression of nationally-based parties; and a one-unit federalism in which the province of Croatia had a privileged autonomous status. Each of the three was rejected by the political elite of at least one of the three constituent nations of the country. The Croat Peasant party, the largest Croat party, consistently denied the legitimacy of the first two models. The Slovene People's party, the largest Slovene party, intermittently did so too. The leaders of most Serb parties rejected the third, federalist arrangement partly because they regarded it as an undemocratic and unconstitutional political deal. This apparent conflict between a unitarist (or centralist) and federalist conception of the common state hid a rather crude competition for monopoly of political power. The unitarist parliamentary model was an instrument for maintaining the monopoly of power of the political leaders of the two major Serb parties and restricting the access to power of all other parties, irrespective of their constituency. After 1929, under the Yugoslav centralist model the crown became the most powerful political agent in the country capable of forming and controlling governments irrespective of parliamentary majorities. Under the one-unit federalism, the Croat Peasant party leadership gained complete control of a large semisovereign state of Croatia and became the second most important political factor in Yugoslavia. Thus this ostensible federalist solution was in effect a power-sharing arrangement between the crown and the Croat Peasant party leaders from which the highly fragmented Serb parties had nothing to gain.

As the leaders of all the major parties saw no need to bring these constitutional arrangements to a parliament, whose rules of procedure would be accepted by all parties, or to a referendum, it appears that they regarded them primarily as arrangements for distribution of political power among themselves. As the benefits of a particular constitutional arrangement would accrue primarily to particular political and, to some extent, social elites of the three constituent nations, the national ideologies which were used to legitimise such arrangements were primarily instruments for mobilising mass support for these political elites in their struggle for power. The national ideology of the Radicals and Democrats which insisted on the need for a strong, centralised state to counter the ever-present threats from abroad appealed to their Serb constituency scarred as it was by the Balkan wars and World War I. But the party leaders conveniently overlooked the fact that their centralist ideology effectively weakened the new state as the Slovene and Croat parties denied the legitimacy of a centralised state from its very start. The Croat Peasant party's slogan of 'one is to enjoy one's own' likened the enjoyment which a peasant has (or should have) of his land to the need for the Croats to have full political control of the historic lands in which they live. This ideology of folksy self-government no doubt appealed to the party's rural constituency and ensured its continuing support for the party. In the wake of the outbreak of World War II, the Croat Peasant party finally came to enjoy a complete control over its constituency and over the civil service jobs and contracts patronage in an enlarged Croatia; what benefits, if any, this brought to their wider rural constituency is quite unclear.

The first Yugoslavia was destroyed by a formidable Axis military machine which was able to crush much larger and politically more stable countries than was Yugoslavia. The Axis attack would have had the same result irrespective of the country's constitutional arrangement in 1941. However, the Axis occupation, resistance to this occupation and the civil war after April 1941 brought into play political movements whose political ideologies differed greatly from those of the major players in the pre-1941 period. The victory of the most revolutionary of these movements – the communist-led one – in the ensuing civil war precluded the restoration of the Kingdom of Yugoslavia in any of its pre-1941 constitutional arrangements.

# 3 World War II

## THE UPRISINGS AGAINST THE AXIS AND THE CIVIL WAR

The capitulation and surrender of over 300 000 men and officers of the royal Yugoslav military in April 1941 did not end the war in Yugoslavia. Colonel Dragoljub-Draža Mihailović disobeyed the orders of his superiors to surrender to the German army and in May 1941 raised an armed rebellion in central Serbia against the German occupying forces. In June 1941, following the German attack on the USSR, the underground Communist party of Yugoslavia issued as well a call for an uprising against the occupiers. The communist forces, called Partisans, were commanded by the Soviet-trained general secretary of the Communist party, Josip Broz Tito. The forces of colonel Mihailović took an older Serb appellation for guerilla fighters, Chetniks. These guerilla units, at times in co-ordinated attacks, cleared most of western Serbia, including several towns, from the weak German army of occupation. In November 1941 the royal Yugoslav government-in-exile in London, delighted at Mihailović's resistance, promoted him to the rank of general and appointed him commander-in-chief of the armed forces in the homeland and, later, minister for war. The first British Special Operations Executive mission arrived at Mihailović's headquarters a little earlier and the British wartime propaganda portrayed him as a great hero of the first resistance movement in Europe. While Tito was at the time unknown in the West, he maintained regular radio contact with the Comintern headquarters in Moscow.

In October 1941 fighting broke out between the Chetnik and Partisan forces, which, interrupted only by a brief armistice, flared up again in December. This was the beginning of the civil war which effectively ended only in 1945 by the annihilation of the Chetnik forces by the victorious Partisans. In an operation lasting from September to December 1941, the German army (consisting of two front-line divisions brought over from the front in the USSR) assisted by quisling forces defeated the demoralised Partisan and Chetnik units. In an attempt to eradicate popular support for the guerillas the German army interned the entire population of several towns and undertook mass shooting of civilian hostages in reprisals for the killing of German soldiers.[1] In the face of defeat, Mihailović allowed many of his units to transfer allegiance, at least nominally, to the German quisling administration of Serbia while he retained a small headquarters which he frequently moved to escape German pursuit.

In Montenegro a mass uprising against the Italian occupation in July 1941 was led by royal Yugoslav army officers as well as by the communists. In October the communists proclaimed a soviet republic on the territory they controlled and staged mass executions of their potential opponents among the resistance fighters. By December 1941 the royal officers who led the uprising declared their allegiance to Mihailović, drove out the Partisans from Montenegro and concluded an agreement with the Italian occupation authorities who, in addition to arms and ammunition, handed over to them full control of the countryside. There was no general uprising in Bosnia–Hercegovina and Croatia until the Croat Ustashe authorities in June 1941 embarked on its three-pronged campaign of forced conversion of the Serbs to Roman Catholicism, their deportation to Serbia and large-scale massacres. Although the Ustashe first eliminated the local Serb leaders – Orthodox priests, members of the intelligentsia and merchants – in August 1941 the Serb villagers rose in arms and cleared large parts of Serb-populated areas of Croatia and Bosnia–Hercegovina of the Ustasha forces. In November, the civil war between Chetniks and Partisans spread to these areas as well and the Serb insurgent militias – split into Partisan and Chetnik detachments – started fighting each other. In Slovenia, Macedonia and Kosovo, there was no mass uprising; an underground resistance movement operated mainly in the Italian zone of occupation in Slovenia while the quisling Albanian militias equipped and supported by the Italian forces effectively controlled Kosovo.

The German offensive in autumn 1941 drove the Partisan high command out of Serbia, first to Montenegro and then into Bosnia. Disregarding the Comintern instructions, Tito, in December 1941 in a town in east Bosnia, formed his first proletarian brigade, commanded by a Spanish civil war veteran, Koča Popović, a Serb communist who was a noted surrealist poet; this small unit formed out of the remnants of the Serbian Partisan units was the nucleus of the future Partisan mobile army. With this unit, Tito marched, over the snow-covered mountains, to western Bosnia where the Partisans were able to recruit a large number of Serb peasants fleeing the Ustasha terror. Most of the remaining Partisan units in Serbia were destroyed by the Serbian quisling forces which incorporated many former Chetnik units.

By early 1942, the three principal[2] sides of the civil war in Yugoslavia were:

- the *Partisans:* a resistance movement led by the Communist party and recruiting from all nations and nationalities of Yugoslavia;[3]
- the *Chetniks*: a resistance movement under the nominal command of general Mihailović, representing the government-in-exile in London; the movement was joined mostly by Serbs with only token participation of Croats, Muslims and Slovenes;
- the *Ustashe*: a pro-fascist movement ruling the puppet-state of Croatia whose armed forces were made up of Croats and Muslims, trained and equipped by the German army.[4]

Throughout the war all three sides fought against each other. Of the two resistance forces, the Chetniks came under sustained attack from the German army but generally collaborated with the Italian forces and with the quisling government officials in Serbia. In 1942 the Partisan forces were the smallest in number and operated under persistent attacks by all the Axis forces, the quisling forces and the Chetniks.

## NATIONAL IDEOLOGIES AT WAR

The paradox of the civil war in Yugoslavia is that both the pro-fascist Ustashe and the resistance movements resorted to the national liberation ideologies in their efforts to mobilise the masses and recruit fighters for their armed forces.

In the *Ustashe*'s view Yugoslavia was an artificial creation which the Serbs imposed on the Croats to deny them their freedom; therefore, to attain their national liberty the Croats have to destroy this state and to free themselves from Serb domination. But the Serbs had not only robbed the Croats of their historical liberties but they also contaminated, with their presence, the purity of the Croat race. Following an older theory on the racial origin of the Croats, the Ustashe ideologues held that the Croats are by origin Goths and thus racially superior to their Slav neighbours, the Serbs. Serbs are thus an alien Oriental (that is, Byzantine) element in the Croat lands which needs to be eliminated. Like the Jews to the Nazis, the Serbs were for the Ustashe not only exploiters but representatives of degraded humanity. The hatred of Serbs came to be the core emotional element of the Ustasha ideology. Together with its racism, Ustasha ideology developed a mystical fascination with rituals of violence and terror similar to other extreme nationalist and racist ideologies of the 1930s. During the war, this symbolism was ritually acted out by gruesome methods of killing of their

Serb, Jewish and Gipsy victims. As in many similar ideologies, the hatred and rituals of violence co-existed with an ostensible respect for the Christian and patriarchal values of the peasant smallholder family. But unlike the German Nazis and the Italian Fascists, the Ustashe had initially no programme of social engineering. It was primarily their racism, their anti-Semitism, their fascination with violence and the cult of their leader or *poglavnik* Ante Pavelić, that linked them with the ideologies of their political patrons, the Nazis and the Fascists.

Most of the Croat government and police – as well as the Croat Peasant party members – initially heeded Maček's[5] call and cooperated with the Ustasha regime. The Croat opposition to the Ustashe came principally from the communists, the left wing of the Croat Peasant party and the Yugoslav-oriented intelligentsia, all of whom were brutally persecuted by the regime. As the Ustashe held Bosnian Muslims to be the descendants of Croat nobility who converted to Islam during Ottoman rule, their ideology attracted various strata of the Muslim population[6] including many of the Muslim (and Croat) peasants from the impoverished mixed population areas of Bosnia–Hercegovina. Their insistence on Croat (that is, Muslim/Croat) racial superiority over the Serbs apparently appealed to the latter group whose self-esteem was bruised not only by their hopeless economic plight but also by their life in royal Yugoslavia under Serb-dominated officialdom. Apart from the plunder which it produced, the systematic murder of Serbs to some of them might have appeared a way of asserting their superiority and recovering their self-esteem.

In contrast to the Ustashe, the *Chetnik* movement had no single ideology nor political programme. In raising the rebellion against the German occupiers, colonel Mihailović was continuing the Serb tradition of armed insurrection against foreign occupation under the rather old-fashioned slogan 'With faith in God, for the king and fatherland'. For most of the rank and file the Chetnik movement stood for the traditional peasant way of life as well as obedience to the traditional authority, the king; or, in other words, it stood for patriarchy and a return to the pre-war social order. This was reflected in the Chetnik methods of recruitment and chain of command: the local notables, usually middle-aged regular or reserve royal officers, recruited peasants in their region of birth thus forming militias of personal followers over which Mihailović had little effective control. The efforts of a few Serb intellectuals who joined his headquarters to form a central propaganda and political organisation was frustrated by the lack of interest of Mihailović and his military staff. Moreover, in late 1942, during

Mihalović's move to Montenegro and eastern Hercegovina, a Chetnik congress endorsed a radical Serb nationalist programme which envisaged a Chetnik military dictatorship after the war, total political dominance of the Serbs in a unitary Yugoslavia, expulsion of all minorities, the re-education of the Croats and a collective revenge for the massacres of the Serbs. Partisan propaganda and their supporters in the Allied capitals used this programme to portray the Chetniks as a fascist movement. To counter this, Mihailović, after protracted negotiations, convened, in January 1944, a congress in the Serbian village of Ba attended by representatives of the Radical, Democratic, Agrarian, Socialist and Republican parties as well as token Croat, Slovene and Muslim delegates. While endorsing the monarchy, the congress proposed the formation of a federal parliamentary state consisting of Serbian, Croat and Slovene units with wide economic, cultural and social autonomy. At the congress Mihailović publicly repudiated any dictatorial aspirations and rejected all collective revenge.[7] However, the absence of an effective political organisation from 1941 to 1944, the openly anti-democratic and Serb nationalist stance as well as the policy of collective revenge against the Croats and Muslims greatly narrowed the Chetnik political base, severely hindering their recruitment efforts and thus contributing to their ultimate defeat.

The *Partisan* movement – or, by its official appellation, the National Liberation Movement of Yugoslavia – was, in theory, a movement of Yugoslav patriots, regardless of their nationality, committed above all to the liberation of the country from foreign occupation. Led and controlled by the Communist party, this was obviously an anti-establishment, if not openly revolutionary, movement which promised a more egalitarian world for the peasants. In particular, the communists' propaganda emphasised the treachery and cowardice of the king and his politicians who fled the country and left the ordinary folk to be slaughtered by the enemy. The Partisans were clearly not fighting for the king and they had no faith in God. The principal Partisan slogan of 'the brotherhood and unity of the peoples of Yugoslavia' projected a vision of equality and harmony of all nations, and not of domination by one or more nations over others. In practical terms, this meant that the Partisans welcomed members of all nations and nationalities to their ranks and systematically opposed any collective revenge against any nation. In addition, the Partisan assembly AVNOJ[8] in 1943 elevated the Montenegrins and the Macedonians to the status of constituent nations of Yugoslavia, increasing the number of constituent nations to five. Their recognition was meant to give members of these nations a stake in the liberation of the country and to recruit them for Partisan units. Apart from emphasising the distinctness and autonomy of Macedonians from both Serbs and Bulgarians, the Partisans took over the cause, propagated by the Internal Macedonian Revolutionary Organisation before the war, of the unification of all Macedonians into one state. This was a call for the creation of greater Macedonia, incorporating territories of Bulgaria and Greece where Slav-speaking Macedonians lived. The unification would offer this group both national recognition and a political voice denied to them in all the states, including royalist Yugoslavia, in which they lived.[9] In general, the Partisans' image as the only all-Yugoslav movement accorded well with the Allies' plans to re-establish Yugoslavia after the war.

In contrast to the Chetniks, the Partisan movement systematically organised national liberation committees in every liberated (and many as yet unliberated) village, putting their supporters in positions of power. In addition, there was a mass youth organisation, a women's organisation as well as various professional associations (for example, of doctors and teachers). A successful mobilisation of students and younger intelligentsia from poorer backgrounds provided the Partisans with an unconventional and youthful officer corps as well as dedicated propaganda and education workers. Education courses set up by the Partisans spread literacy and propaganda and trained half-literate peasant lads and girls for military and political tasks. Thus a variety of political organisations and education courses supplemented the Partisan units as conduits for the social mobility of peasant youths who were given an opportunity of a rapid military or Communist party career.[10] This grand endeavour of popular mobilisation raised the self-esteem and political consciousness of the peasantry in the backward, mountainous areas of Bosnia–Hercegovina and Croatia and enabled them to assume positions of power which previous political regimes had always denied to them. The 'brotherhood and unity' policy and the political emancipation and mobilisation of the peasantry probably explain why the Communist party, a small and clandestine organisation before the war, succeeded, during the war, in attracting the broadest segment of the population in Yugoslavia. The centralised and hierarchical organisational structure of the Communist party also enabled the Partisan high command to impose a high degree of control and discipline in its units, thus increasing its over-all military effectiveness.

In contrast to the Partisans' modernising ideology of 'equal nations' both the Chetnik and Ustasha movements appealed to the patriarchal values of the peasantry and claimed that their respective nations' survival required the defeat (or, in the Ustasha case, the elimination) of the opposing national group. The conflict among these three movements during World War II could be viewed as a conflict between a modernising 'equal nations' type of nationalism and two mutually conflicting ideologies of the 'dominant nation' type.

## THE PARTISANS AND THE ALLIES: TOWARDS VICTORY

As the Partisan proletarian brigades operating in 1942 in Bosnia–Hercegovina threatened the Axis communications and repeatedly captured towns from the Ustasha forces, the German and Italian military – together with Ustasha and, at times, Chetnik forces – launched a series of attacks, attempting to encircle and annihilate them. Having already broken through several encirclements, in 1943 the Partisan commander Tito attempted to stave off further Axis attacks by offering his cooperation to the Germans against the British and the Chetniks. The German army command used the negotiations with Tito to prepare and launch its fiercest attack on the Partisan forces which annihilated several Partisan brigades and their central hospital but failed to net their high command.[11]

The British military missions, parachuted to the Partisan headquarters in 1943, could not fail to note their determination to fight and their military capabilities. In the same year the British government decided to supply the Partisans with arms and war material primarily in order to maintain their capability of tying up Axis forces which would otherwise be deployed against the Allies. But later British decisions to switch all of their aid to the Partisans and, finally, to abandon Mihailović altogether were influenced by other reasons as well. The British Special Operations Executive officer in charge of the Yugoslav desk in Cairo was a dedicated British communist who waged a successful anti-Mihailović and pro-Partisan campaign in British official circles, by, among other things, suppressing British mission reports of Chetnik military actions.[12] But, irrespective of the suppressed reports, the British government was also aware of Mihailović's post-1941 policy of avoiding large-scale actions against the German forces (in order to minimise his forces' casualties and avoid German reprisals against the local population) as well as his narrow Serb political base.

In their endeavour to take over the role of legitimate government in Yugoslavia, the Partisan leaders, on 29 November 1943, called an assembly, generally referred to by its acronym AVNOJ, which appointed a provisional government, resolved to form, after the war, a federal state of five equal nations and numerous nationalities, banned the king's return to the country until at least the end of the war and promoted the Partisan leader Tito to the (previously non-existent) rank of marshal. Although at the time these decisions appeared rather far-fetched, in 1944 the British government initiated the formation of a coalition government consisting of the royal government representatives from London and Tito's ministers.[13] After the Soviet and Partisan forces liberated Belgrade in October 1944, Tito and his Partisan army had secured control over large areas of the country and the ministers from the royal government in the coalition faded into insignificance. Having achieved international recognition for his regime through this coalition government, Tito clearly had no further need for it.

At the end of the war, the Partisan army annihilated the remaining Chetnik forces in Bosnia–Hercegovina using British and Soviet supplied arms. Mihailović refused to leave the country and remained in hiding until 1946 when he was captured, put on a show trial for his alleged collaboration with the enemy and shot. The Ustasha leader Pavelić fled the advancing Partisan armies to find refuge in Spain. The military victory of the communists was, as expected, crowned by an election in November 1945. No opposition party contested the election and, as a result of widespread intimidation of voters and rigging, it produced the desired 90 per cent vote for the communist-controlled Popular Front.[14] From then on the communists were free to subject the country to their favoured experiment of social engineering.


THE LEGACY OF WAR

The war resulted in the victory of the Communist party and the establishment of a one-party state modelled on the Soviet Union. The war also brought much more extensive damage to the country than World War I: most of the communications and transport infrastructure as well as that of industry was destroyed. Millions of people were forced to abandon their homes or were rendered homeless and around one million (out of 16 million inhabitants of Yugoslavia in 1941) lost their lives during the war. The worst human losses were recorded in Bosnia–Hercegovina and Croatia where the Serb population was exposed to systematic massacres by the Ustashe and the Muslim population to Chetnik massacres. Around 300 000 Serbs (as well as smaller numbers of Jews and of Gipsies) from Croatia and from Bosnia–Hercegovina were victims of the former massacres.[15] As this amounts to approximately every sixth Serb living in this region, it means that almost every Serb family had a member killed in the war, mostly by the Ustashe. The Ustasha massacres were unprecedented in this region or for that matter anywhere else in Yugoslavia; no regime or movement in Yugoslavia had ever attempted to wipe out a whole national or ethnic group. The only comparable atrocities, committed by the Ottoman and Bosnian Muslim forces during the 1875 uprising in Bosnia–Hercegovina, were an orgy of punishment of the rebellious Christians but not an attempt to annihilate the whole Christian population. Similarly, the policy of reprisals adopted by the German army in Serbia in 1941, which led to the death of around 100 000 Serbs from Serbia, was an attempt to terrorise and punish the population for its support of the resistance forces.

The sudden and unprovoked Ustasha assault on the acquiescent civilian population left deep traces in the collective memory of the Serbs in Croatia and Bosnia–Hercegovina. In particular, it has produced a feeling of insecurity and fear of any government which, like the Ustasha one, insists on the Croat domination over Serbs. The communist regime was able to assuage these fears during and after the war, by enabling the Croatian and Bosnian Serbs to achieve full control of their local government and to have an influential voice in the Communist party as well as government in Croatia and Bosnia–Hercegovina. This is why the Communist party, until its collapse in January 1990, had been regarded by many Serbs from Croatia and Bosnia–Hercegovina as the principal guarantor of their security in the region.

The Chetnik massacres of Muslims in eastern Bosnia as well as Muslim and Croat villagers elsewhere (allegedly carried out in revenge for the Ustasha massacres of Serbs) created a similar insecurity and fear of the Chetnik Serb forces, in spite of the attempts by Mihailović to conciliate local Muslim leaders. The Partisans, in contrast, not only welcomed Muslims and Croats into their units but formed Muslim and Croat brigades commanded by Muslim and Croat members of the Communist party. The Muslim population thus came to see the Partisan regime as its protector against the revenge of the Serbs. As the ultimate defeat of the Axis and the Ustashe was in sight, this is how many Croats came to see the Partisans as well.

In accordance with its 'brotherhood and unity' policy, the communists, after the war, attributed all war crimes to the Nazi and Fascist collaborators, arguing that it was their collaboration with the enemy that made them criminal and led them to commit those crimes. This made the Partisans the only force allegedly untainted by war crimes and enabled the Partisans to taint any adversary during the war – Chetniks and Ustashe alike – as perpetrators of war crimes. While using the wartime massacres of civilians for purposes of its own propaganda, the postwar communist regime not only failed to carry out a systematic investigation of these crimes but also forbade the relatives to rebury and to pay their respects to the members of their families who fell victim in the massacres.[16] Although the Partisan forces refrained from any large-scale massacres of civilians during the war, they ruthlessly eliminated their enemies, real or potential, during and immediately after the war. In particular, they massacred tens of thousands of Croat and Slovene home guard conscripts as well as Chetnik fighters which the Allies handed over to them after the end of the war. During 1945 under the guise of the elimination of enemy collaborators, they executed a great number of merchants, wealthier peasants and members of the intelligentsia, in particular in Serbia, thus eliminating a potentially influential 'class enemy'.

The communist recipe for national reconciliation after the war was quite simple: national unity has been forged through the Partisan struggle of national liberation in which all the nations and nationalities of Yugoslavia equally participated and in which all the forces of national hatred and conflict were successfully defeated. To protect the newly forged national unity it is sufficient to cultivate its tradition and to continue to build socialism under the leadership of the Communist party, which will eliminate all inequalities, including national ones. National reconciliation was thus firmly tied to the myth of the national liberation struggle and the communist ideology. Once their ideology and the attendant myth of the national liberation struggle collapsed in the late 1980s, no other ground for postwar national reconciliation remained. In fact, the national ideologies which re-emerged in the late 1980s called not for a national reconciliation but for the final settling of old scores. The re-emerging Serb national ideologies assumed that Croats and Muslims were collectively responsible for the wartime massacres of Serbs and called for revenge and/or admission of guilt by the Croats and Muslims. In contrast, the Croat national ideologies, as we shall see in Chapter 7, minimise Croat responsibility for the massacres of Serbs and Jews, portraying them as minor and relatively normal wartime phenomena in which some Serbs and Jews willingly participated. The collapse of one, communist, mythical representation of the Yugoslav civil conflict during World War II thus led to the re-emergence of a score of old myths and the creation of new ones, all of which were in turn used for the mass mobilisation during the civil wars which started in 1991–2.

The civil war among Chetniks, Partisans and Ustashe during World War II, was, in part, a struggle for the re-establishment of Yugoslavia as well as for the postwar control of the whole of the country. The civil wars in Croatia and Bosnia–Hercegovina, which started in 1991–2, have been fought primarily for control over areas of Croatia and Bosnia–Hercegovina with mixed Croat, Serb and Muslim population which had experienced both the heavy fighting as well as civilian massacres during the 1941–5 civil war. Prior to the outbreak of the recent civil wars, political leaders of these three nations mobilised their respective peoples' support by stirring up popular fears which are grounded in the experiences of the previous civil war. For this purpose, the old national myths and ideologies appeared particularly convenient: in the framework of each of these national ideologies, the other nation(s) living in the area is viewed as a permanent threat to the survival of 'one's own' nation or culture. In contrast to the 1941–5 period, in 1991 pan-national Yugoslavism, transcending the separate national ideologies, was so firmly linked to the collapsed regime that it attracted very little support anywhere. Not only did the nationalists of each nation blame the communist regime for the ills which allegedly befell their nation, but, more importantly, the pan-national and pro-Yugoslav parties (some of which were successors to the communists) were not able to dispel the rising fears of the electorate of yet another bloodbath and to assure, as the communists had done before them, the safety of all national groups in the mixed population areas. In the atmosphere of rising fears, the field was left to the parties promoting separate national ideologies as the only guarantors of the safety of the national groups which they targeted. It is these resurrected and opposing national ideologies which have fuelled the most recent civil wars (see Chapter 10).

# 4 The Second Yugoslavia

## A FEDERATION AND ITS INTERNAL BORDERS

The first post-World War II constitution, passed by the communist-dominated Constituent Assembly in January 1946, abolished the monarchy and proclaimed the Federal People's Republic of Yugoslavia, the first in the series of people's republics constituted on the Soviet model in Eastern Europe under Soviet control. True to its revolutionary ideology, the Communist party of Yugoslavia set out to create a new state and a new society which bore no relation to the Kingdom of Yugoslavia except for its name. Accordingly, the new state found its origins in the rather mythical acts of self-determination of its five constituent nations – Croats, Macedonians, Montenegrins, Serbs and Slovenes – allegedly performed at the meeting of the Partisan assembly, AVNOJ, on 29 November 1943, and at other meetings of regional national liberation committees. In this fictive account, the five nations – or their members, irrespective of the federal republic in which they lived in Yugoslavia – exercised once and for all their right of self-determination by uniting into the federation established in January 1946.[1]

Following the 1936 USSR constitution, the six republics – Croatia, Bosnia–Hercegovina, Macedonia, Montenegro, Serbia and Slovenia – held the honorific title of 'states', while Vojvodina was an autonomous province and Kosovo–Metohija an autonomous region within the republic of Serbia. In actual practice, political power, once again on the Soviet model, was concentrated in the highly centralised Communist party and its highest executive organ, the Politburo, whose members were chosen by the Party's general-secretary Tito. Since his appointment to this highest position in the Party by the Comintern in Moscow in 1937, Tito had picked for the top Party positions those members who were personally loyal to him. During the war, the Partisan propaganda created a 'personality cult' of Tito, extolling him, through various marching songs and propaganda sheets, as the great leader of the Yugoslav struggle for liberation. Until 1948, this cult of Tito was second only to the cult of Stalin; after the break with Stalin in 1948, Tito's cult had no rival. Likewise, from 1948 until his death in 1980 Tito had no serious political rival in the Yugoslav Communist party or in the country at large: he was the undisputed Party leader who governed the country through a coterie of handpicked officials.

Like its model the USSR, Yugoslavia was a centralised one-party state displaying the trappings of a federation based on a fictive self-determination of its nations. In such a state, the borders between the federal units were of little practical political importance. This in fact was made clear by Tito in a speech during his first postwar visit to Zagreb:

> These [federal] borders... should be something similar to those white lines on a marble column... What is the meaning of federal units in today's Yugoslavia? We don't consider them a group of small nations; rather they have a more administrative character, the freedom to govern oneself. That is the character of independence of each federal unit, full independence in the sense of free cultural and economic development.[2]

Although there has been no official explanation of how the borders between the new republics were drawn in 1946, most (but not all) of them roughly follow the pre-1914 international as well as Austro–Hungarian provincial borders, almost none of which coincided with the boundaries between the national groups. Thus the border between Bosnia–Hercegovina and Serbia followed the international border between the Ottoman (later, Austro–Hungarian) empire, to which Bosnia–Hercegovina belonged, and the independent kingdom of Serbia. The borders between Bosnia–Hercegovina and Croatia followed, with only minor corrections, the border between the Ottoman and Austro–Hungarian empires, which, with the Austro–Hungarian annexation of Bosnia–Hercegovina in 1908, became a provincial boundary within Austria–Hungary.[3] In a few places the communist leaders substantially modified the old borders to take into account the nationality of the majority populations in the particular area. Thus the border between Croatia and Serbia (in the northern province of Vojvodina) was modified so as to allow some (but not all) Serb-majority areas (such as Srem) to be transferred to Serbia and a Croat-populated area, Baranja, to be transferred to Croatia. In a similar way the south Adriatic area of Boka Kotorska with a majority Serb or Montenegrin population was assigned to Montenegro. The former Austro–Hungarian province of Dalmatia and the pre-1945 Italian province of Istria were also incorporated into the federal republic of Croatia presumably on the ground that Dalmatians and Istrians belong to the Croat nation.[4] These modifications appear to have been rather arbitrary, given the range of similar modifications which could also have been made. In a similar

48

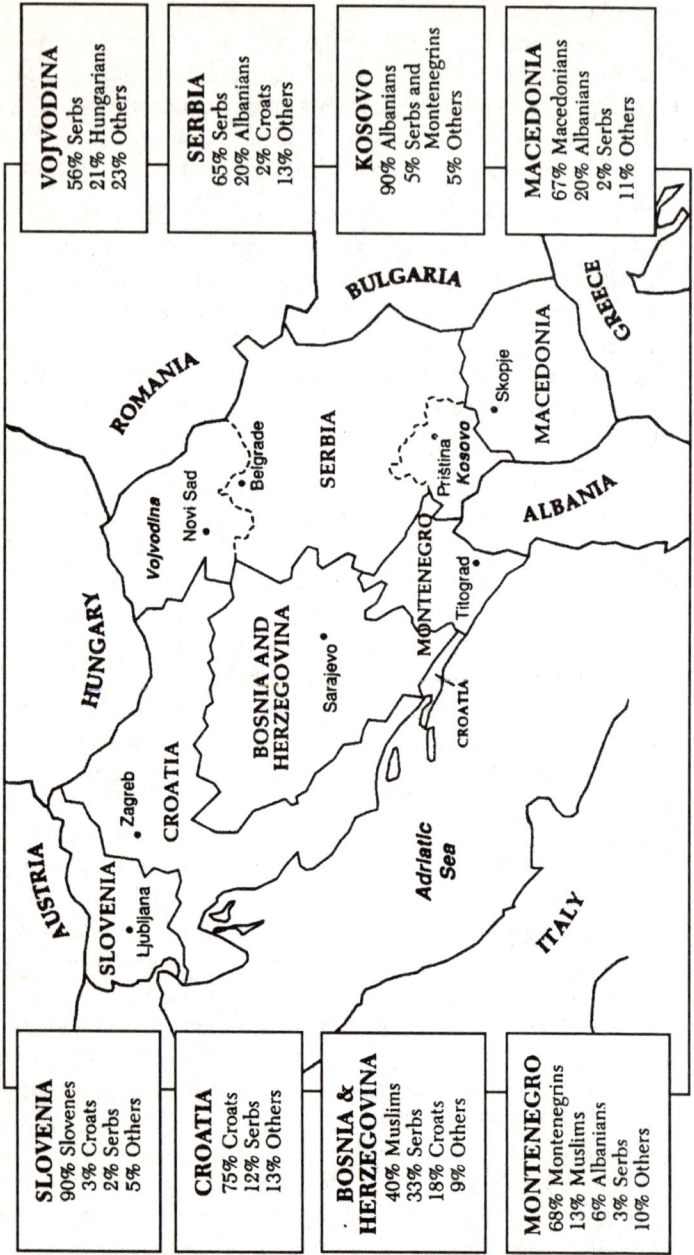

*Map 2* Distribution of national groups by republic and province (1991)
*Source:* P. Mojzes, *Yugoslavia's Inferno*, New York: Comtimuum Publishing, 1994.

**VOJVODINA**
56% Serbs
21% Hungarians
23% Others

**SERBIA**
65% Serbs
20% Albanians
2% Croats
13% Others

**KOSOVO**
90% Albanians
5% Serbs and
Montenegrins
5% Others

**MACEDONIA**
67% Macedonians
20% Albanians
2% Serbs
11% Others

**SLOVENIA**
90% Slovenes
3% Croats
2% Serbs
5% Others

**CROATIA**
75% Croats
12% Serbs
13% Others

**BOSNIA & HERZEGOVINA**
40% Muslims
33% Serbs
18% Croats
9% Others

**MONTENEGRO**
68% Montenegrins
13% Muslims
6% Albanians
3% Serbs
10% Others

manner, for example, the Austro–Hungarian (or Ottoman) borders of
Bosnia–Hercegovina could have been modified so as to include a few

TABLE 1  *National groups in Yugoslavia in 1991*

| Total population: | | 23 528 000* | Percentage of the total |
|---|---|---|---|
| **Croats** | | 4 636 000 | 19.7% |
| out of which in Croatia | 3 708 000 | | |
| in Bosnia-Hecegovina | 755 000 | | |
| in Serbia | 130 000** | | |
| (the remainder in other republics) | | | |
| **Macedonians** | | 1 372 000 | 5.8% |
| **Montenegrins** | | 539 000 | 2.3% |
| **Muslims** | | 2 353 000 | 10.0% |
| out of which in Bosnia-Hercegovina | 1 905 000 | | |
| in Serbia | 237 000 | | |
| (the remainder in other republics) | | | |
| **Serbs** | | 8 526 000 | 36.2% |
| out of which in Serbia | 6 428 000 | | |
| in Bosnia-Hercegovina | 1 369 000 | | |
| in Croatia | 580 000 | | |
| (the remainder in other republics) | | | |
| **Slovenes** | | 1 760 000 | 7.5% |
| **Yugoslavs** | | 710 000 | 3.0% |
| out of which in Serbia | 317 000 | | |
| in Bosnia-Hercergovina | 239 000 | | |
| in Croatia | 104 000 | | |
| the remainder are in other republics | | | |
| (Yugoslavs are those persons who declared their nationality as Yugoslav in the census) | | | |
| **Albanians*** | | 2 178 000 | 9.3% |
| out of which in Serbia | | | |
| (Kosovo and other parts of Serbia) | 1 686 000 | | |
| in Macedonia | 427 000 | | |
| (the remainder in other republics) | | | |
| **Hungarians** | | 378 000 | 1.6% |
| Others and unknown | | 1 070 000 | |
| (including other nationalities and those who refuse to declare their nationality) | | | |

* Figures rounded to a thousand.
** The figure includes Bački Bunjevci who were in the 1981 census counted as
   Croats.
*** Most Albanians boycotted this census. The figures are estimates by the
    federal census office.
*Source*: R. Petrović, 'The National Composition of Yugoslavia's Population',
*Yugoslav Survey*, vol. 33, 1 (1992) pp. 3–22.

border areas of Croatia (such as Krajina) where Serbs predominate while the Croat-populated areas of west Hercegovina could have been easily incorporated into Croatia.[5] Perhaps the communist leaders made only a few modifications to the historical borders simply because, in drawing the federal borders, they obviously did not intend to create six nation states. In fact, all federal republics of Yugoslavia, except Slovenia, were left with nationally mixed populations in various proportions. As a consequence of following the borders of the multinational Austria–Hungary, approximately 30 per cent of Serbs and 20 per cent of Croats were in 1946 left out of 'their' respective republics, Serbia and Croatia.

In any case, the new federal structure ensured that the largest and most dispersed nation in the country, the Serbs, would not be given so large a republic[6] as to be able to dominate the others. The equality of all nations – which in a one-party state serves largely symbolic purposes – demanded that no nation, Serbs or others, could dominate the rest in any way. By appealing to the national pride either of the newly emergent nations, such as the Macedonians, or of the nations such as the Croats, who had in pre-war Yugoslavia sought to achieve autonomy, this ideology of equality of all nations was used to mobilise support among these national groups for the Communist party and its leaders.[7] As the regime allowed no public dissent on any issue, it is difficult to estimate how wide was the support in 1946 for the new communist federal structure. During the late 1940s, the regime faced the opposition of small bands of guerillas (which were routinely branded either as Chetniks or Ustashe) in the mountains of Bosnia–Hercegovina, Serbia and Croatia as well as of Albanians in the Kosovo–Metohija region, whose mass uprising against its reincorporation into Yugoslavia started in 1944 and was suppressed, by massive military force, only in 1946. In view of the unrest among Kosovo Albanians which re-emerged in 1968 and has continued into the 1990s, it is doubtful that the federal structure which confined the Albanian population to the status of a national minority and Kosovo–Metohija (later Kosovo) to a sub-federal unit (province) has ever won wide acceptance among Kosovo Albanians or their educated elites. Apart from this, it is now impossible to gauge the extent of Serb *ressentiment* in the late 1940s at the separation of Macedonia from the pre-1914 territory of Serbia and the creation of two autonomous provinces within Serbia. This *ressentiment*, especially over the creation of the two provinces, displayed openly only among a few dissident intellectuals in the 1960s, became the major driving force behind the spread of Serb nationalism in the 1980s. It is unlikely, however, that disaffection with the federal structure in 1946 was very widespread in the rest of Yugoslavia; after so much bloodshed, most people accepted these federal arrangements as they would have any other ones which promised a modicum of peace.

The communist policy of national equality found its most successful implementation in the Party recruitment of its members and cadres. From a nominal membership of 12 000 in 1941 (of which 9000 died during the war) the Party expanded to around 140 000 by 1945 and to 500 000 in 1950.[8] The Party recruited its members and cadres (trusted party members appointed to supervisory and managerial posts at all levels) from all constituent nations more or less proportionally. As a result, the Party membership increased from 1949 to 1963 at a very similar rate in all republics and among all of the five constituent nations.[9] In fact, Party recruitment of new cadres could be regarded as both a channel of upward mobility of the under- and uneducated as well as a means of emancipation of the previously neglected strata and of unrecognised ethnic groups such as Macedonians, Muslims and, later, Kosovo Albanians. Although the number of Serbs and Montenegrins in the Party in the late 1950s grew out of proportion to their respective populations, this increase did not lead to their increased participation in the highest Party or federal government bodies. The recruited cadres were employed and promoted in their republic of origin while an attempt was made to achieve either proportional or equal representation of all nations in the federal representative bodies and in most federal ministries. From early on, a Party cadre or a budding official knew that his (or, more rarely, her) career was most likely to be tied to the cadres of his (or her) republic, even if he (or she) were to be temporarily transferred to a federal body. This policy created separate and well-defined political constituencies, consisting of Party cadres and officials from each republic with shared career and political interests. The cadre constituencies were the main beneficiaries from the communist regime and, therefore, its main pillar of support; they also formed a power-base for the future national and republican communist elites which came to the fore in the early 1960s. In this way, a successful policy of equal national recruitment and political representation led, in the long run, to the creation of national communist elites who in the late 1960s successfully dismantled the highly centralised Communist party structure and created, in the early 1970s, a semiconfederation of republics (see Chapter 5).

## COMMUNIST MOBILISATION AND CONTROL OF THE POPULATION

The Yugoslav communists took effective control of large parts of the country even before the end of the war. The Party nominally shared power with other parties until the elections of November 1945 when it dispensed with the need for any power-sharing arrangements. A small parliamentary opposition was effectively neutralised during 1946. From 1947 the Party established its control, through nationalisation and confiscation, over large industry, banking, transport and communications as well as in political life and education. Its drive to collectivise agriculture, started in 1948, was an attempt to extend its control over peasants which appeared to be the most recalcitrant group of all. Although the Party was able to mobilise, during the war, impoverished segments of the peasantry in some areas of Croatia and in Bosnia–Hercegovina, the smallholder peasants in other, agriculturally more developed, areas had nothing to gain from the compulsory sale of their produce to the communist government at the government-fixed prices or from the effective confiscation of their land through the collectivisation.

On the Soviet model, politics was practised as a form of administration from above. No public debate over any issue, including the nationalities policy, was needed or allowed. The debate, if any, was confined to the highest Party policy-making body, the Politburo or, at best in its Central Committee. All other bodies, including the legislatures, were in effect charged with the implementation of these policies. Every institution – from housing estates and municipal services to the army and government departments – had Party cells of varying size (in the immediate postwar days they were small – from three to ten members – but later they increased in size). Heads of the Party cells regularly received directives from and reported to their superiors, usually organisation secretaries of the district Party committees. Party directives, communicated to the members by their cell secretaries, ordered and exhorted members to perform specific tasks and offered explanations, in terms of the official ideology, of the current Party line and policies. Party members were, in turn, supposed to supervise and exhort non-members at their work, and, at times, at their place of residence.

While the principal task of Party members was to mobilise the population and supervise its work, the principal task of the secret police was to control the population by identifying and punishing recalcitrant citizens and by 'weeding out' enemies. Founded in 1943 by Aleksandar Ranković, a former tailor and a local cadre from Belgrade whom Tito personally promoted to the upper echelons of the Party in 1937, the secret police, at first known by its acronym OZNA,[10] was modelled on its Soviet counterpart. From its early days it created a network of informers in all places of work and residence and a vast archive of dossiers not only of suspects and enemies but also of loyal Party cadres;

apart from weeding out enemies of the communist regime, it served as a huge vetting organisation for all posts of importance.

## THE YUGOSLAV ROAD TO SOCIALISM

In spite of their evident loyalty and obedience, Stalin and the Soviet Communist party early in 1948 accused the Yugoslav communist leaders of ideological deviation and sliding back into capitalism; as Tito and his colleagues denied the accusations, the Soviet party called on the Yugoslav communists to remove their leaders. In order to identify potential supporters of Stalin, each Yugoslav Party member was asked to declare his or her opinion of the Soviet Communist party's charges. Many of those who sided with the Soviets had no firm ideological reasons for doing so but simply could not bring themselves to denounce so suddenly the previous official idols, Stalin and the Soviet party. Ranković's secret police rounded up hundreds of thousands of suspected pro-Stalinists, many of whom were victims of false denunciations. Tens of thousands of them were sent to labour camps, set up by Yugoslav secret police, to undergo brutal re-education at the hands of their fellow-inmates. In an unprecedented move, the Yugoslav Party Politburo in 1948 published their correspondence with the Soviet Communist party leaders, presenting their case as a defence of national independence from foreign interference. The clash with Stalin thus provided a second opportunity for the Yugoslav communists to mobilise popular support as defenders of national independence. Responding to the rallying call for the defence of the country, thousands joined the Party after 1948 and even those who did not, came to regard Tito's regime as a defender against the Soviet menace.

As the Soviet Union cut its extensive credits, exports and technical support after the break in 1948, the Yugoslav economy faltered. To exhibit its political and ideological correctness, the Yugoslav leadership attempted until 1950 to maintain Stalinist economic policies, including the highly unpopular and forced collectivisation of agriculture. The latter proved an utter disaster which, in addition to a severe drought, led to the Yugoslav request in 1950 for food aid from the US and its West European allies. As the grain sent to Yugoslavia averted a threatening famine, the Yugoslav government negotiated in 1951 an economic aid package with the USA, France and Britain and a military aid package with the USA; the latter involved the stationing of a US military assistance group in Belgrade. From 1950 to 1955 total US official economic aid amounted to 598 million US dollars (only 55 million of which were in repayable loans and the rest in grants); US military aid totalled 588 million dollars.[11] Of course, the Western economic and military aid was at the time justified in geopolitical and geostrategic terms: at the height of the Cold War and in the midst of the Korean War, the US and its European allies were in this way propping up an ally against the USSR. In response, the Yugoslav government in 1953 signed a pact of military cooperation with two NATO members, Greece and Turkey, forming the so-called Balkan Pact and, sometime later, settled its dispute over the city of Trieste with Italy. As a result of the break with Stalin, Yugoslavia, of all East European countries, was the recipient of the largest amount of Western economic and military aid. Foreign aid in the period from 1951 to 1960 became the source of 42.6 per cent of the all investments in Yugoslavia.[12] This huge inflow of foreign investment, mostly in a non-repayable form, could not fail to boost the Yugoslav economy, probably causing its take-off in the early 1960s. A variety of trade agreements with Western countries had also opened Western markets to its mineral and, later, agricultural products.

In 1950 the juncture at which the Yugoslav economy, as a result of the Soviet economic blockade, reached a crisis point, the Yugoslav communist leadership halted its drive for the collectivisation of agricultural land and decided to involve its working class in the running and management of their enterprises. The law on self-management enacted in 1950, the first in a long series of legislative acts dealing with self-management, required all larger enterprises to elect a workers' council of between 15 and 120 members which, in turn, would elect a management or executive board charged with the daily running of the enterprise. The workers' council was supposed to exercise an overall supervisory role, reviewing all the plans of the enterprises and electing and dismissing the executive board, of which the enterprise director was the only non-voting member. In practice, the workers' council was dominated by Communist party members who would ensure their election to the key positions. Although in fact instruments for the implementation of Party policies, these self-managing bodies proved to be less coercive and more participatory than any other instruments of the communist regime. Moreover, elections to the workers' councils, regular meetings and briefing of the workers, instilled, over the years, a sense of participatory rights and of personal worth to most Yugoslav workers. Every worker was entitled to the honorific title of 'self-manager' which put him or her on a par with Party bosses and enterprise directors with whom he or she was now to rub shoulders at the workers' council or executive board meetings.

Probably because of its non-coercive and participatory nature, the system of self-management came to be regarded as an effective tool for increasing economic efficiency. The underlying idea appeared to be quite simple: as the workers, apparently by their own will, made decisions regarding their output and productivity as well as partial distribution of profits, it was in their interest to carry these decisions out themselves. In the process they were supposed to grasp how the growth of their income is related to their productivity and output. As workers' councils provided non-members and Party members alike with a forum to air their views on strictly local issues, the arena for debate on public issues was somewhat widened as well. The system of self-management also slowly changed the way Party cadres operated. As the Party had to procure the assent of elected bodies in which at times it had no absolute majority, Party cadres as well as enterprise managers had to learn how to achieve this without overt coercion. In response to this need, the local Party bosses created patronage networks: in return for personal favours, their 'men' (and women) with whom all the elected bodies would be stacked, would deliver the vote on demand. The local Party bosses and their cadres would join a similar patronage network of a district Party boss and so on up to the very top of the republican and the central Party leadership.

As part of these reforms, the Yugoslav Communist party at its sixth congress in November 1952, changed its name to the League of Communists of Yugoslavia[13] and ostensibly transformed itself from a 'direct operative manager and commander in economic, state and social life' to a mere guide and benevolent supervisor of these aspects of life. In fact, the Party never shed its role of 'commander' until its effective dissolution in January 1990. However, its 1952 statute and programme replaced its Soviet Stalinist organisation with a less coercive and more broadly based type of organisation. From 1953, the year Stalin died, the Party's and secret police's surveillance of everyday life became more selective as well. The death of Stalin appeared to eliminate the threat of Soviet subversion; in consequence, the convicted Stalinists were released from prison camps and the practice of summary non-judicial imprisonment largely discontinued. However, the relaxation of control of everyday life did not mean the relaxation of the Party elite's grip on political power. When in 1953 the chief Party ideologist Milovan Djilas, in a series of articles, attacked the Party elite of which he was a member, he was forced to recant and later expelled from the Party.[14]

After 1952 the Stalinist model in art and science was also rapidly abandoned. The prohibition of 'bourgeois' science and art was lifted, allowing Yugoslav scholars and writers not only to quote and imitate freely Western authors and artists, but also to travel to study in the West, primarily Britain and France. The younger generation of writers and painters turned to Western artistic models, arguing for the autonomy of art from any political ideology. By the early 1960s the Party leadership relinquished control of artistic production, restricting itself only to prohibition of overly critical political works of art.

In addition to the relaxation of Party control, the Yugoslav road to socialism came to embody a foreign policy of nonalignment, which meant the refusal to align one's country to either of the two existing military and political blocs. The early adherents to these policies were found among the recently decolonised countries of Africa and Asia, such as Egypt, India and Indonesia. An active promoter of nonalignment, Tito travelled in state to nonaligned countries in an attempt to forge a movement of the nonaligned as a third, balancing force in the bi-polar world. In early 1961 his diplomatic activity was crowned with the first conference of the nonaligned movement held in Belgrade.[15] In the process he assumed his third public persona – the one of which he was obviously most fond – that of a world statesman. The previous two – the heroic resistance leader and a fiercely independent communist leader – were, in part, the roles he took on in order to gain and to maintain himself in power. The third – that of world statesman – was not instrumental in keeping him in power. It was, one may say, somewhat decorative, enabling him to mingle with foreign potentates and celebrities without bringing much tangible benefit to his countrymen.

## THE YUGOSLAV ROAD TO DEFENCE

Confronted with the threat of Soviet military intervention, the Yugoslav government from 1948 to 1953 kept a half-million strong conscript army at a high degree of combat readiness. While the army's numbers and combat readiness decreased after the death of Stalin and Khruschev's retraction, in 1955, of Stalin's charges against Tito, Yugoslavia maintained a large armed force of over 250 000 men until the late 1970s. In keeping with its nonaligned policy it also developed self-reliance in armaments and military equipment. Even before US military aid was terminated in 1958, the Yugoslav arms industry had expanded considerably. Most of the military equipment from the 1960s onwards, except for heavy armour, advanced aircraft and missile defences, came to be home-produced.[16] Military planning in Yugoslavia based on the

Partisan resistance experience envisaged a protracted war fought in the mountains of Bosnia–Hercegovina, Montenegro and Serbia. Accordingly, large supplies of arms and ammunition were (in particular from 1968 onwards) stored, at times underground, in these and other locations throughout the country. At the early stages in the civil war in Bosnia–Hercegovina in 1992, most of the Yugoslav federal army (the Yugoslav People's Army as it was officially called) depots in that republic were either evacuated to Serbia or taken over by the Bosnian Serb military providing it with a formidable array of weaponry and ammunition.

In 1969, partly as a result of the threat posed by the Soviet invasion of Czechoslovakia, the Yugoslav military devised a new concept of 'general national defence' to enable rapid and full mobilisation of the population in the event of a foreign invasion. Every person, including women, from 15 to 65 years of age was made subject to military or civil defence call-up. A second-tier territorial defence force was formed of reservists, commanded by local reserve officers and armed from their own local arms depots.[17] For this purpose the territorial defence depots, containing small arms as well mortars and light anti-aircraft and anti-tank weapons, were established at all larger industrial enterprises as well as municipal offices. All sides in the civil wars which started in 1991 were armed, at least in part, from these territorial unit depots. The Slovenian armed forces in June 1991 and the bulk of the Bosnian army formed in 1992 by the Bosnian Muslim government of Alija Izetbegović, were made up of the territorial defence units armed from such depots; so were the forces of Serbs from Croatia and from Bosnia–Hercegovina.

The Slovenian and Croatian governments in July 1991 proclaimed independence from federal Yugoslavia while commanding large, albeit lightly armed forces formed mainly from these territorial defence units or from reserve police units. Thus they were able not only to challenge the frontline federal defence forces – the much better armed Yugoslav People's Army – but also to exert effective control over all of their territory. Were the new Slovene and Croat national elites who came to power in April 1990 unable to create their own military forces using the territorial defence infrastructure and supplies, it is not clear whether they would have been ready to proclaim the independence of their republics so soon after their ascent to power. The system of a territorial defence force with its local supply base, however, merely facilitated the break-up of the federation and the subsequent civil wars. It was the fragmentation of Yugoslavia's constitutional structure and the devolution of power to the nationally-based political elites which started in the early 1960s, that had laid the constitutional and political groundwork for the final break-up of the federation in 1991.

# Part II
# The Homeland Fragmented

# 5 From a Centralised State to a Semiconfederation

## INTELLECTUALS AND THE REVIVAL OF OLD NATIONAL DEMANDS

During the 1950s Yugoslavia, in spite of its federal structure, was much more of a centralised state than it probably ever was since its creation in 1918. The introduction of self-management did not immediately change the centralism of the Party organisation nor did it lead to the devolution of decision-making onto the federal units. On the contrary, the Constitutional Law of 1953 which enshrined the first self-management principles and rights, abolished a separate Chamber of Nationalities in the Federal Assembly, no longer described the federal republics as 'sovereign' and deleted the rights of national self-determination including secession.[1] These constitutional changes were part of a general abandonment of the Soviet state model on which the first constitution of 1946 was based. However, they clearly indicated that the Party leadership at the time did not plan any further federalisation of the country.

These constitutional changes provoked a debate about the nature of federalism in Yugoslavia. Some Croat jurists pointed out that the republics had no right to self-government and that they, in consequence, had no real powers. Their arguments hinted – but did not state openly – that federalism in Yugoslavia was a sham. They and their Macedonian colleagues found the rescission of even purely formal attribution of the republics' sovereignty undesirable.[2] This first postwar public debate on federalism, restricted as it was to the legal scholarly journals in 1952–4, indicated that there were highly divergent views on the issue even among communist legal scholars and that the old division between the centralists – usually Serbs – and the federalists – usually Croats – survived the communist takeover and was re-emerging.

While reducing the formal rights of the republics, in the early 1950s the Party leadership initiated a campaign to instil Yugoslav national consciousness and to create a common Yugoslav culture. At the time Yugoslav national consciousness was firmly tied to the Partisan ideology of 'brotherhood and unity', according to which a Yugoslav patriot can identify himself or herself as a Macedonian or a Croat or a Serb or (...) *and* a Yugoslav, ready to sacrifice his or her life for the whole of the country. In this two-tiered approach to national identity, Yugoslavism was thus conceived as a rather vague supranational identity transcending but not abolishing basic national identities. In this vague form it provided no functional national markers: it was not possible to tell a Yugoslav from a Croat or a Macedonian or a member of any other established nationality. At the Party's seventh congress in 1958, Yugoslavism was further defined as a 'socialist Yugoslav consciousness' which is to be developed, in future, through the creation of a common Yugoslav culture. In attempting to create the latter, new all-Yugoslav cultural and professional organisations, providing new sinecures for approved intellectuals, had already been created and common Yugoslav school curricula and textbooks were planned. In 1954 in Novi Sad leading Yugoslav linguists had also concluded an agreement, establishing a common literary Serbo–Croat standard, with equal Eastern (Serbian) and Western (Croatian) variants. Apart from an official orthography guide, based on the agreement, the campaign for a common Yugoslav culture produced nothing of lasting value; no common Yugoslav school textbooks or school curricula were ever produced in Yugoslavia. Attempting to explain this apparent failure, in 1961 Dobrica Ćosić, one of the most prominent communist Serb writers – and the future president of the Federal Republic of Yugoslavia (1992–3) – hinted that the development of a common Yugoslav culture was hindered by the federal republics and their bureaucracies. In a brief but vitriolic polemic a prominent Slovene literary critic accused Ćosić of returning to the pre-war Serbian cultural unitarism and centralism (which, it was pointed out, was also endorsed by the Chetniks).[3] As in the nineteenth century and again in the interwar period, in 1961 many Croat and Slovene intellectuals obviously regarded Yugoslavism as a threat to their separate national identities. This is probably why they identified Yugoslavism with Serb hegemonism and dismissed it as a mask for Serb political and cultural domination.

Nationalist polemics in the early 1960s moved to the field of economics as well. Predictably, economists as well as politicians from the economically more developed Croatia and Slovenia argued that the decision-making on capital investments should be taken away from the federal government and that their republics should have control over their contributions to the economic development of the less developed republics. In this and all subsequent debates the Yugoslav economy was no longer viewed as a single economy but as a sum of its republics' economies. In this framework, the old question of economic 'exploitation' of the developed regions – Croatia and Slovenia – by the less developed ones was easily resurrected as well.

History, the favourite field of national ideologues, was next. In 1963 in a polemic with a well-known communist Serb historian, Croat historians – including Franjo Tudjman, the future president of the Republic of Croatia (1990–) – sought to establish that the state sovereignty of Croatia was preserved in the process of the formation of the communist Yugoslav federation and to rehabilitate various Croat national movements as progressive.[4] Croatia has always had a distinct and unique sovereignty which, they argued, had been retained in the communist federation. This, of course, was the old ideology of Croat historic state rights adapted to the new circumstances. The Croatian Party's reprimand of the Croat historians – including Tudjman – for their attacks on the official history of the Communist party did not deter major Croat cultural organisations from issuing, in 1967, a declaration rescinding the 1954 Novi Sad agreement on the Serbo-Croat literary standard and demanding the constitutional separation of the Croat literary language from the Serbian. This was, in fact, a declaration of full Croatian cultural sovereignty and uniqueness which openly repudiated any common Yugoslav culture. The declaration provoked a response by Serbian writers who, while agreeing to the separation of the two languages, demanded that the Serbs in Croatia be free to use Serbian (and the Cyrillic alphabet) and that Cyrillic be adopted in Belgrade television broadcasts and print media. While the Party's official reaction to both declarations was predictably negative, already in 1964 the new Party programme dropped any reference to socialist (or any other) Yugoslav consciousness and to a common Yugoslav culture: as an official communist ideology, by 1964 Yugoslavism was dead.[5]

## NEW COMMUNIST NATIONAL ELITES IN ACTION

As the intellectuals who signed the above declarations were only mildly punished for their transgression, it was obvious that at least some communist leaders found these new expressions of nationalism politically useful. By the early 1960s the communist leaders – members of Tito's old guard – in each republic had created their national clientele and patronage networks of middle- and lower-ranking communist cadres. As in the late 1950s younger university-educated Party cadres started to replace the older generation of Partisan cadres, they and the republics' leaders, their patrons, no longer shared the common experience of

Partisan struggle and endeavour. The only alternative experience they
shared was that of cultural background, language and nationality. Thus
from the early 1960s a budding Party cadre needed to share the nationality of his Party patron or at least be fully 'acculturated' in his nationality. As Yugoslavism was no longer the official communist ideology,
those who declared themselves as Yugoslavs only, found that they were
ineligible for any elective Party or government positions. In the late
1960s the Croatian Party leaders, launched a successful campaign to
secure equal national representation in the non-elective professional
positions in the federal Party and government administration as well.
From then on in order to get a job as a professional – for example, an
economist or a lawyer – in the federal administration, one had to belong to the approved national group whose representation quota had
not been filled. This rule did not apply in two areas only: the middle-
and lower-ranking posts in the foreign service and the Yugoslav People's Army, the two federal institutions under Tito's personal control.[6]

In this context, the traditional national demands, voiced primarily by
Croat and Slovene intellectuals in the early 1960s, could be viewed as attempts to rally the support of the communist cadres, the intelligentsia
and the general reading public in each republic for the communist elites
emerging from the new nationally based clientele networks. As each of
these elites aimed at the control of their own republic's economy, culture
and police, any federal institution or ideology interfering with these
aims was, by definition, hostile. In consequence, the ideology of a common Yugoslav culture as well as the federal secret police and federal
planning and investment bodies were considered obstacles to their
aims. In particular, the federal secret police under the Serb communist
Ranković was interfering, through its system of security vetting, with
the appointments and promotions of the Party cadres in the republics,
which the republican Party bosses considered their exclusive domain.

At a special meeting of the Party's Central Committee at Tito's residence on the island of Brioni in July 1966, Ranković was accused not
only of abuse of power through his secret police apparatus but of Serb
nationalism masked under unitarist Yugoslavism as well as of bugging
Tito's own bedroom. The last charge – which was denied by Ranković's
deputies[7] – was brought in to alienate Tito from his trusted prewar
comrade while the accusation of Serb nationalism was intended to discredit Yugoslavism by associating it with an aggressive nationalist
ideology and a repressive secret police apparatus. In spite of the Serbian communists' dutiful support of the charges against Ranković, his
fall was, at the time, generally viewed among communists and non-

communists alike, as a defeat of a Serbian bid to control the Yugoslav Party and the whole country. However, in the early 1980s many Serbs came to regard Ranković as the only Serb communist politician of Tito's era who protected Serb interests in Yugoslavia.[8]

As a result of his fall and the purge of his supporters from the secret police, the communist leaders of each republic gained full control of their own republic's secret police; each republic, through its secret police, became free to target its own internal enemies. In the late 1970s this devolution of secret policing made life somewhat easier for certain political dissidents: intellectual dissidents targeted by secret police in Croatia or Bosnia–Hercegovina often found refuge and employment in Serbia (but almost never the other way around) because the Serbian secret police did not see any danger in the political dissidents coming from these republics. As the reorganised secret police shed most of its huge informer network, life was also made easier for ordinary people and Party cadres alike who no longer had to fear retribution for any chance critical remark or a political joke they made. Moreover, with the abolition of secret police vetting of passport applications, every adult citizen became, in principle, entitled to a passport and to travel abroad. From the late 1960s an estimated one million persons, mostly as temporary 'guest workers', left the country, mainly for Germany, France and Sweden but also for North America and Australia. The emigration of labour – unprecedented among the communist-ruled countries at the time – not only relieved the country's unemployment problem but contributed to the further decrease in rural population. As a result of this wave of emigration as well as the industrialisation in the 1950s, by the late 1960s most of the Yugoslav population lived in urban centres and drew their income from non-agricultural employment. The unprecedented increase in the standard of living which all strata experienced at the time was probably a combined result of the increased government investment in consumer-oriented industries (often financed from foreign credits), the inflow of foreign currency earnings from Yugoslav 'guest workers' abroad; and a rapid expansion of tourism and hospitality industries in the Adriatic area (which, after the guest workers' remittances from abroad, was the largest source of foreign currency earnings).

## NEW NATIONS AND NEW NATIONAL MOVEMENTS

In the late 1960s the new communist elites now firmly based on their national clientele networks, moved to consolidate and expand their power in the republics and in the province of Kosovo and to increase their share of power at the federal level. Endeavouring to mobilise mass support for their policies, the new elites transferred old (and new) nationalist demands from the sphere of intellectual debates to that of mass politics.

The first to do so was the new Muslim communist elite: in May 1968 the Central Committee of the Communist party of Bosnia–Hercegovina proclaimed the Muslims a separate nation, the third constituent nation in this republic and sixth to be recognised in Yugoslavia.[9] The new constituent nation is a Slav ethnic group, speaking Serbo-Croat (or in Macedonia, Macedonian), whose members either profess Islam or who come from an Islamic background. After World War II they were encouraged to declare themselves as Yugoslavs, or to declare themselves as either Serbs or Croats or, if all fails, to state their nationality as undeclared. Only in the 1960s were they given the option of declaring themselves as 'Muslims in the ethnic sense'. As at the time they surpassed in number either Serbs or Croats in Bosnia–Hercegovina, they had formed their own communist intellectual and political elite in this republic. While the Muslim intellectuals offered marxist explanations of the evolution of the Muslims into a separate national group (see Chapter 7), their political elite sought to lobby Tito and his closest advisers for their recognition as a constituent nation.[10] This recognition ensured them compulsory representation in the administration and political bodies both in their republic and at the federal level. Tito's appointment of a first self-declared Muslim from Bosnia–Hercegovina to the post of Yugoslav federal prime minister in 1971, indicated that yet another nation had arrived in Yugoslavia.

After the fall of Ranković, political power in the province of Kosovo-Metohija passed to a younger generation of Kosovo Albanian leaders who, freed from the restraint of Ranković's secret police, quickly expanded its new clientele network of Kosovo Albanian cadres. In November 1968, coinciding with Albania's National Day, well-coordinated and in some cases violent Albanian demonstrations broke out in a number of towns in Kosovo and in western Macedonia. Led in some cases by Albanian students from the newly established university faculty of Priština (which offered instruction in Albanian), the Albanian demonstrators demanded that their province Kosovo be transformed into a separate republic. This would also mean that, like the Muslims a few months earlier, the Albanians (at the time a national minority of around one million) should be elevated to the status of a constituent nation of Yugoslavia. In practice, this elevation would give the new Kosovo Albanian political elite – like the national elites in the existing republics – full control over

Kosovo's economy, education and secret police. Coordinated demonstrations on this scale could not have been organised without the knowledge and tacit support of the Kosovo Albanian communist leadership. But, as the suppression of the demonstrations led to a loss of life, the latter was forced to distance itself from the demonstrators' demands for a republic. The new communist leaders in Serbia – who were installed in power only in 1967 – responded to the Albanian national movement in Kosovo by increasing the level of industrial, educational and infrastructure investment in the province. In the view of the young and well-educated communist leaders, Latinka Perović and Marko Nikezić, Serbia as well as Kosovo needed a modern economy, based on large and profitable industrial firms as well as a modern broadly based (albeit still one-party) political system. While undoubtedly modernising, their response did not change the Albanian demands for a republic of Kosovo nor stop their dissemination: small-scale Albanian demonstrations under the same slogan 'Kosovo – republic!' were organised in Kosovo several times[11] after 1968 and the Serbs and Montenegrins continued to emigrate from the province (see Chapter 6).

While the role of Kosovo Albanian communist leaders in the rise of the Albanian national movement in Kosovo was, at the time, not subjected to any scrutiny, the Croatian communist leaders in 1970 came to lead openly a mass national movement whose long-term aim was the attainment of sovereignty for Croatia and the confederalisation of Yugoslavia. Like its Serbian counterpart, the Croatian government and party leadership was at this time rejuvenated with the elevation of Mika Tripalo and Savka Dabčević-Kučar to top Party posts in the republic. Their patron, the senior Croatian Communist party boss Vladimir Bakarić initiated, in December 1969, a campaign against (Yugoslav) unitarism which, according to him, was still the main enemy of democratic socialism and of Croatian national interests. In defence of the latter, he made clear, the Croatian Communist party needed to mobilise the Croat masses.[12] Accordingly, the new Croatian leaders began a mass recruitment drive of Croats into the Communist party of Croatia and into various cultural organisations (such as *Matica Hrvatska* – the Croatian Hive) which were transformed into mass organisations[13] with a nationalist cultural and political agenda.

The rhetoric of the leaders of the new mass organisations in many respects resembled the rhetoric of the prewar Croat Peasant party with its principal slogan 'one is to enjoy one's own'. They argued that since Croatia had until recently been trampled upon, it needed to recover its true identity, by adopting not only its traditional state symbols (without the red star) and its own separate language (purified of Serb influences) but also by having its own territorial army (with the proviso that Croat recruits to the federal army serve only in Croatia). In addition, the foreign currency earnings of Croatia and the Croats working abroad should be allocated to Croatia and not to the Yugoslav federation. Moreover, the overrepresentation of Serbs (from Croatia) in the Party, government, media, industry and police needed to be rectified by replacing Serbs with Croats. Although the Croatian Party leaders did not accept all these demands, they initiated an ethnic purge (called recounting) through which a significant number of Serbs from Croatia were dismissed from managerial posts and replaced by the ethnic Croat supporters of the Croatian Party leaders.

After Tito's endorsement of the Croatian leaders' new policies in September 1971, the nationalist leaders in the student organisation and in *Matica* stepped up their demands, (including the revision of the definition of Croatia's sovereignty to include the right of secession and the incorporation into Croatia of parts of Hercegovina and Montenegro)[14] and attacked Bakarić himself. Reacting to the increasing Croatisation of public life, the local Serbs in Croatia demanded guarantees of their continued links with Serbia and started, quite publicly, to arm their population in the Krajina region in expectation of a possible conflict. After Zagreb University students went on strike in support of their favourites, Tripalo and Dabčević-Kučar, their erstwhile patron Bakarić and other Croatian communist leaders, in late November 1971, persuaded Tito to dismiss the two. In the wake of violent demonstrations of Zagreb University students protesting their dismissal, the principal leaders of the mass national movement were arrested and later sentenced to prison terms. Thousands of Tripalo and Dabčević-Kučar supporters were purged from their Party and managerial posts. This time, however, the new Communist party leaders, sensitive to the issue of Serb domination, did not replace the purged Croats with Serbs from Croatia.

Having purged the Croatian Communist party, Tito turned to the Slovenian and Macedonian Party leaders whom he purged without much difficulty. The Serbian communist leaders, Perović and Nikezić, accused of 'liberalism' and 'technocratism', resisted the purge by rallying their communist cadres from all over Serbia. In October 1972, an enraged Tito confessed in a newspaper interview that during the four days of inconclusive meetings of the Serbian Party's Central Committee he was confronted not only by a united opposition but by 'unfavourable and impermissible' comments about himself. After the two leaders were replaced by Tito loyalists, around 6000 of their supporters throughout the Party and managerial posts were also purged. Tito's purges of the younger generation of communist leaders and their clientele networks in these four republics in 1971–2 did not, however, result in the recentralisation of government and Party institutions but only in the recentralisation of political power in his hands and the hands of a coterie of officials which he selected and controlled. His reassertion of authority in this way, one can argue with the benefit of hindsight, set Yugoslavia on the road to its eventual disintegration if not to the civil war.

## A SEMICONFEDERATION UNDER TITO'S PERSONAL RULE

The Yugoslavia which disintegrated in 1991 was in fact a semiconfederation constituted in 1974 by its fourth post-1945 constitution. The drafting of the constitution started in 1972, soon after the purges of the republics' leaderships were completed. Its avowed aim was to extend the principles of self-management into all aspects of political, economic and social life. In pursuit of this, the constitution – then the longest one in the world – created a pyramidal structure of self- managing bodies at the apex of which stood a two-chamber federal assembly whose deputies, elected in complex indirect elections, were primarily responsible to their republican or provincial electoral bodies.

The top decision-making body in Yugoslavia became the state presidency, consisting of one representative from each republic and province, which elected its president, in a pre-determined order, on a rotating yearly basis. A parallel but larger presidency had already been installed as the governing body of the Yugoslav Communist party. The office of president of the republic, to which Tito was duly elected for the duration of his natural life, was to expire with the death of its only holder and to be replaced by the state presidency. The constitution gave Tito an almost unlimited right to conduct foreign policy as well as to command the military forces. The few other areas of competence of the federal government – common monetary policy, custom duties collection, funding of undeveloped regions and federal transport and communications – were all controlled by the republics' leaders through the state presidency and federal cabinet. As the state presidency had to reach most of its decisions by consensus, each republic and province, regardless of its size and contribution to the federal budget, was virtually given the power of veto which could be effectively overridden only by Tito. The members of the first collective presidency, chosen by Tito from his old guard, were drawn together by the bonds of their shared revolutionary struggle as well as their loyalty to Tito. In contrast to the loyalty binding all these leaders to Tito, the institutional bonds drawing the republics together were quite weak. Each republic had so wide a range of sovereign rights and powers that, in spite of the explicit attribution of some sovereign rights to the nations of Yugoslavia, the republics did appear to be both the sources of state sovereignty and centres of political power. The only areas over which the republican leaders exercised no control were those in Tito's personal domain, namely, the military and foreign affairs. By assigning only these two areas of state competence to an authority (that is, Tito) independent of the republics, the constitution of 1974 had made Yugoslavia into a semiconfederation of semisovereign republics.

Despite a complex web of self-managing bodies and councils, the way the Yugoslav president exercised his political power was likened to that of a semiconstitutional monarch. The ageing Tito (82 in 1974) aloof from daily politics for long periods, ruled through a small coterie of his old Partisan comrades and a few handpicked younger functionaries. While his chosen comrades ruled over their republics as their personal fiefdoms, the old marshal's undisputed domain was the military. In fact, in the late 1970s there was no Party or government body which could check or resist Tito in his exercise of power. Not only his exercise of power but also some aspects of his lifestyle came to resemble that of a monarch. In addition to his official residences in Belgrade and Zagreb, he used several hunting lodges (a few of which previously belonged to the Karađorđević dynasty) as well as a whole Adriatic island, Brioni (with a private zoo, among other amenities) to which Party and government bodies as well as individual officials would be often summoned for meetings.[15] It was there that Tito liked entertaining both foreign celebrities[16] – including film stars – and well-known Yugoslav intellectuals and artists. Often his travel from one of these residences to another resembled a royal progress during which the local populace and their leaders were expected to stage prolonged effusions of adulation. However, unlike other communist potentates, Tito had no use for nepotism; neither his two sons nor any of his relatives were given any high official posts.

## THE SEMICONFEDERATION AND THE CONFLICTING NATIONAL DEMANDS

In spite of their constitutional equality, the uneven level of economic development among the six republics and two provinces created persis-

tent disagreements among their leaders about the allocation of economic aid for underdeveloped regions. The poorer republics and
provinces – Macedonia, Bosnia–Hercegovina and Kosovo – continually demanded a higher allocation of aid from the central federal fund
whereas the Croatian, and, in particular, Slovenian leaders, refused to
countenance a continual drain on their resources for purposes of finan-
cing grandiose and often unprofitable economic projects in the underdeveloped republics (see Chapter 6). In addition, in the constitution of
1974 created a dual status for the autonomous provinces of Vojvodina
and Kosovo; these provinces were both constituent parts of the federation and of the republic of Serbia. In practice, the republic of Serbia
was virtually federalised: the provinces had full legislative autonomy
and their legislatures could, in principle, veto Serbian legislative acts
by refusing to endorse them. Even Tito's obedient placemen who took
the top posts in the Serbian Communist party in 1972 attempted to
find some way of redressing this constitutional anomaly. Although
their initial timid efforts intensified after Tito's death in 1980, the constitutional duality of the provinces' position remained unchanged. It
was left to Slobodan Milošević in 1987 to make the reunification of a
dismembered Serbia his battle-cry with which he swept Serbia and created a mass nationalist movement which surpassed anything seen in
communist Yugoslavia (see Chapter 8).

While the constitutional confederalisation of Yugoslavia met many
of the demands of the Croat and Slovene national movements, it raised
in an acute form the Serb national question. As the Belgrade philoso-
pher and legal theorist Mihailo Ðurić noted already in 1972:

> It is obvious that the borders of the present-day Socialist Republic of
> Serbia are neither the national nor the historic borders of the Serb
> people. In general, the borders of all present-day republics in Yugo-
> slavia... have more of an administrative than a political character.
> When they are understood as the borders of national states it be-
> comes evident that they are inappropriate, arbitrary, and untenable.[17]

Since the 1971 constitutional amendments (and their sequel, the 1974
constitution) aimed at creating national states out of republics, the
Serbs, he argued, need to re-examine their fatuous attempt to create a
single state for themselves in Yugoslavia and to struggle once again for
their 'national integrity', that is, unification. For these views he was arrested and received one year in prison. This harshest sentence meted
out to any Serb intellectual since the early 1950s probably indicated an
awareness of how destabilising the idea of Serb unification was to the

communist regime in Yugoslavia. The idea of Serb unification in one state implied that Serb loyalty lies primarily with the state which they share with all other Serbs. If Yugoslavia is no longer a state which they share with other Serbs, Serbs in other republics (and even in Serbia) need no longer acknowledge the legitimacy of the communist leaderships of these republics (because their republics were not part of the state of all Serbs). Even more dangerously, in striving for their renewed unification, the Serbs may demand that the republics' borders be changed to reflect their desire to live in a single state. This would imply not only a considerable reduction in power and territorial control of the already well-established national communist elites in Croatia and Bosnia–Hercegovina but would also create a huge and dominating republic. In 1988 the new communist leader of Serbia, Slobodan Milošević, incorporated this vision of Serb unification in his nationalist revival programme. As the opposition to his programme would show, no non-Serb political elite in Yugoslavia – whether communist or not – could agree to such a redistribution of power and territory.

Moreover, the traditional demand for the unification of all Serbs, conflicted with the traditional ideology of Croat historic state rights: the unified Serb state would naturally include Serb-populated territory of the republic of Croatia which, according to the Croat ideology, is a historical part of the Croat nation-state. The demand of each of the traditional national ideologies for a national state of its target nation would also require at least a partition of Bosnia–Hercegovina along national lines. The constitution of 1974 offered no mechanism for the resolution of the potential conflict of re-emerging national ideologies. On the contrary, one can argue that by abolishing any legal source of political power and legitimacy independent of the republics and provinces (except Tito's office of president) it ruled out the possibility of any effective arbiter of or check on their conflicting demands.

Further, the 1974 constitution exacerbated this potential conflict by leaving unclear who were the subjects of national self-determination in Yugoslavia. The constitution of 1974, like the first communist constitution of 1946, acknowledged the right of each (recognised) nation to self-determination 'including the right to secession' but then proceeded to state that on the basis of this right, the nations of Yugoslavia 'had united in a federal republic of free and equal nations and nationalities. . .'.[18] As with the 1946 constitution, this constitution also implied that this right had been exercised once and for all through the nations' unification in one federal state. The nations and nationalities of Yugoslavia, the constitution stated, exercise their sovereign rights in the republics and pro-

vinces in which they live, except for those rights which the federal constitution specifically identifies as coming under the federal jurisdiction.
The right of national self-determination had been exercised, the constitution implied, by the Yugoslav nations prior to the establishment of the
framework of the republics and is thus independent of this framework.
As the Yugoslav federation was not created through a unification of republics but through a rather fictive national self-determination of its nations, the Yugoslav federation was never defined as an association of
republics.[19] Thus the decision of the EC Arbitration Commission in December 1991 to assign the right of self-determination not to the six
nations of Yugoslavia but to the nationally mixed population of each
republic had no basis in the 1974 or any previous Yugoslav constitution
(see Chapter 10). In asserting the right to national self-determination of
the six constituent nations, the 1974 constitution suggested that any potential states to be formed on the territory of Yugoslavia could be based
on the right of self- determination of these nations, irrespective of the
republics in which they reside. This principle would, naturally, support
the drive for integration of the dispersed nations such as the Serbs and
the Croats and the consequent abolition of the existing federal units.
But by attributing sovereignty and statehood to the federal units, that is
republics, the constitution also appeared to suggest that they need to be
regarded as sovereign nation-states, in spite of the nationally mixed
populations of most of them. The conflict between the principle of
sovereignty of individual nations and the principle of sovereignty of
federal republics was neither brought into the open in the constitution
nor was any suggestion made how it could be resolved. The constitution
thus appeared to have suggested both the possibility of the formation of
six independent states out of its six federal units and an alternative kind
of state-formation which would not follow the federal units' borders and
which would be based on the national self-determination of its
dispersed nations. As the constitution did not address the possibility of
the dissolution of the federation in any way whatsoever, it did not
provide any legal or political mechanism for the resolution of conflicts
either over these two kinds of state-formation or over the territory of the
future independent states.

## TITO'S FRAGMENTATION OF YUGOSLAVIA

In the constitution of 1974 the communist national elites and their
leaders in each republic and province received constitutional guarantees of full control over their respective republics and provinces. The

fragmentation of Yugoslavia into six quasi-states and two lesser-than-a-state federal units thus appears to be directly linked to the evolution of the republics and provinces into powerbases for the leading Party officials. Naturally, the Communist party leaders, and Tito himself, could have tried to prevent this by creating an all-Yugoslav body of communist cadres – a constituency of communist managers and officials – capable of operating in all republics of Yugoslavia. Indeed, the promotion of Yugoslavism in the early 1950s might have been motivated by a desire to create such a body of Yugoslav cadres whose primary loyalty would be to the Yugoslav Communist party. This supranational Yugoslavism was, however, successfully suppressed and then finally discredited by its association with the effective head of the secret police Aleksandar Ranković.

The only leader who could have profited from the creation of an all-Yugoslav body of Party cadres – especially after the fall of Ranković – was Tito himself. However, he was so assured of the loyalty of the Party members and cadres of all national groups that he had no need to create a separate group of Party cadres with an all-Yugoslav national identification. He was also well aware of the opposition among most of his trusted, old guard comrades to Yugoslavism as a substitute national identity, and he clearly preferred using his old guard and their personal clientele networks as conduits of his power than antagonising them by the creation of an independent power base for himself alone. In order to replace the fragmented political elites with a single unified one, Tito would have needed a revolutionary political vision as well as revolutionary political zest and energy such as he had displayed in his younger days. After the acknowledgment of his victory over Stalinism in the mid-1950s, Tito had lost both; by this time he ceased to be a revolutionary and transformed himself into an elder world statesman, the role which apparently gave him more satisfaction than any other. The constitutional fragmentation of the country presented no obstacle to his rule and entrenched him in power for life. Moreover, the 1974 constitution, by replacing the office of president, after his death, with the collective state presidency, assured him a unique place – that of the last president – in the history of the country which, however, disintegrated only eleven years after his death.

# 6 The Loss of Legitimacy 1980–9

The politics of Yugoslavia from 1974 until Tito's death in 1980 was marked by the continuity of the rule of his chosen coterie of functionaries as well as by a proliferation of legislation codifying increasingly arcane and complex self-managing practices. Thus in 1976 all institutions and enterprises (including the secret police) were broken up into 'basic units of associated labour' which were linked to other such units through self-managing agreements governing all exchanges of services, goods and money. Shielded from the competition and the possibility of bankruptcy by interlocking agreements of this kind, unprofitable enterprises of all kinds were enabled to survive and even flourish. In this hierarchical world of self-management bodies all interests were to be 'harmonised' through discussion and agreement: the ultimate goal was harmony in a world of happy producers. The illusion of successful harmonisation was no doubt fostered by the absence of any overt friction among the republics' leaders belonging Tito's inner circle. Since Tito had made it quite clear, after the 1971–2 purges, that he would no longer tolerate any dissension, his obedient coterie obliged not only by avoiding disagreements among themselves but by denying any dissenting voices access to the public. In contrast to the period preceding the purges, in the 1970s contentious political views were barred from the official press.

The self-imposed harmony could not prevent the long-standing differences from reappearing in debates on the distribution of federal funds for economic development of undeveloped regions. The total transfers through federal funds to the undeveloped regions (comprising of Bosnia–Hercegovina, Montenegro, Macedonia and Kosovo), amounted to 3 per cent of the social product of the developed republics (Serbia, Croatia and Slovenia), which was deemed to impose a heavy burden on the latter.[1] In spite of this, in the 1970s and 1980s the undeveloped regions, with the exception of Macedonia, failed to improve their relative economic performance. This failure was due to the relatively high birth rate of the undeveloped regions (in particular, Kosovo) as well as to the widespread mismanagement of the investment funds by recipient republican or provincial governments.[2] The latter was one of the reasons the Croatian and Slovenian governments demanded the abolition of the central federal fund for undeveloped regions; instead of the fund, they proposed that the donor republican governments retain control over their contributions by directly investing in selected development projects in the undeveloped republics.[3] In the late 1980s the failure to meet their demands for reform of this system was increasingly used as an argument for the full confederalisation of Yugoslavia or, failing that, for Slovenia's and Croatia's secession from Yugoslavia.

The last years of Tito's rule were, however, not marked by premonitions of disharmony among his chosen successors but by a petty intrigue at his 'court' which resulted in his separation from his third wife Jovanka. In removing her Tito's coterie clearly wanted to ward off any initiative to remove them from power before his death: their position in power at his death, they believed, would secure them continued enjoyment of the same thereafter. Indeed, Tito's prolonged illness – from January to May 1980 – enabled them to organise a smooth transfer of power to the collective state and Party presidencies which they dominated. The spontaneous outpouring of popular grief at the news of his death on 4 May 1980 in Ljubljana certainly surprised the critics of his regime. The mourning crowds in Zagreb, as the train with his cortege passed through on its way to the capital Belgrade and the hours people from all walks of life waited in Belgrade to pay their last respects to him, undeniably exhibited the extent of his personal popularity. This probably encouraged his successors to believe that the political system created while he was in power was equally popular. The role they chose to play was that of faithful guardians of the system: their main mission, well encapsulated in the slogan 'After Tito, Tito', was to keep the system unchanged. But the economic crisis in which the country plunged in 1980 and the escalating national conflict in the province of Kosovo appeared to be insoluble within the semi-confederal self-managing political system they wanted to preserve. By 1988 the great majority of Tito's chosen coterie of republics' leaders had been replaced with leaders who had no common loyalties (to Tito or to anyone else) and a rapidly diminishing number of political interests in common. By that time, however, both the Yugoslav federation and the Yugoslav Communist party – the League of Communists – which nominally ruled the country had lost much of their legitimacy.

## THE ECONOMIC CRISIS AND THE LOSS OF LEGITIMACY

In his lucid account of this period, *Yugoslavia in Crisis,* Harold Lydall points out that from 1979 to 1985, the economy of Yugoslavia, in all respects except employment, showed downward trends: while the real social product (the Yugoslav equivalent to gross domestic product), investment and productivity plunged, employment grew by 16.1 per cent. Not surprisingly, average net personal income per worker in the same period fell by over 26 per cent. The downward trend in the economy was aggravated by a large foreign debt which, in 1982, stood at over 18 billion US dollars, amounting to half of Yugoslavia's annual social product.[4] Most of the debt was owed to Western banks and governments which, after 1973, went on a lending spree to many countries of Eastern Europe including Yugoslavia. The massive waste of foreign loans (raised in the 1970s) in non-productive or unprofitable investments[5] made the repayment of so large a debt very difficult. In 1982 the Yugoslav federal government's belated reaction to the rapidly growing foreign debt was to impose wide and severe import restrictions. These restrictions reduced the already declining domestic production and exports, making the repayment of the debt even more difficult than before. From 1980 to 1987 the Yugoslav federation was able to pay the interest but very little of the principal from this debt. Unable to meet its interest payments in 1987, it asked for a rescheduling of its obligations which was granted in 1988. In addition to falling production and a huge foreign debt, from 1981 the Yugoslav economy suffered from accelerating inflation. Periodic but relatively brief price and/or income freezes imposed by the federal government only accelerated the pace of inflation and discredited the government. Only in late 1989, under the new prime minister Ante Marković, did the government impose the necessary restrictions on the money supply which belatedly ended the inflation (see Chapter 8).

While some of the economic difficulties Yugoslavia and other East European countries experienced in the early 1980s could be explained by the world recession and the resultant loss of markets and increasing interest rates, the major source of the continuing economic crisis in Yugoslavia was to be found in the combination of the semiconfederal constitutional structure and self-management at the local level. As Henry Lydall succinctly put it:

> When socialist self-management is combined with federalism, it creates a whole range of new problems. For now each commune, with all its power over local enterprises, is combined with a 'national'

(republican or provincial) one-party state. In Yugoslavia each of these states claims the right to direct its own economy, to formulate its own plans, to determine its own investment priorities, to raise its own taxes, to control its own national bank, and even to establish its own balance of payments with the outside world...The consequences of this 'feudal socialism' are disastrous for the Yugoslav economy. Investment projects are duplicated, enterprises in one republic or province are protected from competition from enterprises in other republics and provinces, there is more trade with the outside world than with other republics or provinces within the country, obstacles are put in the way of financial flows across republican and provincial borders, and each republic and province tries to hold on to as much as possible of the foreign exchange for 'its' exports.[6]

The fragmentation of the Yugoslav economy, however disastrous it may have been, was a necessary concomitant of the devolution of political power to national communist elites in control of each republic and province; these elites naturally refused to implement any economic reform which would have resulted in the loss of their control over the major sources of their patronage in jobs and sinecures. Only when threatened with massive social unrest in 1988 and the resultant loss of political control over the population, were they ready to implement an economic reform which, in March 1989, they entrusted to a new federal government under prime minister Ante Marković (see Chapter 8).

The protests against the economic conditions in the country were gathering pace after 1982. The number of sporadic workers' strikes was steadily increasing until 1987 at which point 1570 strikes involving 360 000 workers were recorded, four times more than in 1985.[7] In 1987, as a result of yet another round of income freezes, the strikers attempted primarily to adjust their incomes to the rising inflation. Their main demands were rises in pay (often from 50 to 100 per cent) and removal of incompetent or unpopular managers and directors. The strikes clearly exhibited the failure of the much vaunted self-managing system to deal with the workers' demands. As self-management was one of the principal sacred pillars of the Yugoslav political system, its obvious failure to fulfil even the minimal expectations of the working population seriously undermined its legitimacy.

The wave of strikes in 1987 were not the only factors undermining the legitimacy of the system and its ruling elites. A series of financial scandals culminated, in August 1987, in the largest recorded financial scandal in communist Yugoslavia: the disclosure that promissory notes equivalent to 500 million US dollars had been issued without collateral by Agrokomerc, one of the largest firms in Yugoslavia, located in the towns of Bihać and Velika Kladuša in northwest Bosnia. The investigations into the scandal revealed a clientele network leading to the top Bosnian communist leader, the Muslim Hamdija Pozderac, which enabled the firm and the local bank to issue a seemingly limitless amount of promissory notes and thereby systematically to flout the law. Hamdija Pozderac was forced to resign after long and distinguished service to the Yugoslav Communist party while the director of Agrokomerc and a member of the Central Committee of the Communist party of Bosnia–Hercegovina, the Muslim Fikret Abdić, after a lengthy trial, was given only a suspended sentence and virtually cleared of all wrongdoing, to the rejoicing of his large constituency in the region around Bihać.[8] The Agrokomerc scandal, which received wide publicity in all Yugoslav media, undermined the legitimacy of the official political and financial institutions of Yugoslavia by exposing private and illegal institutional networks which top politicians used to enrich themselves and their supporters.

Faced with the continuing economic crisis, the Yugoslav state presidency, even before the Agrokomerc scandal, proposed to amend the Yugoslav constitution of 1974. The amendments – passed, after prolonged and bitter debate, in November 1988 – aimed at strengthening the legal guarantees of the unified Yugoslav market as well as federal control over the country's foreign currency dealings. As this largely symbolic exercise had no impact on economic performance, the Yugoslav constitutional arrangements no longer appeared to offer any way out of the worsening economic crisis which the country was experiencing since 1980. But the long-lasting economic decline and the resulting social unrest were not the only factors pointing to the possibility of the collapse of the Yugoslav political and constitutional system. More crucial was the rise of nationalisms which threatened to destroy the division and balance of power among the recognised national elites codified in the 1974 constitution.

In the March and April 1981 riots in Kosovo large numbers of ethnic Albanians, demanding the status of a republic for Kosovo, in effect demanded an unprecedented change in the Yugoslav constitutional structure. With hindsight, one could argue that the riots signalled the failure of the 1974 constitutional arrangements to satisfy the growing demands of the newly emergent communist elites and their constituencies, as in the case of the Kosovo Albanians, for political autonomy and control over 'their' territories.

## KOSOVO: THE HARDEST TEST OF THE YUGOSLAV FEDERATION

Since the late 1960s the province of Kosovo had an average annual natural increase in population of around 29 per cent, the highest in Europe. This growth was recorded only among the Albanian population of the province which from 1948 to 1981 more than doubled in size.[9] However, the increase in the proportion of Albanians in the population of Kosovo (from 63.7 in 1948 to 77.4 per cent in 1981) was only partly attributable to its high rate of natural growth; since 1967 – and in particular since 1981 – the emigration of Serbs and Montenegrins from the province had also significantly accelerated. The communist authorities had never attempted to control the birthrate of the Albanian population, and until 1981, it did nothing to halt the emigration of Serbs and Montenegrins from the province. However, the Yugoslav federal government had, from 1967 onwards allocated to Kosovo the largest proportion of funds from the Yugoslav federal fund for undeveloped regions: in the peak period 1986–90 Kosovo was receiving over 48 per cent of the allocation of the whole fund.[10] As a result, Kosovo in the early 1970s recorded the fastest economic growth of all regions in Yugoslavia. However, in spite of later increases in the total federal allocation to Kosovo, its economic growth throughout the late 1970s and 1980s lagged behind the more developed Yugoslav republics. Because of slower growth and an extraordinary increase in population, Kosovo remained by far the least developed region of Yugoslavia with the highest rate of unemployment of all. In 1986, according to the official statistics, the unemployment rate stood at 55 per cent of the workforce employed in the 'socialist' (that is, state) sector.

The unemployment problem was not alleviated by the founding of a university faculty in 1967 and the University of Priština[11] in 1970 at which most subjects were taught in Albanian. While from 1967 to 1978 the number of tertiary students increased sevenfold,[12] two-thirds of the graduates were in nontechnical professions with limited employment opportunities outside government and the educational system. Thus, the least developed region in Yugoslavia had by the end of the decade probably the largest number of tertiary students per capita. One could imagine that many of the unemployed or underemployed Albanian humanities and social sciences graduates found their plight particularly insulting since, in their view, the Kosovo Albanians had only in 1966 – after the fall of Ranković – been freed from intellectual and political subservience to the Serbs.

Apart from endemic economic underdevelopment, the region has, since the middle of the nineteenth century, been exposed to recurrent cycles of political and ethnic violence. From that time until 1912 its Serb and Montenegrin inhabitants sent a steady stream of complaints, detailing continual pillage, rape, murder and kidnapping by unruly Albanian warlords and their tribal followers, to the Serbian and various European governments. The Serbian conquest of Kosovo, in the first Balkan war of 1912, against the armed opposition of its Albanian population, ended this cycle of violence but initiated a reverse one in which the Albanians were expelled and harassed as opponents of the new Serbian authorities. After a large uprising of several Albanian tribes was quelled by military force in 1918–20, the Belgrade government imposed a Serbian administration in the region and settled over 60 000 Serb colonists on the properties expropriated from Albanian landholders. This as well as continual harassment of Albanians and other Muslims was intended to 'encourage' them to emigrate to Turkey. During the Axis occupation of Yugoslavia 1941–5, tens of thousands of Serbs and Montenegrins were expelled from Kosovo by Albanian quisling militias under nominal Italian authority. In 1946 after the suppression of the Albanian mass uprising (see Chapter 4) the Yugoslav secret police took effective control over the province, bringing Serb and Montenegrin officials in, wiping out the small Albanian intelligentsia, and 'encouraging' once again Albanians and Muslims to emigrate.[13] The fall of Ranković in 1966 ended the Serb and Montenegrin domination, as the Albanian cadres rapidly took over the majority of official posts, including those of the security apparatus. At this point Serbs and Montenegrins started to emigrate from the province, alleging Albanian pressure and harassment.

The Albanian demonstrations first erupted in 1968 (see Chapter 5) and were then repeated every few years (though on a much smaller scale) until 1981 when the demonstrations, started in early March at the University of Priština, later spread to major industrial centres in the province. Throughout early April 1981 violent riots involving more than 20 000 Kosovo Albanians engulfed almost every district of Kosovo. As before the principal slogan was 'Kosovo – republic!' although demands for unification with Albania were also made.[14] In some cases, demonstrators exchanged shots with police and, in others, used small children as shields. In response, the Yugoslav federal government proclaimed a state of emergency in the province and sent armoured military units and police to suppress the riots; the final death toll was officially put at 9 persons while the unofficial figures go up to a thousand.[15]

Although the worsening economic situation and the attendant unemployment were generally recognised to have contributed to the riots, the Yugoslav Party presidency, on the initiative of the Macedonian leaders,[16] dismissed the top Albanian and Serb Party leaders in Kosovo, initiated the first in a series of purges of the Kosovo Party organisation and authorised a police crackdown which resulted in the imprisoning of around 1000 Albanians accused of participating in the riots. It appears likely that in March 1981 the Kosovo Albanian communist leaders, like their Croat counterparts in 1971, encouraged or at least condoned the demonstrations, in the hope that, under their impact, the republican status of Kosovo would be brought on to the agenda of Yugoslav Party bodies. However, as the protests got out of hand and were transformed into riots, the Yugoslav Party leaders were united in their rejection of the Albanian demand for a republic of Kosovo. They probably feared that the demand, if granted, would spark a whole series of similar demands for changes in the established federal and provincial boundaries and that, as a republic, Kosovo would gain the right to secede from Yugoslavia and unite with the adjacent Albania.

The continuing disturbances and violence led to an accelerated exodus of Serbs and Montenegrins from the province. As the Party and government bodies could no longer ignore this trend, the official media started to publish monthly statistics of the Serb and Montenegrin emigration from Kosovo along with stories of intimidation, beatings, rape, property and crop destruction as well as the desecration of graves of Serbs and Montenegrins. The Kosovo Party organisation was instructed to implement measures which would stop the migration and a special combined unit of police forces from all republics was sent to the province to end violence and guard state property. Kosovo Albanian communist leaders resented the attention paid to the alleged harassment of non-Albanians and to their emigration, arguing that non-Albanians were emigrating in search of better employment opportunities and not because of alleged harassment. But the Kosovo Albanian leaders' access to the media outside their province was limited and their denials, in view of the increasing emigration, appeared as an exercise in damage-control. Moreover, offensive (albeit private) remarks of one of the Kosovo Albanian leaders about Serb women, when published, gave a distinct impression that he and his colleagues were not concerned with the maltreatment of Kosovo Serbs.[17] Whether really concerned with the plight of Kosovo Serbs and Montenegrins or not, the Kosovo Albanian leadership did not succeed in slowing down, let alone halting, the emigration of Serbs and Montenegrins. And, although they continued to prosecute Albanians for their participation in illegal demonstrations and underground opposition, until 1988 they successfully protected both the political autonomy of Kosovo and the dominance of the Albanian elites in the provincial Party bureaucracy. In the continuing purges of Albanians from managerial positions following the riots of 1981, dismissed Albanians were almost invariably replaced by other Albanians and not by Kosovo Serbs or Montenegrins. In this way, the Kosovo Albanian communist leadership preserved the support of its Albanian cadre constituency as well as the Albanian masses.

In 1985, however, the Serbs in Kosovo started to organise their protest movement outside the official Kosovo Party organisation. In early 1986 a petition of 2011 Kosovo Serbs to the presidency of the Serbian Communist party, demanding radical measures to stop the continuing harassment of non-Albanians, was published in a Belgrade literary weekly. After the first protest rally of a hundred Kosovo Serbs staged in 1986 in Belgrade, similar rallies, with greater numbers of participants, were organised in Belgrade as well as Kosovo and Serbian cities. The organisers of these protests were Serb and Montenegrin farmers, skilled workers, teachers and low-ranking communist officials.[18] This gave the movement the look of an anti- elite, grassroots movement of harassed Serb and Montenegrin minorities in Kosovo.[19] While the Belgrade media gave wide coverage to the protest rallies, the Serbian Party leadership, under Ivan Stambolić (see Chapter 8), was rather uneasy about them, because they reminded the public of the impotence of the Serbian Party to stop the harassment of Serbs and distracted attention from the officially set political agenda.[20] Naturally, the Kosovo Albanian communists strongly criticised the Serb protest rallies but, as the Serbian Party leaders did nothing to halt them, the Kosovo Serb movement went on to gather supporters and widespread sympathy among Serbs throughout Yugoslavia. The old grizzled Serbs in their poor peasant garb and distressed Serb mothers who travelled to the rallies became potent symbols of the suffering of the Serbs and the Party's indifference to their plight. In late 1986 their protests acquired a clear political turn as individual Kosovo Albanian politicians came to be targeted and demands made for the reintegration of Kosovo within Serbia.

In April 1987 this movement gained a most powerful supporter, the president of the Serbian Party's presidency, Slobodan Milošević.[21] As he arrived at a meeting with the Kosovo Party leadership in a small town near the capital Priština, around 15 000 Serbs and Montenegrins gathered to demand the end of their harassment. As the crowd surged forward to storm the building, the police – mostly Kosovo Albanian – beat them back with batons. Responding to the cries 'They are beating us...' from the demonstrators, Slobodan Milošević uttered the words which, in retrospect, appear to have changed the nature and course of Yugoslav politics and political discourse: 'No one is allowed to beat you'.[22]

Ecstatic to find a protector, the crowd responded by chanting his first name (which in Serbo-Croatian means 'the one who is free'). Having delivered an unprepared and stirring speech (see Chapter 8), he spent almost 10 hours listening to their grievances and returned the next day to Belgrade, an emotionally changed man, to urge the Serbian Party presidency to enact immediate measures for the protection of Kosovo Serbs and Montenegrins. Symbolically, Milošević's guarantee 'no one is allowed to beat you' took these two national groups out of the political 'jurisdiction' of the Kosovo provincial Party leadership and thus broke the post-1974 division of power between the Serbian Communist Party leadership and the communist leaders of Kosovo and Vojvodina.[23]

Couldn't he also take all other Serbs in Yugoslavia – those of Bosnia–Hercegovina as well as Croatia – out of the political 'jurisdiction' of the communist leaders of these republics? Couldn't he become the protector of all Serbs in Yugoslavia? At the time the communist leaders in other republics did not raise these questions – at least not publicly – partly because, in 1987, Kosovo, with its prolonged history of political unrest, was generally considered to be a special case. As the increased policing of Kosovo and repeated purges of its Party organisation neither slowed down the Serb and Montenegrin emigration nor halted the Albanian political protests and violence, the Yugoslav Party leaders appeared to have no answer to the continuing Kosovo crisis. To some of them Milošević's move probably appeared to be an effective way of removing from the Yugoslav Party and its federal government any further responsibility for the crisis. However, the inability of the Yugoslav communist leaders to find solutions for the continuing crises both of Kosovo and of the Yugoslav economy greatly undermined the legitimacy of their regime. In this context Milošević's move might have been viewed as a bold measure to re-establish the trust in and the legitimacy of the Serbian Party leadership. Unlike the Yugoslav federal government and Party bodies, in April 1987 the Serbian Party under his leadership appeared ready to try to solve the most protracted and violent political crisis in the history of the second Yugoslavia.

# 7 The Rise of Nationalism: From Dissidence to Power 1980–90

In addition to rapid economic decline and the outbreak of violence in Kosovo, in the 1980s Yugoslavia experienced a veritable renaissance of nationalist ideologies of the 'dominant nation' type. As we have seen, arguments based on national ideologies of this type reappeared in intellectual and political debates in the late 1950s and 1960s. However, in the aftermath of the suppression of the mass national movement in Croatia in 1971, the publication of any texts of vaguely nationalist content was effectively banned in all parts of Yugoslavia, except in Kosovo. While ending public polemics by national ideologues, the ban confined nationalist polemics to the closely watched realm of intellectual dissidence. All intellectual dissidents aimed primarily at the delegitimisaton of the existing communist regime in Yugoslavia. Nationalist – as opposed to liberal – dissidents argued that this regime had betrayed the principal national goals of their respective nations and thereby lost the right to rule over that particular nation. Each of the national ideologies claimed that the communist regime intentionally belittled and disadvantaged 'its' nation and benefited its competitor nation or nations. However absurd these claims may appear when taken together, they reveal how limited was the target of each national ideology: it was targeting only 'its' nation in its attempt to prove that the communist regime had failed that nation alone and should not have the right to rule over it. Apart from nationalist dissidents, marxist academics, contributors to the international philosophy journal *Praxis,* which was banned in 1975, formed an internationally well-known group of dissidents both in Belgrade and Zagreb. A smaller group of liberal political theorists and writers was also active in these two capitals as well as in Ljubljana. Although they often held opposing views, all of them were in the early 1980s united in their rejection of the communist regime. Many of them – especially nationalists and marxists – in the 1970s and early 1980s attacked the communist regime with the same ardour with which they earlier – from 1945 to the middle 1960s – supported it as its official apologists.[1]

As the regime, after Tito's death, appeared to be losing popular support, the dissidents were able to raise their public profile again. Revisionist historical works were published questioning the official views of the National Liberation Struggle and of the immediate post-World War II period. A leading publishing house in Belgrade, by an oversight, published in 1981 a collection of poems including several with transparently anti-Tito verses. The Party officials reacted by banning the offending works and at times gaoling their authors. But these actions brought much wider publicity to the dissidents than they could have hoped otherwise. Although they never commanded a significant following, their target audience, the intelligentsia, developed a growing sympathy for their views, especially as their dissidence appeared to attract – at least in Slovenia and Serbia[2] – only limited punishment. Intellectual dissidents, however differing might have been their views, appeared to offer a fresh and different approach to the problems confronting Yugoslav society which the Yugoslav ideology of socialist self-management could hardly explain let alone solve.

From September 1987 when Milošević started to purge the Serbian communist elite, the position of most dissidents – first in Serbia and then in Slovenia and finally in Croatia – radically changed. First they were allowed access to the mainstream media and, then, their republican communist leaders and media started to use the rhetoric of the dissident – primarily nationalist – programmes. This takeover of nationalist rhetoric was clearly an attempt by the communist leaderships in almost all republics to regain legitimacy through a change in their ideological image. In this new field of nationalist politics, communists-turned-nationalists soon faced formidable opposition from the very dissidents who first articulated nationalist ideologies. In late 1989 and early 1990 dissidents of all persuasions turned into party politicians, becoming leaders and founders of new opposition parties. In the first multiparty elections of 1990, in all republics, except Serbia and Montenegro, former nationalist dissidents won power. In Serbia and Montenegro the communist parties were able to retain power, in part, by taking over the dissident nationalist programme first made public in 1986. In retrospect, the 1980s in Yugoslavia could be viewed as a slow but steady march of nationalist ideologies from dissidence to power.

## KOSOVO ALBANIAN NATIONALISM

The Kosovo Albanian riots of 1981 were the first large-scale – and violent – manifestation of nationalism in Yugoslavia since the Croat mass nationalist movement in 1971. Like Croat nationalism, Albanian nationalism is based on Albanian historic rights derived from the alleged direct descent of Albanians from the ancient tribe of Illyrians who populated the Balkans before the settlement of the South Slavs. This is the argument from historical precedence: Illyrians, that is, Albanians, were there first and all the others – in particular, Serbs – are later conquerors who do not rightly belong to the territory inhabited by Albanians.[3] Within the framework of this ideological conception, the patriotic Albanian historians in Kosovo since the early 1970s engaged in research aiming to demonstrate the main premise of the argument, that the Illyrians or Albanians preceded the Serbs and other South Slavs in Kosovo and in Macedonia. In addition, Kosovo Albanian historians also wanted to demonstrate that the Kosovo Albanian contribution to the Partisan struggle and to the liberation of Yugoslavia was proportionate to the other nations of Yugoslavia. These two historical arguments were intended to prove the right of the Albanians to Kosovo and the right of Kosovo to be a republic separate from Serbia. Since, by virtue of their historical precedence, Kosovo rightfully belongs to the Albanians, there is no reason for Kosovo to be part of Serbia. As they fought for the liberation of their province and of Yugoslavia as did all other constituent nations, they should form a constituent nation with its own homeland – the republic of Kosovo.

Another aspect of Albanian nationalism – the demand for the unification of all Albanians into one state, Albania – was, for obvious reasons, confined to underground or dissident groups. The demand for unification or for an integral Albania was regarded in Yugoslavia as irredentism and separatism and was officially banned. But if one grants that Albanians are direct descendants of the ancient Illyrians then should not the whole territory on which they live belong to Albanians and not to any allegedly later settlers like Serbs or Macedonians. If this is granted, Albanians should have a historic right to their own state on their own land which would include Albania, Kosovo and western Macedonia.

In the above form, this is an argument from the primordial settlers' rights which one finds in almost all Balkan – and not only Balkan – national ideologies. As it identifies the possession of land with possession of statehood and sovereignty, its primary target are smallholder farmers, until the early 1980s the most numerous segment of Kosovo's Albanian population. In addition, the argument aims to convince individuals of the target nation that a denial of their 'primordial settlers' rights' – that is, the denial of a sovereign state for their nation – personally humiliates them and makes them into second-class citizens. In the context of Kosovo, the argument may also appear to justify any action taken to induce the 'later settlers' – Serbs and Montenegrins – to leave Kosovo; their emigration may help the alleged primordial settlers to get control over their land as well as over their state.

It was this emigration of Serbs and Montenegrins and not the spread of Albanian nationalism that provided a stimulus for the surge in dissident Serbian nationalism. As Albanian nationalism was confined to texts in Albanian, it was inaccessible to the great majority of Serbs. The extensive media coverage, in particular after the 1981 Kosovo Albanian riots, of the intimidation of and violence against Kosovo Serbs naturally demanded an explanation of these anti-Serb actions. The official Party explanation attributing these actions to fringe groups of extreme Albanian nationalists lost its plausibility as the violence appeared to spread and continue in spite of increased policing of the province. Serb nationalist ideologies appeared to many Serbs to provide a more appealing if not plausible explanation.

## SERB NATIONALISM

In contrast to Albanian nationalism which was, in one of its aspects, officially sanctioned, Serb nationalism was, until 1987, confined to dissident circles. In its early 1950s form, the Serb nationalist stance was strongly anti-communist. The communist takeover, it was argued, negated major Serb historic achievements: it overthrew the Serbian dynasty and it took away from Serbia its medieval lands (Kosovo and Macedonia) which were regained 'by Serb blood', that is, as a result of military victories in the Balkan wars and World War I. According to patriotic Serb historiography, Serbs in these two wars liberated their South Slav brethren from foreign oppressors. In communist historiography, however, Serbs were transformed from liberators into oppressors and the World War II royalist resistance movement, the Chetniks, was often branded as collaborationist and fascist as the Croatian Ustasha movement. In the process, communist historiography allegedly played down the magnitude and scope of the Ustashe massacres of Serbs.

The principal complaint – that the Serbs were the greatest losers and victims of the communist regime – was further reinforced by the provisions of the 1974 constitution which attributed virtual statehood to the republics and equal federal status to Kosovo. The Serbs, Serb nationalists argued after 1974, were divided among three states – Croatia, Bosnia–Hercegovina and Serbia – and were virtually made into a minority in their own ancestral land of Kosovo–Metohija while this province, under the truncated name 'Kosovo', had acquired a status equal to that of Serbia. The communist leaders further let the Albanians coerce Kosovo Serbs into leaving their land and thus helped create an overwhelmingly Albanian province 'ethnically cleansed'[4] of Serbs and Montenegrins. This systematic policy of revanchism against the Serbs was a result of a conspiracy of the top Yugoslav communist leaders, the Croat Tito and the Slovene Kardelj, against the Serbs. They simply continued the pre-1930s policy of the Comintern which branded the Serbs as the chief oppressor of other South Slavs. Moreover, the communists in fact collaborated with the Vatican in the subjugation of non-Catholic and anti-communist Serbs by the Catholic nations in Yugoslavia – Slovenes and Croats. In this framework, the forced emigration of Serbs from Kosovo was regarded as a continuation of World War II genocide against the Serbs: just as the Roman Catholic Ustashe and their Muslim allies massacred and expelled the Serbs, so the present-day Muslim Albanians are forcing the Serbs from their ancestral home of Kosovo–Metohija.

The main document of revived Serb nationalism in the 1980s, the draft memorandum of the Serbian Academy of Arts and Sciences, elaborated on the two main nationalist themes – the victimisation of Serbia and Serbs and the conspiracy of non-Serb communist leaders against Serbia.[5] The document, originally intended for the highest Yugoslav and Serbian Party bodies, also proposed a return to the 'integrative democratic' federation originally established by the AVNOJ assembly in 1943. Although it firmly rejected the constitution of 1974, the draft argued for the reunification of Serbs within a reconstituted Yugoslavia still ruled by the Communist party. Only at its very end, did the document concede that if other nations in Yugoslavia do not accept this solution, Serbs should consider alternative options apart from the reintegration of Yugoslavia.

In 1988 the Serbian communist leader Slobodan Milošević and the new communist elite he brought to power took over the draft's diagnosis of the Serb predicament and its proposed cure. He pledged to undo the consequences of the alleged anti-Serb revanchism and to unify the Serbs, once again, into one state, if possible, a 'democratic integrative' Yugoslavia. However, in his mass mobilisation of Serbs through a series of rallies and mass 'celebrations' in 1988–89 Milošević used almost all available Serb nationalist themes and symbols, including religious rituals (see Chapter 8). A series of historical events – in particular the six-hundredth anniversary of the Kosovo battle in June 1989 – were officially celebrated with mass rallies, political speeches and religious ceremonies bringing together 'The People, the State Authorities and the Church'.[6]

As the effect of the unification of Serbs in an 'integrative democratic' Yugoslav federation would be a Serb numerical predominance over the other nations, many non-Serbs regarded such demands as a transparent ploy for ensuring Serb political domination over other nations in Yugoslavia. Of course, this was not what most Serb dissidents – both liberals and nationalists – demanded in the early 1980s. However, the Bosnian Serb academic Dr Vojislav Šešelj in 1984 proposed a territorial division of Yugoslavia by its only three 'true' nations – Serbs, Croats, and Slovenes. This division would ensure Serb supremacy over large parts of Croatia, Bosnia–Hercegovina, Kosovo and Macedonia. This first open statement of 'dominant' Serb nationalism earned its author almost two years in jail. But, in 1988 Slobodan Milošević's rhetoric of resurgent pride in Serb military glory and historic achievement appeared to express the traditional Serb nationalist belief in Serb superiority over other Yugoslav nations, the belief on which the Serb claims to political dominance in Yugoslavia had been based in the past.

As communist Yugoslavia started to disintegrate early in 1990, the unification of Serbs outside the Yugoslav federation appeared to many Serbs as the option which was being forced on the Serbs by the separatism of Slovenes and Croats and not chosen by Serbs themselves. At that point Serb national ideologues started to argue that the creation of Yugoslavia in 1918 was a costly mistake embroiling the Serbs in a national conflict which could have been avoided by creating, in 1918, a Serb state out of the lands populated by the Serbs.[7] This mistake forced the Serb nation at the end of the twentieth century, to seek to establish a national state of its own while most other European nations already had such states for some time; in view of this, it was not surprising that the other nations strongly opposed the belated Serb moves towards Serb unification. In its insistence on a Serb nation state, Serb nationalism was returning to the nineteenth century idea of Serb unification of the Serbs in a national state, excluding their Croat and Slovene 'brethren'. As communist Yugoslavia started to disintegrate, the Yugoslav idea appeared to have finally lost its usefulness as a vehicle for Serb unification.

## SLOVENE NATIONALISM

The basis for Slovene nationalism was, traditionally, the belief in the linguistic and cultural distinctness of the Slovene nation. This belief was created in the nineteenth century by the Slovene men of letters who standardised the language and created a high-brow literature in the newly standardised tongue. The current Slovene men of letters – intellectuals – often considered themselves as successors to the creators of Slovene nationhood, whose main task was to guard, vigilantly, its cultural and linguistic distinctness. From their point of view the federal republic of Slovenia, and its legislative and political autonomy was the chief political instrument in this task.

A return to an 'integrative' Yugoslavia, as proposed in the leaked draft memorandum of the Serbian Academy of Arts and Sciences in 1986, would – in the view of the intellectual guardians of Slovene autonomy – present not only a threat to the autonomy of Slovenia but also to the distinctness of the Slovene nation. Partially in response to the draft, in 1987 the editors of the Ljubljana journal *Nova Revija* requested from a diverse group of Slovene intellectuals their views on the Slovene national programme. In spite of obvious differences in approach, style and content, almost all of the 16 papers argued for a sovereign state of the Slovene nation. In addition to the traditional argument from the Slovene linguistic and cultural distinctness, various philosophical, historical, economic, social and even religious reasons were advanced in support of Slovenian statehood. As the clearest indication of the lack of Slovene sovereignty, several contributors pointed to the absence of Slovenian armed forces and argued for the need to assert Slovenia's sovereignty through its own armed forces.[8]

All authors – among whom the future minister Dimitrij Rupel and the future candidate for president of Slovenia Jože Pučnik stood out – took a fairly strong anti-communist stand, either criticising Bolshevism or simply dismissing it. However, for most authors the most important question was not 'Why has Slovenia not become a sovereign state as yet?' but, rather, 'How is Slovenia to become a sovereign state now or in the near future?' In this the Slovene essays radically differed from the Serbian Academy's draft: they were primarily dealing with the future and not with past wrongs. Moreover, some of the Slovene authors, anticipating possibly their role as opposition politicians, offered surprisingly detailed political programmes, outlining the type of civil society and liberal political institutions they would like Slovenes to develop. But none of them dwelt much on Slovenia's future relations with the other nations or republics in Yugoslavia. They all saw Slovenia more or less separated from Yugoslavia, evolving on its own as a sovereign state. In fact, this separatism appeared to be shared by all of these otherwise highly different contributions to the Slovene national programme.

In spite of the initial – and predictable – condemnation of the document by the Slovenian Party leaders, within a year of its publication, some of the arguments put forward by the *Nova Revija* contributors found their way into the Slovenian Party press and became part of official Party rhetoric and policy. Already in September 1988 the Slovenian Party initiated new legislation to assert Slovenia's sovereignty and started transforming its territorial defence units into a state army. By 1989 most of the contributors to this issue formed their own political groups or parties which were committed to making Slovenia a sovereign state. From April 1990, those *Nova Revija* contributors who became ministers in the first postcommunist government in Slovenia were also given the opportunity to put their separatist national programme into action and to create a sovereign Slovene state with its own armed forces.

## CROAT NATIONALISM

In contrast to Slovene nationalism, which openly preached separatism, Croat nationalism, in the 1980s, mainly continued the tradition of the Croat nationalist movement from the 1970s in demanding a thorough confederalisation of Yugoslavia. Yugoslavia needed to be transformed into an association of truly equal and fully sovereign nations. Sovereignty for each nation demands its full control of all aspects of its life. Like their Slovene counterparts, Croat national ideologues viewed the creation of national armed forces as an essential aspect of national sovereignty. But unlike their Slovene counterparts, the Croat ideologues were also able to refer to the myth of the unbroken historical line of Croatian statehood, starting in the tenth century (see Chapter 1). In the 1980s this unbroken line came to include both the pro-fascist Independent State of Croatia (1941–5) and the post-1945 federal republic of Croatia. The argument of the unbroken line of Croatian statehood, in the past, was used to support the demands for outright Croatian independence and for a sovereign Croatia in a confederal association. While the former demand had never been abandoned, the principal national ideologues of the 1980s, such as Dr Franjo Tudjman,[9] opted for the latter, at least in the short term. As international factors – including the European Community countries – would not favour outright secession, Croatian sovereignty should be achieved through an association of nations and states modelled on the European Community.

But if the Ustasha state is included in the unbroken line of Croat statehood, then one could argue that the future sovereign Croatia, like the Ustasha state, should also include Bosnia–Hercegovina. While this claim was rarely made in public statements, there was no doubt that at least Croat-populated areas of this republic were ear-marked as part of the planned Croatian state.[10] But even if limited to the minimal claim of the Yugoslav federal republic of Croatia, the planned national state would include a sizeable Serb minority. This Serb minority, in the eyes of Croat nationalists, in communist Yugoslavia was given a privileged status in Croatia on the grounds that it was in World War II a target of Croatian Ustashe genocide. This privileged status was not only codified in the Croatian constitution – according to which both Serbs and Croats were the constituent nations of Croatia – but manifested in the highly disproportionate numbers of Serbs in the Croatian Communist party. In order to establish the Croatian right to treat Serbs as any other national minority, it appeared necessary to refute the claim that Serbs were a special target of the Croatian Ustashe genocide during World War II. One of the leading Croat dissidents, the historian Dr Franjo Tudjman, from the early 1970s took it upon himself to refute this claim. His argument was that the total number of victims of the Ustashe terror during World War II was not more than 60 000 and that most of the victims were of non-Serb nationality – Jews, Gipsies and anti-fascist Croats. While Ustashe terror was undoubtedly criminal, it did not differ much from either the Chetnik or Partisan terror nor from the Allied bombing of the German and Japanese cities.[11] This explanation of the Ustashe terror is, in Dr Tudjman's work, embedded in a general philosophy of history according to which mass terror and genocide are permanent features of human history: a nation, such as the Jews, which was once a target of genocide, often proceeds to commit genocide against others (Jews against Palestinians).[12] Neither were the Serbs the unique target of Ustashe terror nor was this terror in its historical context unique. Anyone who argues to the contrary, Dr Tudjman claims, is a Serb nationalist attempting to denigrate the Croat nation.

In the view of Dr Tudjman and his followers, this argument disposes of any special rights which Croatian Serbs could claim on the basis of their historical experience. Serbs in Croatia, in their view, have always been a minority like any other. Since no minority in European states has a right of self-determination, Serbs in Croatia – whatever its final borders – have no such right either. For example, to claim for the Serbs of Croatia a right to choose to unite with their co-nationals in Bosnia and Serbia – or even to form their own mini-state within Croatia – is only an attempt to expand the state of Serbia beyond its historical and 'natural' borders on the river Drina. Thus, any right of self-determination of Croatian Serbs is regarded only as a cover for greater Serbian expansionism. In Croatia, however defined, only the Croat nation has the right of self- determination or the right to statehood.

Through this re-evaluation of the Croatian Ustashe past and removing the stigma of genocide Dr Tudjman was also recovering the rightful dignity of the Croat nation: no longer will a Croatian child have any reason to say 'I do not want to be a Croat' from shame at the Ustashe crimes.[13] But such a re-evaluation of the past also revives the memory of the (alleged) genocide committed against the Croats by the Chetniks and Partisans. This memory, in turn, warns of the need for a sovereign state with an armed force capable of protecting the Croat nation. But unlike Serb nationalism of the 1980s, Croat nationalism went beyond the re-evaluation of the past in its project for a future confederation of equal and sovereign nations modelled on the European Community.

Upon his election as president of Croatia, in April 1990, Dr Franjo Tudjman and his government proceeded to carry out the nationalist political programme contained in his earlier writings. First, the Croatian government instituted a thorough purge of Serbs in governmental, managerial and media positions. Then it proceeded to change the constitution, deleting the reference to Serbs as a constituent nation of Croatia and returning the historic symbols of Croatian statehood, also used by the Ustasha regime. Finally, it began creating its own national armed forces while at the same time proposing, together with the Slovenian government, the transformation of Yugoslavia into a confederation of sovereign states.

## MUSLIM NATIONALISM

In Bosnia–Hercegovina Muslim national ideologies developed in two quite distinct forms. The first was an officially sanctioned non-religious ideology which explained and vindicated the belated recognition of the Muslim nation as the sixth constituent nation in Yugoslavia in 1968. The second was a pan-Islamist national ideology which continued the tradition of the religious and political movement Young Muslims (*Mladi muslimani*) formed in March 1941 in Sarajevo. Unlike the first, the second form was officially banned and its adherents imprisoned in the 1980s.

According to the officially sanctioned ideology, the Muslims 'affirmed their socio-ethnic identity through the creation of a synthesis of spiritual traditions and new spiritual, literary, political and cultural features',[14] The process of affirmation culminated in communist Yugoslavia with the recognition of Muslims, first through the introduction, in 1948, of the census category of 'Muslims of undeclared nationality', which was finally transformed into the 1971 census category of 'Muslims' under the 'stated nationality' rubric. Without the support of the Yugoslav Communist Party, the official account implied, the Muslims of Yugoslavia would not have achieved their nationhood nor the recognition it required. But since on a marxist account, the religious affiliation could not be the key or persistent marker of a national group, Islam could have only served as an initial stimulus in the genesis of this nation.

In contrast to the official version, the pan-Islamist version of Muslim nationalism regarded Islam as the immutable core of Muslim national and political identity. From its beginning in 1941 in the Young Muslims, this ideology emphasised the education of Muslims in the correct Islamic spirit, the creation of a true Islamic society and the liberation and unification of the Islamic world.[15] While the communist authorities were able to suppress the organisation in the late 1940s by imprisoning and even executing some of its members, two of them, Alija Izetbegović[16] and Omer Behman, emerged in the late 1960s as leaders of informal discussion groups consisting mainly of students of Muslim *medresa* or seminaries. In 1970 Izetbegović wrote and circulated among members of this circle a short treatise entitled *The Islamic Declaration: A Programme of the Islamisation of Muslims and Muslim peoples.*[17]

The aim of this program was to emancipate Muslim peoples from foreign – communist (Eastern) and capitalist (Western) – influences through a revival of an authentic Islamic consciousness. The main premise of the work is that Islam offers a comprehensive and distinct model of individual, social and political life which the Muslim faithful should embrace without having to look for any other non-Islamic models. In its insistence on the revival of the original Islamic model, the programme resembles other fundamentalist Islamic programmes as well as revivalist nationalist programmes in other parts of the world. Although the details of Islamic political organisation are left quite vague, the following three 'republican' principles of political order are deemed to be essential: '(1) The electibility of the head of state (2) the accountability of the head of state to the people (3) the obligation of solving communally general and social issues.'[18] However, the 'attainment of the Islamic order /is/ a sacrosanct goal which cannot be overridden by any vote'. In other words, while the above 'republican' principles are applicable in an Islamic state, the ultimate goal of establishing such a state is not

subject to a democratic procedure of any kind; the institution of an Islamic state is a divinely proclaimed historical goal.

But an Islamic movement can take over political power only when it is
morally and numerically sufficiently strong not only to overthrow the existing non-Islamic authority but also to build a new Islamic one.[19] The Islamic order would prohibit all forms of 'alcoholic intoxication of the
people', public and secret prostitution, all forms of pornography, casi-
nos, night and dancing clubs as well as other forms of entertainment
which are incompatible with Islamic moral precepts.[20] Given the treatise's insistence on the introduction of Islamic law, it is not clear whether
it envisaged any political participation of non-Muslims in an Islamic
state; its application of Islamic legal and moral precepts would obviously restrict non-Muslims' civil rights and liberties. For the main
principle of Islamic order, the unity of faith and politics, leads, among
others, to the following 'first and most important' conclusion:

> There is no peace or coexistence between the 'Islamic faith' and non-
> Islamic social and political institutions. The non-functioning of these
> institutions and the instability of regimes in Muslim countries, which
> is manifested in frequent changes and coups d'etat, is most frequently a
> consequence of their a priori opposition to Islam. Claiming its right to
> order its own world alone, Islam clearly rules out the right and the
> possibility of the application of any foreign ideology in its own region.
> There is, therefore, no lay principle, and the state ought to be a re-
> flection of and to support the moral concepts of the religion.[21]

Since Islam is a supranational religion, an Islamic state would not be
a national state. Yet it is to be established in any country – such as Paki-
stan – in which Muslims form a majority.[22] In 1970 in Bosnia–Hercegovina Muslims formed a relative but not an absolute majority of slightly
less than 40 per cent of the population. But as the Muslim birth rate
was the highest of all three principal national groups in Bosnia–Hercegovina and the Serb and Croat rates of emigration from the republic
were much higher than the Muslim one, the Muslims could be expected to reach an absolute majority in the foreseeable future.[23]

But regardless of any demographic predictions, Izetbegović's programme linked Muslim national identity with politics in a simple and
easily intelligible way. It is a person's Muslim religion which defines
their national identity; and as it defines the core of their identity, it
also defines their political preferences. A Muslim's true allegiance is to
an Islamic movement which aims at the affirmation of Muslim religious and moral conceptions in all spheres of life, including politics.

In 1990, Izetbegović and the members of his circle founded the Islamic political movement which Islam, in their opinion, required. This was the Party of Democratic Action (*Stranka demokratske akcije* – *SDA*) which in the elections of 1990 in Bosnia-Hercegovina won a relative majority in the parliament enabling its leader Izetbegović to be elected the president of the republic's collective presidency (see Chapter 8). While affirming Islamic values, this party avoided any commitment to the creation of an Islamic state in Bosnia–Hercegovina. Its goals were restricted to the spiritual regeneration of the Muslim nation, its political and social organisation and to the takeover of positions of power in all Muslim-populated areas of Yugoslavia. This 'takeover of power'[24] was to serve further affirmation of the Muslim nation and its Islamic values in all spheres of life. In terms of the *Islamic Declaration* (reprinted, in 1990, in 10 000 copies), this is the work preparatory to the creation of an Islamic society. The affirmation of Muslim religious and moral conceptions within a project for the creation of an Islamic society was, for many Serbs and Croats in Bosnia–Hercegovina, associated with the Ottoman social order in which the Muslims held political power and owned most of the land. In this Islamic society, the non-Muslims – Serbs and Croats – were second-class citizens with no political and restricted civil rights. In this context, the affirmation of an Islamic religiously-defined identity in politics was viewed, by many Serbs and Croats, as a drive towards renewed political and economic dominance by the Muslims in Bosnia–Hercegovina.

## THE CONFLICT OF NATIONALISMS

One of the primary aims of each of the dissident national ideologies was to reaffirm the sovereignty of 'its' nation over the territory that was claimed for it. The Croat and Slovene national ideologues saw the reaffirmation of sovereignty necessitating the creation of national armed forces within a new Yugoslav confederation or outside Yugoslavia. The reaffirmation of the sovereignty of the Muslims was to be carried out first through the reintroduction of Islamic values in public life and politics and eventually in the creation of an Islamic state. Albanian sovereignty was to be achieved first in a separate Yugoslav republic and then, possibly, in unification with Albania. Serb sovereignty was to be reaffirmed in the unification of all Serbs in a reorganised 'democratic integrative' Yugoslav federation; if this proved to be impossible, in a Serb state without other Yugoslav nations. All these programmes were in effect asserting the right of a single nation to dominate within 'its' territory. Moreover, from the point of view of all non-Serb national ideologies, the proposal to return to a 'democratic integrative' Yugoslavia, within which Serbs would be in a relative majority, was regarded as a denial of 'their' nation's fundamental right to self-determination and independence. In fact, any unification of all Serbs in one state – whether an 'integrative' Yugoslav federation or a state of Serb-populated lands – would appear to deny the Croat, Albanian and Muslim inhabitants of these lands the right to form their own state on the same territory.

Thus the conflict of national ideologies became a conflict over the control of territory which each ideology claimed for 'its' nation. The Croat, Albanian and, later Muslim, ideologues claimed territory populated by the Serbs on the basis of 'their' nations' alleged historic rights: they were the lands which either belonged to the medieval kingdoms believed to be the precursors of their national states or the lands which their nations, allegedly, settled before the Serbs. This 'historical' view of national rights clashed with the Serb claim to the 'democratic' right of national self-determination of the Serbs on territory which they inhabited for centuries. This conflict of claims was further complicated by the Serb ideologues' claims to territories from which Serbs had been forcibly expelled in recent history – during World War II and under communist rule. These were territories in Croatia, Bosnia–Hercegovina and Kosovo–Metohija.

Within the framework of the Croat, Albanian and even Slovene 'dominant nation' ideologies,[25] the Serbs and their political demands were perceived as the principal obstacle to the reaffirmation of sovereignty of these nations. This perception then easily generated a fear of Serb domination over other nations – the fear which also fuelled nationalist polemics in pre-1941 Yugoslavia: the Serbs thus became, once again, the prime target of fear, and, later, of hate. Under the rule of the communist 'equal nations' ideology, such fears of domination were mostly out of place, since the resulting federal system prevented the domination of any single nation over others. With the delegitimisation of the communist ideology and its 'equal nations' approach in the late 1980s, the stage was set for the generation of fears of the domination not only of the Serbs but of other nations (for example, of Croats over Serbs in Croatia). These fears, generated by the 'dominant nation' type of ideologies, were then successfully utilised in the drive for the mobilisation of popular support for nationalist parties in all republics of Yugoslavia. What started as a revival of romantic or traditional nationalism within dissident delegitimising ideologies in the 1970s, became, in the late 1980s, a powerful tool for political mobilisation.

# 8 The Rise of New National Elites 1987–90

## ECONOMIC REFORM IN A DISINTEGRATING FEDERATION

Unable to control galloping inflation and massive labour unrest, the Yugoslav state presidency in March 1989 appointed Ante Marković, a Croat electrical engineer and a leading Croatian politician, as the federal prime minister. Circumventing the established republican Party networks he chose a cabinet of technocrats – economists, engineers and managers like himself – committed to radical economic reform and pushed through the federal parliament a package of long-term economic reforms whose ultimate aim was the introduction of a free market of goods and labour and privatisation. As the reduction of the federal budget and restrictions on federal borrowing in the first part of 1989 failed to curb hyperinflation – reaching 3000 per cent – in December 1989 Marković implemented a 'shock therapy' based on an economic model partly drawn up by the Harvard economist Jeffrey Sachs. While introducing a price and wage freeze, Marković's government imposed strict monetary and credit restrictions, pegged the local currency, the dinar, to the German mark and made it convertible into foreign currency. The competition from less expensive foreign imports – allowed by Marković – started to break up the long-established monopolies and led, as expected, to a spate of bankruptcies among the established loss-makers in most republics.

The most vociferous opposition to these reforms came from Milošević's government in Serbia, which organised large-scale demonstrations in Belgrade against Marković's policies, portraying him as a pawn of Slovenian and Croatian communist leaders. In fact, Marković's principal support in 1989 came from the Slovene president of the Yugoslav state presidency Dr Janez Drnovšek[1] and the Slovene communist leaders to whom Marković's promotion of a free market and integration into Europe was particularly appealing. At the time Marković apparently held that successful economic reform and modernisation, together with political and economic integration into Europe, might counter the processes of disintegration of the Yugoslav federation which

99

were, by the middle of 1989, in full swing. When in January 1990 the Slovene and Croatian Party delegations walked out of the fourteenth extraordinary congress of the Yugoslav Communist party thus effectively dissolving the Party, there was no all-Yugoslav political party remaining to support the Yugoslav federation. Apparently unconcerned Marković claimed that the end of the Communist party of Yugoslavia did not mean the end of Yugoslavia.[2] One reason for his lack of concern was, perhaps, a phenomenal surge in his personal popularity. As the annual inflation rate dropped from 3000 per cent to around zero in mid-1990, Marković became the most popular politician in Yugoslavia.[3] As the opinion polls made clear, his policies had most support among the educated and managerial strata of the population.[4] Marković's reforms, by dismantling the old self-management system of decision-making, freed enterprise managers and the technical expert teams from the shackles of self-management bodies and agreements and effectively gave them control over the running of their enterprises. Moreover, Marković's second-tier package of reforms lifted all restrictions on private ownership of companies (while retaining the limit of 30 hectares for individual land ownership), enabling more than 50 000 private firms to be set up in the first year of his term. The standard of living of the primary beneficiaries of these reforms – the middle-class managers, professionals and entrepreneurs – rose dramatically as the convertibility of the dinar and the free imports of consumer goods gave them a full taste of West European lifestyle.

But by May 1990 the political support for Marković was rapidly eroding: Dr Drnovšek was replaced by a Milošević appointee and the new postcommunist governments of Slovenia and Croatia, elected in the April–May multiparty elections (see below), began their boycott of the Yugoslav federal fiscal bodies, by refusing to transfer their tax allotment to the federal treasury. As a result of the boycott, many citizens, fearing the end of the local currency's convertibility, made a run on the banks changing the local into foreign currency and transferring it abroad. Forced repeatedly to devalue the dinar, in the autumn of 1990 Marković's anti-inflationary policies appeared to crumble. By June 1990 Marković's government was caught in a cross-fire between the Serbian government's insistence on reaffirming the powers of the federation and the Croatian and Slovenian governments' insistence on their republics' sovereignty.

It was only at this point that Marković decided to mobilise his natural constituency – the middle-class beneficiaries of his reforms throughout Yugoslavia – into a political party, the Alliance of Reform

Forces of Yugoslavia – a rare all-Yugoslav party among the multitude of separate national parties. Unlike the latter, his party stood for a Yugoslavia with 'a unified market, currency, foreign policy, frontiers and defence of the country'.[5] However, Marković's party, like its founder, left the constitutional arrangements of Yugoslavia completely open, to be decided by some future 'democratic agreement of its citizens'. Being an all-Yugoslav party it appeared well placed to contest any future multi-party elections for the Yugoslav federal assembly. However, the republican leaders – first those of Slovenia and, later, from Serbia and the other republics – repeatedly blocked Marković's proposals to hold multi-party elections for the Yugoslav federal parliament. Founded after the April–May 1990 multiparty elections in Slovenia and Croatia and denied legal registration in Croatia, Marković's party, split into separate republican branches, contested elections in Bosnia–Hercegovina, Macedonia, Montenegro and Serbia. Many Serb politicians regarded Marković's party as a part of a Croat plot to divert the vote of Serbs and (self-declared) Yugoslavs from the Serb national parties in Bosnia–Hercegovina and in Serbia. Apart from a television station he founded himself, and a daily newspaper with a very limited audience, principally in Serbia, no other media outlet offered support to his party. The local leaders of his party, often members of the ex-communist intelligentsia, lacked the requisite electioneering skills and clientele networks. Its relative success in Bosnia–Hercegovina (8.46 per cent of the vote and 11 seats) and, in particular, in Macedonia (9.17 per cent of the vote and 11 seats)[6] was explicable, at least in part, by its reliance on the clientele network of its ex-communist local leaders. Finally, the main beneficiaries of Marković's reforms formed a very small stratum of the urban population. To all others, facing the uncertainty of the imminent collapse of the federation and the prospect of unemployment and even civil war, Marković's party, like his government, offered little if anything. The dismal failure of Marković to transform his high popularity rating into electoral success thus appears to be due to his party's restricted electoral appeal and the lack of a grassroots organisation.[7]

## MILOŠEVIĆ'S MASS MOBILISATION OF THE SERBS

The first communist politician to make use of the re-emerging nationalist ideologies was Slobodan Milošević, then the president of the Communist party of Serbia. In using Serb nationalism to gain control first of the Serbian party apparatus and then of the Kosovo, Vojvodina and Montenegro Party apparata, he effectively purged the communist elites of Serbia and Montenegro and replaced them with new elites.

In 1984 Ivan Stambolić – who was Milošević's friend and patron – was elected to the post of president of the Communist party of Serbia, previously held by his uncle, Petar Stambolić, a member of Tito's old guard. Starting from his family patronage network Ivan Stambolić promoted members of the Belgrade communist intelligentsia – academics and journalists – to important Party positions while giving, at the same time, considerable access to the media to Party deliberations and political decision-making. As in 1986 Stambolić was elected president of the presidency of Serbia, Milošević replaced him as president of the Serbian Party. At the time Milošević's political style – with the obligatory self-management jargon and monotonous delivery – did not differ from other communist cadres. But in his unplanned response to the Serb demonstrators (see Chapter 6) who burst into the meeting-hall near the Kosovo capital Priština on 24 April 1987, Milošević suddenly adopted the rhetoric of Serb national and historical responsibility:

> This is your land, your houses, your fields and gardens, your memories. Surely, you will not leave your land, because life is difficult on it, because you are oppressed by injustice and humiliations. It was never characteristic of the spirit of the Serb and Montenegrin nations to halt in the face of obstacles, to demobilise when they ought to be fighting, to be demoralised when they find it hard going. You should remain here for the sake of your ancestors and of your descendants.[8]

No communist politician in Yugoslavia, before or after World War II, openly appealed to the national traditions and national pride of the Serb and Montenegrin nations. As Milošević's appeal proved an instant success, he spread, during 1988, his message of the restoration of Serb national pride throughout Serbia. It was a novel, simple and directly personal appeal breaking the 45 years of communist-imposed taboos. The glorious past of the Serb nation and its pride was, he stressed in his speeches, the inalienable patrimony of every individual Serb, which demands of every Serb individually to prove themselves worthy of their ancestors. In the context of the alleged humiliation of Serbdom by the Kosovo Albanians – in Kosovo, the scene of the first traumatic Serb historical humiliation in the Battle of Kosovo in 1389 – this personal appeal proved to be very potent.

The encounter with the Serb demonstrators near Priština convinced Milošević of the need to take quick and resolute action to resolve the Kosovo crisis, by coercion if necessary. The Stambolić faction – in particular, one of Stambolić's closest aides, Dragiša Pavlović – opposed such measures, preferring to continue using the Kosovo Albanian Party leaders to stabilise the crisis. In September 1987 Milošević organised an unprecedented, fully televised, ritualistic verbal bashing of Pavlović at a Central Committee meeting in which 91 speakers participated. Totally demoralised, the Stambolić group was ousted without a fight; in December 1987 Ivan Stambolić was finally dismissed from his post of president of the Serbian presidency. Milošević's coup led to a small-scale Party revolution. The Central Committee members from the provincial posts who were recruited for the assault on the Stambolić faction, rapidly replaced the Belgrade party elite in top Party posts and the media. The smooth Belgrade drawl – which by the 1960s had become the dominant speech of the politicians and journalists – was replaced by the uneducated speech of the new communist cadres from central and south Serbia. The sole source of power and influence of this new elite was Milošević and his network. In carrying out his orders they proved to be obedient, resolute and ruthless – the qualities which Milošević needed in his drive to reshape the constitutional structure of Serbia and, eventually, of Yugoslavia.

Soon after the coup the Serbian media started to run stories regarding the corruption under Tito's regime as well as injustice and discrimination against the Serbs during and after World War II. Under the guise of revealing the secrets of the past, the popular press ran a coordinated campaign of delegitimisation of Tito's rule and its constitutional foundations. As part of this campaign, Belgrade intellectual journals were allowed to discuss many former taboo questions and, as a result, in 1988 open anti-communism or anti-Titoism became the latest intellectual fashion. Leading dissident intellectuals were given access to the popular media to air their – previously banned – criticism of the communist rule of Yugoslavia. By enthusiastically participating in this campaign of delegitimisation of Tito's rule, many nationalist and neomarxist dissidents as well as previous apologists of Tito's regime offered open or tacit support for Milošević's 'new course'.[9] Moreover, Milošević systematically incorporated former dissident ideas – nationalist as well as neomarxist ones – into the official rhetoric. Thus 'united, single Serbia' – one of the major tenets of the draft memorandum of the Serbian Academy of Arts and Sciences – became the principal slogan of Milošević's campaign of mass rallies lasting from May until November 1988. The mass rallies, organised by local Party committees and the Kosovo Serb protest movement, were held in all major towns of Serbia. Hundreds of thousands of people participated, carrying Serbian and Yugoslav flags and pictures of Milošević, Lenin and Tito. As the series of rallies progressed, Tito's and Lenin's pictures were replaced by those of Serb national heroes and the Yugoslav insignia were replaced by Serb national emblems. New patriotic songs, in particular the militant 'Who says, who dares to lie that Serbia is little?' as well as chants extolling Slobodan Milošević as a national hero provided the required emotional foci, while extensive media coverage, full of human interest stories, aimed to show that Milošević's mass support came from all strata of the Serbian population, young and old, educated and uneducated.

The rally fever, called the 'happening of the people', was crowned by a rally in Belgrade in October 1988 which, according to the official accounts, was attended by more than a million people.[10] The rallies were unprecedented in Yugoslav and Serbian history, greatly exceeding in the numbers of participants and their geographic spread similar mass rallies held by the Croatian Communist party leaders in Croatia in 1971. The campaign placed Milošević in the pantheon of Serb national heroes – to which no Serb communist politician ever belonged – and established him as the most powerful Serb politician in the post-1945 period. Apart from entrenching his rule in Serbia, the rallies were obviously intended to intimidate and demoralise his opposition, primarily the communist leaders of the provinces of Kosovo and Vojvodina. In October 1988 'happening of the people' was organised by Milošević loyalists in the capital of Vojvodina, Novi Sad. After several days of siege of their Party headquarters, the province's Party leaders resigned *en masse* to be replaced by Milošević's appointees (who had organised the demonstrations). With the support of Serb demonstrators in Kosovo's capital, in November 1988 Milošević was able to engineer the replacement of the entrenched Kosovo Albanian leadership – led by one of Tito's favourite youth leaders, Azem Vllasi – by new Kosovo Albanian leaders loyal to him. This, in turn, sparked widespread Kosovo Albanian demonstrations throughout the province in support of their deposed communist leaders.

Similar mass demonstrations – dubbed 'street democracy' – were organised in August and November 1988 in the capital of the Republic of Montenegro and two of its major cities. Unlike their counterparts in the provinces of Vojvodina and Kosovo, the leaders of the Republic of Montenegro controlled the republic's police, which they repeatedly used to disperse tens of thousands of demonstrators demanding their resignations. But by January 1989, Milošević loyalists were able to sway Montenegro's police chiefs and so, in the face of a second wave of demonstrations, the Montenegrin communist leaders, bereft of police protection, resigned. This was the first instance in post-1945 Yugoslavia that a communist leader from one republic was able to replace the leadership of another republic by his appointees. Already in 1988 the communist leaders of the as yet unaffected republics – primarily Slovenia and Croatia – attempted, in vain, to rein in Milošević. After unsuccessful attempts to discredit his policies and appointees at the federal level, in February 1989, the Slovenian press and communist leaders took up the cause of Kosovo Albanian miners striking in support of their deposed communist leaders. At a mass political meeting, organised by the Slovene communists together with their new opposition parties, the Slovene communist leader Milan Kučan[11] argued that the Kosovo Albanian miners were defending the very foundations of Yugoslavia, established by the AVNOJ assembly in 1943, which Milošević had been undermining. Thanks to direct television coverage of the meeting, Belgrade students immediately reacted to Kučan's statement by organising huge demonstrations at Belgrade University which drew hundreds of thousands of demonstrators. The demonstrators' demands were conveniently channelled into a demand for the arrest of the deposed Kosovo Albanian communist leader Azem Vllasi which was duly carried out.[12] This incident signalled an almost total breakdown of relations between the Slovene and Serbian communist leaderships.

Milošević's handling of this incident followed the pattern already emerging in his deployment of 'street democracy' against his political opponents. He used every conflict, whether or not provoked by his actions, to rally popular support through organised rallies and media campaigns and to threaten his opponents with coercion. This type of intimidatory and coercive style of politics could neither be contained nor controlled within the framework of the consensus-seeking federal bodies of Yugoslavia. As each republic was 'sovereign' in its 'internal' affairs, the federal bodies, including the federal Party bodies, had no jurisdiction over each republic's leadership and its policies. Ironically, it was a Serbian leader who was the first to exploit in this way the republics' 'sovereignty' which was promoted by the Slovenian and Croatian communist leaders from the 1960s on. In April 1989 Milošević's government passed amendments to the constitution of Serbia effectively reintegrating Kosovo and Vojvodina into Serbia and stripping the two provinces of their political and legislative autonomy. This act of overt defiance of the Yugoslav constitution of 1974, which granted a dual status to the two provinces (see Chapter 5), was followed, in July 1989, by proposals from a Serbian reform commission which would in effect enable the Serb deputies in the federal parliament, together with any allies from smaller national groups, to outvote Croatian and Slovenian deputies.[13]

Milošević's advocacy of a unified Yugoslavia in 1989 was complemented by mobilisation of Serbs outside Serbia. During 1988-9 his supporters, through their contacts with local Serb intelligentsia and notables in Croatia and in Bosnia–Hercegovina, helped to organise local Serb rallies and Serb cultural organisations which by the end of 1989 formed a loosely-organised pan-Serb national movement. Like the leaders of the Kosovo Serb movement of 1986-8 (see Chapter 6), its leaders were usually prominent local Serb professionals – teachers, doctors, lawyers and the like – who were neither members of the republican communist elites in Croatia and Bosnia–Hercegovina nor professional politicians. In their view, the republic's boundaries artificially divided the Serb nation; only by crossing these boundaries, would the Serb nation be able to achieve the political unity it needed.[14]

The first to oppose Milošević's ascendancy were the Slovene communist leaders who saw in his campaign for a 'unified Yugoslavia' a bid to take over power and recentralise the state; if successful, he would not only have been able to oust the Slovene communist elites but also to strip Slovenia of the political and cultural autonomy it had enjoyed so far. To pre-empt Milošević's bid the Slovenian communist leaders were, in 1988, ready to ally themselves with new Slovene opposition parties and to start the process of gradual 'disassociation' of Slovenia from the Yugoslav federation.

## SLOVENIA: THE RISE OF THE DISSIDENTS

In the early 1980s two distinct groups of political dissidents emerged in Slovenia. The first, the Alternative movement – a conglomerate of single-issue groups (such as the Peace and Ecology movement, a feminist and a gay rights group) – was part of an alternative youth scene of various rock bands and art groups. As the latter were following the latest Western fashions in music and the arts, so the Alternative movement followed the latest fashions in the Western alternative political movements, trying to adapt them to the Slovenian political conditions of one-party rule. Their main outlet was the youth weekly *Mladina* and the student radio station *Radio Študent* both of which were financed and run by the official communist-controlled youth organisation.

The second focus of dissidence in Slovenia was the Society of Slovene Writers,[15] a semi-official organisation which in the early 1980s undertook to promote the concept of a single and distinct Slovene cultural space, embracing all native Slovene speakers. The distinctness and uniqueness of Slovene cultural space would enable Slovenes to disassociate themselves from the 'Balkan Southerners' – primarily Serbs – who lacked the European culture and customs of the Slovenes.[16] In the 1987 issue of *Nova Revija* (see Chapter 7) the idea of a linguistically and culturally defined Slovene space found its political expression in the demand for Slovenia's full sovereignty and independence. In 1986 the Society successfully blocked the election of a Serbian writer as president of the League of Writers of Yugoslavia and in 1988 it severely chastised Serbian writers for their alleged lack of support for the rights of Kosovo Albanians.[17]

In early 1988 *Mladina* started to target the Yugoslav federal army by exposing its arms sales to impoverished Third World countries and its corruption. In early March 1988 just as the weekly was preparing to publish transcripts of Party and military meetings discussing the arrest of Slovene dissidents, the Yugoslav federal army arrested three of its journalists and a Slovene sergeant-major who procured the secret documents for them. One of the journalists, Janez Janša,[18] was a prominent activist of the Alternative movement's peace branch. His friends from the Alternative movement, immediately upon his arrest, founded the Committee for the Defence of Human Rights, consisting of dissidents from the youth Alternative movement and from the Slovene Society of Writers.[19] The Committee, with the active support of the Slovene Communist party, the communist-controlled media and the Roman Catholic church, organised a widespread campaign of protests against the arrest of the 'Ljubljana four' as they came to be called. According to one of its members, the Committee in a short time gained over 100 000 members from all walks of life and organised daily demonstrations against the Yugoslav federal army.[20] These continuous protests reached a crescendo with the decision of the Yugoslav federal army military court to conduct its proceedings in Serbo-Croatian, the language of military command in the army. Although the Yugoslav constitutional court ruled the decision to be constitutional, the Slovene Communist party leader, Milan Kučan strongly remonstrated against it saying that 'Slovenes cannot regard as their own any state that does not secure the use of their mother tongue and its equality, and in which the freedom, sovereignty and equality of the Slovene people is not guaranteed'.[21]

The trial – at which the four were found guilty and sentenced to prison terms ranging from four years to five months – brought together not only the Slovene communist leadership and the dissident groups but also all strands of Slovene nationalist symbolism: the arrest and sentencing of Slovene citizens by the Yugoslav military authorities symbolised the breach of Slovene state sovereignty by a 'foreign' force while the use of Serbo-Croatian symbolised the 'foreign' oppression of Slovene culture and a denial of Slovene sovereignty. The astounding success of the Committee for the Defence of Human Rights in creating a mass national movement and mobilising Slovene public opinion encouraged various groups within the Committee to form their own 'political identities' and, ultimately, separate political parties. The first alternative political party, the Slovene Democratic Alliance, was established already in January 1989. Its founder Dimitrij Rupel, in his contribution to the 1987 *Nova Revija* issue on the Slovene national programme, argued for Slovenia's political as well as cultural independence (see Chapter 7). Soon afterwards another *Nova Revija* contributor, Jože Pučnik, formed the Slovene Social Democratic Alliance, committed to the drafting of a new Slovene constitution and institutionalising the republic's sovereignty. They were followed by the Slovene Christian Democratic party, the Green Alliance and the Slovene Craftsmen's party and, later, the Slovene Farmers' Alliance. As many of the leaders of these new parties had already worked together in the Committee for the Defence of Human Rights, they had no difficulty in forming, in January 1990, the opposition coalition bloc known by its Slovene acronym DEMOS.

As a result of its participation in the national movement in 1988, the Communist party of Slovenia rapidly transformed itself into a Slovene national party. As one member of the Committee points out, in the process the Communist party appears to have 'highjacked' the national cause from the Committee for the Defence of Human Rights for its own purposes.[22] Already in December 1988, the communist leader Milan Kučan had asserted Slovenia's right to secede from the Yugoslav federation.[23] This was followed, in September 1989, by a series of constitutional amendments passed by the Assembly of the Republic of Slovenia enabling the republic's organs to proclaim a state of emergency in the republic (independently of the Yugoslav state organs) and codifying the Slovenian state organs' duty to defend and protect the republic against any federal organs.[24] This was the first in the series of legislative moves asserting full Slovenian sovereignty over its affairs and 'disassociating' the republic from the Yugoslav federation.

In November 1989 the multiparty political system was finally legalised and the stage set for the first multiparty elections in April 1990.

The Slovene Communist party delegation walked out of the fourteenth Extraordinary Congress of the Communist party of Yugoslavia in January 1990, refusing to be outvoted on its proposal to confederalise the Yugoslav Communist party. The Slovene Communist party, immediately upon its delegation's return, abandoned marxism, changed its name, programme, flag and image. Under its new slogan 'Europe now' it presented itself as a national party of all Slovenes which was ready to find a place for Slovenia, as a fully sovereign state, within a new confederal Yugoslavia. While the opposition DEMOS parties differed greatly among themselves in their ideological programmes, they were united in their rejection of Yugoslavia as an 'exhausted concept'. In the elections for the lower chamber of the Slovenian assembly in April 1990 (in which 80 per cent of the electorate turned out to vote), the ex-communist Party of Democratic Renewal got the most votes by a single party (17 per cent) followed by the ex-communist Liberals (15 per cent). They were followed by the parties of the opposition bloc DEMOS: the Christian Democrats (12.9 per cent), the Farmers' Alliance (12.5 per cent), the Slovene Democratic Alliance (9.9 per cent), the Greens (8.9 per cent), the Slovene Social Democratic Alliance (7.3 per cent) and the Slovene Craftsmen's party (3.5 per cent). As the DEMOS coalition parties together gathered 55 per cent of the vote, in April 1990 the coalition formed the first postcommunist government in Yugoslavia with the prime minister Lojze Peterle (the leader of the Slovene Christian Democrats) and all other ministers former dissidents. However, in the second round of voting for the president of the republic the ex-communist leader Milan Kučan won against the ex-dissident Jože Pučnik (with 58.3 per cent against the latter's 41.7 per cent of the vote).

The former dissidents now in government, while holding widely divergent political views, were primarily united in their principled commitment to Slovenia's independence and secession from Yugoslavia. For them this was an article of faith which allowed no compromise. They set about to achieve it with all the organisational ingenuity which they displayed in their dissident days.


## THE DISSIDENTS' TAKEOVERS IN OTHER REPUBLICS

### Croatia

In contrast to the Slovene communists, the Croatian Communist party leaders neither supported the dissident movement's drive towards Croa-

tian independence nor did they successfully 'highjack' the Croatian national cause. The Croatian communist leaders in the late 1980s belonged to the anti-nationalist wing of the Croatian Party which came
into power in 1971 to replace the nationalist communists purged by
Tito. Remaining true to their anti-nationalist stand, up to 1988 they
continued to persecute and discredit the Croatian dissidents. However,
in the prolonged conflict between the Slovene communist leaders and
the Milošević elite in Serbia, the Croatian communist leadership rather
reluctantly took the side of their Slovene colleagues. Like their Slovene
comrades, they must have perceived Milošević's programme of recentralisation of Yugoslavia and his pan-Serb mobilisation as a direct threat
to their hold on power; in an attempt to widen their popular support,
they, like their Slovenian counterparts, found in late 1988 a new toler-
ance for nationalist dissidents.

The Croat nationalist dissidents quickly followed in the steps of their
Slovenian counterparts and on 28 February 1989 Dr Franjo Tudjman
founded the first opposition party – the Croatian Democratic Union,
widely known under its Croatian acronym HDZ.[25] Although the great
majority of its founders were university educated (proudly noting their
degrees), there was a significant number of entrepreneurs – for example, restaurant owners – and a small number of tradesmen.[26] These
strata of self-employed entrepreneurs and tradesmen would provide the
financial and organisational backbone to the party in its march to
power in April–May 1990. Its initial platform called for the development of Croat national consciousness, unifying all its past diverse
strands,[27] and for a confederal reorganisation of Yugoslavia on the basis
of the existing AVNOJ borders among the republics. It also advocated
the development of a free market economy, a democratic political system reintegrating the Croat diaspora abroad and Christian (that is, Roman Catholic) family values. While the party was declared open to
Serbs and other nationalities, it emphasised that all other nationalities
need to respect their common homeland – Croatia.[28] From the very
start the HDZ claimed that for the Serbs in Croatia there is only one
homeland – Croatia – and thus denied to them any territorial autonomy or the right to consider Yugoslavia as their homeland.

Focusing on the writings and speeches of some of its founders, the
communist-controlled media in Croatia and Serbia attacked the HDZ,
routinely linking it with the Croat mass national movement in the
1970s and pro-Ustasha revisionism. Its anti-communist reputation
firmly established, the party gained the largest following amongst emigré Croats who belonged to a variety of nationalist and anti-communist

political organisations. Tudjman's semi-rehabilitation of the Ustashe Croat state (1941–5) as 'not only a quisling creation and fascist crime, but also an expression of the historical strivings of the Croat nation'[29] was widely acclaimed among Croat emigrés as a reflection of their common political principles. Having found in the HDZ the party of their unity and purpose, Croat emigrés poured millions of dollars into its campaign coffers.

The principal leaders of the Croat national mass movement of the early 1970s did not join the HDZ but formed their own parties – Croatian Social Liberal party, Croatian Democratic party, Croatian Peasants' party, and the Social Democratic party of Croatia. On 1 March, together with four other parties, they formed an eight-party Coalition of National Accord which emphasised the need for a peaceful restructuring of the Yugoslav federation into a confederation.[30] The Serb Democratic party, founded in February 1990 by Dr Jovan Rašković, a psychiatrist and author, initially demanded Serb cultural autonomy and 'ethnic sovereignty' within Croatia and strongly opposed the separation of the Serb-populated areas of Croatia from Yugoslavia. In addition to the Serb party with its power based in Serb-populated regions of Krajina and Slavonia, Istrian and Dalmatian regional parties were formed as well. After their walk-out from the Yugoslav Communist Party Congress in January 1990, the Croatian communists quickly changed their name and, like their Slovene counterparts, transformed themselves into a non-marxist social democratic party. In the elections of April–May 1990, the reformed communists faced two coalitions: the eight-party Coalition of National Accord, led by the prominent leaders of the 1970s Croat mass national movement and the most nationally assertive grouping, the six-party Croatian Democratic Bloc led by Dr Franjo Tudjman and his HDZ. The latter's election campaign with huge rallies, the prominent display of national symbols and the cult of its leader resembled Milošević's style of populist mobilisation.

The electoral system, approved by the communist-controlled Croatian Diet before the elections, required an absolute majority of votes in the first round or a relative majority of votes in the second round of balloting to win a seat in the Diet. Under this system of voting, the HDZ with 44 per cent of the vote secured 205 (or 58 per cent) of the 386 seats in all three chambers of the Croatian Diet. The ex-communists together with their allies secured only 101 seats. In the Socio-Political Chamber of the Diet, the most important of the three, with 42 per cent of the vote the HDZ won a two-thirds majority of 54 seats (out of 80). The runners-up, the ex-communists with 34 per cent of the vote got only 19 seats. The Coalition of the National Accord, trailing a poor third, split almost immediately after the elections. The Serb Democratic party won 5 seats altogether.

Thus the first-past-the-post system enabled the HDZ-led coalition to win an absolute majority in parliament without winning an absolute majority of votes. However, HDZ's impressive margin of votes over the ex-communists could be explained, at least in part, by its superior organisation and marketing. During more than a year of its existence, it created an effective clientele network in almost all districts of Croatia, often nominating for its candidates well-known local businessmen who were supported by systematic door-to-door canvassing. Its advertising campaign, generously financed by its Croat supporters abroad, conveyed a simple message: this was a truly Croat party which knew how to take care of Croat interests. With the rising threat of Milošević's domination over Yugoslavia and the continuing Slovenian–Serbian tension, this was a very effective message. The HDZ's success was a victory not only of a nationally-assertive political platform which its dissident leader had propagated for almost two decades but of the social strata – self-employed farmers, entrepreneurs and tradesmen as well as Croat emigrés – which previously had little if any impact in the politics of Croatia. Dr Franjo Tudjman, whom the Croatian Diet proclaimed the President of Croatia (with 281 out of 386 votes), resurrected for them Croat pride in their past and a hope for their future in a state they could call their own. For many of the HDZ faithful he was the true father of their nation.[31]

Having lost power, the ex-communists almost immediately lost a great number of its former supporters and cadres to the HDZ. Many Party cadres – of all ranks – declared themselves to be long-standing HDZ moles in the Party while others sought whatever positions they could get from the new government. Soon after the elections the reformed communists split and gradually became a marginal political force. By the end of 1990 the HDZ, having placed its supporters in almost all key positions in most Croatian institutions, including the media, successfully marginalised all other political forces in Croatia except for the Serb Democratic Party in its Serb-populated Krajina powerbase and the regional party in Istria.

**Bosnia–Hercegovina**

Throughout the 1980s the Bosnian Communist party continued to repress its dissidents most severely, punishing any critics of the communist regime – intellectuals and non-intellectuals alike – with long prison sentences. As a result, in 1988 there were, apart from the Islamic groups (whose leaders, including Alija Izetbegović, had just been released from prison), no other intellectual dissident groups in Bosnia–Hercegovina. In 1988 the purge following the *Agrokomerc* scandal (see Chapter 6) brought to power a younger generation of communist leaders who, following their counterparts elsewhere in Yugoslavia, proved to be more tolerant of dissidence. However, in legalising the formation of other political parties, they attempted to prohibit the formation of political parties based on national or religious affiliation (which in Bosnia–Hercegovina largely coincided) arguing that this would irreparably split the republic. As the republic's constitutional court overruled the prohibition, the Islamic dissidents were the first to found such a party – the Party of Democratic Action (*Stranka demokratske akcije* – SDA) led by Alija Izetbegović. It defined itself as an association of citizens of Yugoslavia who belong to the 'Muslim cultural and historical circle' as well as of others who endorse its programme. In its programme, democracy was defined as the rule of just laws (in contradistinction to the rule of majorities) and it included an 'efficacious restriction of several social ills: the diseases of addictions, trashy literature and pornography'.[32] While granting the Serbs and Croats the right to live in Bosnia–Hercegovina, the party claimed that Muslims are the autochthonous Bosnian nation and, as a Muslim party, it declared its special interest in preserving the republic's unity. In one of the largest election rallies, in the stronghold of former communist party boss Fikret Abdić (see Chapter 6), Izetbegović declared that the Muslims, together with other nations, would defend Bosnia from partition with armed force if necessary.[33] In his interviews Izetbegović and other leaders of his party – among whom there were several prominent Muslim clerics – reiterated both the party's commitment to a state of equal citizens and their demand for a society based on Islamic norms.[34] However, the tension between these two irreconcilable aims apparently led to the split in October 1990 in which one of its founders Adil Zulfikarpašić, left the SDA to form a secular party of Muslims.[35]

The Serb Democratic Party (SDS) was founded by Dr Radovan Karadžić, a psychiatrist, minor poet and businessman who was, in the communist era, imprisoned for alleged embezzlement. The party was committed to the integrity of federal Yugoslavia; if the latter failed, the party would 'seek a democratic response of the Serb nation to any possible new situation'.[36] From the start, it demanded a new administrative division of Bosnia's municipalities (communes) which would not disadvantage its highly dispersed Serb population. Aiming to unite all Serbs in Bosnia–Hercegovina, communists and Orthodox believers alike, it was part of the pan-Serb movement in Yugoslavia supported by Miloš-ević's government and by its twin party in Croatia.

Its Croat counterpart, HDZ for Bosnia–Hercegovina, was a branch of the Croatian HDZ in Zagreb which controlled its finances, person-nel and policies. The Bosnian HDZ aimed primarily at 'securing the right of the Croat nation to self-determination up to the right of seces-sion'[37] within a sovereign republic; in practice, this meant securing a desired level of Croat self-government in the predominantly Croat areas. In contrast to the Serb party, the Bosnian HDZ propagated the confederalisation of Yugoslavia within which the republic would be sovereign and independent. Before the November 1990 elections, the Muslim SDA leaders refused to endorse either the Croat confederal or the Serb federal project of Yugoslavia, preferring to keep their options open. The reformed Bosnian Communist party took a similarly ambig-uous stand. In opposition to the national parties, the reformed commu-nists came out against any form of nationalism and against the 'political instrumentalisation of national and religious sentiments'.[38] They and Ante Marković's Alliance of Reform Forces were the only major parties not based on national affiliation; pre-election opinion-polls and media commentators predicted their victory. In November 1990 the electorate, however, returned an overwhelming majority to the three national parties, each of which secured a proportion of the vote which roughly reflected the 1991 census figures for the respective national groups:

- SDA (Muslims): 37.8 per cent of the vote (43.5 per cent of the popu-lation)
- SDS (Serbs): 26.5 per cent of the vote (31.3 per cent of the popula-tion)
- HDZ (Croats): 14.7 per cent of the vote (17.5 per cent of the popula-tion)

The reformed communists got only 6 per cent (7.6 per cent with their so-cialist allies) and Marković's Alliance 5.6 per cent of the votes cast, while numerous smaller pan-national parties got most of the remaining votes.

With the Yugoslav federation disintegrating and the new Slovenian and Croatian governments set on achieving independence, the major electoral issue in Bosnia–Hercegovina was how to achieve security and peace in a republic with such sharp national cleavages. Given that no national group in the republic commanded either the numbers or the level of force sufficient to ensure its own supremacy and the maintenance of law and order on its own, without any help from outside, the electorate chose the parties which had each already obtained substantial support from outside the republic. Even the Muslims – with no large neighbouring co-national group in Yugoslavia – probably felt assured of support for the Islamic SDA from the Islamic countries with which their leaders had already established close ties. Alija Izetbegović's studious references to his party's ties with the Islamic world, which his political opponents had used in their propaganda against him, probably helped him to attract even the secularised segments of the Muslim electorate. The two principal pan-national parties, the Alliance and the communists, had no backing from any major political players in Yugoslavia or abroad. Izetbegović's SDA was the only political force which seemed capable of protecting the position and security of the Muslims, faced with the two other national parties backed by their co-national sponsors from outside the republic.

After the elections, the three national parties formed a coalition government in which the portfolios were divided roughly according to the election results. The leader of the strongest party, the Muslim Alija Izetbegović, was elected the president of the seven-member presidency of the republic. The prime ministership went to a Croat and the president of the parliament was a Serb. The coalition partners agreed to resolve all major issues, such as those relating to the equality of nations in the republic, by consensus through the already established parliamentary procedure.[39] The distribution of political offices and the consensus-seeking political decision-making procedure aimed at ensuring the avoidance of political conflicts. However, after the outbreak of violence and fighting in neighbouring Croatia, each of the national parties, early in 1991, started to supply its members with arms; in consequence, criminal gangs, engaged in arms smuggling and protection rackets, sought to ally themselves with local leaders of all the three main national parties. The division of political offices enabled these political leaders to protect criminal suspects of their own nationality from the police and the judiciary. As the power of state institutions was undermined, many functions of the state were transferred to the apparata of the three national parties. In fact, in those municipalities (communes) in which a single national party gained a majority, that party took over almost all the functions of the local government. In addition to the distribution of political and high administrative offices by national affiliation, this take-over of local government by national parties assured that political power and administration of the republic was effectively partitioned among the national parties even before the civil war erupted in April 1992.

Already in October 1991, less than a year after the elections, the principle of consensus in major decision-making was breached as the Muslim and Croat parties proceeded to adopt the Memorandum of Sovereignty of the republic in spite of its rejection by the Serb party (see Chapter 11). As Yugoslavia was disintegrating into separate nation-states, the three national parties of unequal electoral strength were not very likely to maintain the consensus required to keep their coalition government working.

**Macedonia**

As in Bosnia–Hercegovina, the formation of new parties in Macedonia followed the break-up of the Yugoslav Communist party in January 1990. The first nationalist party, the Movement for all-Macedonian Action (MAAK) was founded in February 1990 by a writer who was the president of the Union of Macedonian Writers. It pledged to defend the interests of all Macedonians, including those from the Aegean and Pirin parts of Macedonia (that is, of Greece and Bulgaria).[40] Another writer, the 25-year-old Ljupčo Georgijevski founded, in June 1990, another nationalist party – the Internal Macedonian Revolutionary Organisation–Democratic Party for Macedonian National Unity (IMRO–DPMNU). Continuing the tradition of its namesake, the IMRO founded by Goce Delčev in 1893, this party was committed to the formation of an independent Macedonian state and for the unification of all (Slav) Macedonians in one state by non-violent means. It demanded a confederal Yugoslavia, the creation of a Macedonian national army and a Macedonian passport to be issued to all Macedonians in the diaspora who were forced to use Greek or Bulgarian passports.

The Albanian national party – Party for Democratic Prosperity in Macedonia – was also founded by intellectuals but of Albanian nationality. Opposed to Macedonian nationalist parties, this party regarded Macedonia as a state of Macedonians, Albanians and other nationalities living in it; accordingly it demanded the right to Macedonian citizenship of all its residents, irrespective of their national or religious affiliation as well as the right of public education in one's mother tongue. The leaders of the Albanian minority – which probably numbered over 21 per cent[41] of the republic's population at the time – had long complained of the paucity of primary and secondary schools with instruction in Albanian and of the denial of citizenship to the Albanians who had emigrated to Macedonia. Like its counterparts in other Yugoslav republics, the Communist party of Macedonia, after January 1990, changed its name, abandoned marxism and promoted a sovereign Macedonia. Already in 1989, the Party initiated a change in the constitution of Macedonia, making it a 'nation-state of the Macedonian nation' and deleting any reference to national minorities; on the eve of the November 1990 elections, the Party initiated a further constitutional amendment which made Macedonia the protector of Macedonians living in other countries.[42] The 'left' parties' bloc also included Ante Marković's Alliance and a Socialist party.

Only after three rounds of voting in November and December 1990, did the nationalist IMRO emerge as the largest party with 38 out of 120 seats in the unicameral parliament. The reformed communists came second with 31 seats; the Albanian party was third with 17 and Marković's Alliance fourth with 11 seats. All other seats were taken up by smaller parties, most of them either of Albanian or Macedonian nationalist orientation. With no party achieving an absolute majority, the early coalition governments were quite short-lived. After prolonged haggling, in late January 1991 the parliament elected Kiro Gligorov, a Macedonian communist leader who was a member of Tito's chosen coterie, president of Macedonia; in March a cabinet of non-party experts was formed to tackle the dire economic crisis which befell Macedonia's underdeveloped economy. The failure of the nationalist parties to win outright control of the government and the inclusion of Albanian party leaders in successive Macedonian governments probably prevented the escalation of interparty conflict into an interethnic conflict between the Macedonian government and the Albanian minority. Its ex-communist president and government were not supportive of the nationalist parties' moves to proclaim the independence of the republic; only after the fighting escalated in Croatia in July 1991 did the former proceed to organise a referendum, held in September 1991, on independence. On the basis of the pro-independence vote in the referendum, the Macedonian government, in December 1991, requested EC recognition of its independence (see Chapter 10). Following an agreement with the Yugoslav army's High Command, in March 1992 the Yugoslav federal army left the republic without any incident and, in April 1993, the republic, under its temporary name the Former Yugoslav Republic of Macedonia, was admitted to the UN. Partly because of its government's conciliatory stance, Macedonia was the only republic whose secession from the Yugoslav federation did not cause an armed conflict.

## SERBIA AND MONTENEGRO: THE VICTORY OF EX-COMMUNIST PARTIES

Until mid-1990 Milošević and his supporters from Montenegro attempted, in vain, to revive the the Yugoslav Communist party which effectively dissolved in January 1990. In spite of his attempts to keep the one-party system going, the first opposition political parties started to form in Serbia early in 1990. Among the first were the Serb Renewal Movement led by a popular novelist and dissident Vuk Drašković, and the Democratic party, continuing the traditions of its pre-1941 namesake.[43] The former attempted to create a mass anti-communist movement among various strata of the population based on a radical nationalist programme of reunification of the Serb lands into one state while the latter, founded by Belgrade liberals and (former) neomarxists, promoted parliamentary liberalism primarily among the urban intelligentsia. Under pressure to call multiparty elections, in July 1990 Milošević went to a referendum with a proposal to introduce a new constitution for Serbia which stripped the autonomous provinces of their political autonomy and entrenched the supremacy of the president of the republic (the post he held) over any parliamentary bodies.[44]

As expected, the parliament of Kosovo, dominated by Kosovo Albanian communist deputies, refused to endorse the proposed change in the status of Kosovo. Having been locked out of the parliament building, in July 1990 Kosovo Albanian deputies passed their own constitutional declaration at its entrance. Following the model of Croatia and Slovenia, the declaration proclaimed Kosovo an independent and sovereign republic, severing its ties with Serbia. The Serbian parliament responded by dissolving the Kosovo parliament which, in turn, triggered a general strike of Albanians in Kosovo. In September 1990 – as the Milošević-controlled Serbian parliament was passing the new Serbian constitution – Kosovo Albanian deputies of the dissolved Kosovo parliament, at a secret meeting, passed a constitution of the republic of Kosovo, creating in effect a parallel underground state of Albanians in Kosovo. In May 1992 Kosovo Albanians held their own multiparty elections which the Serbian authorities proclaimed illegal. The Democratic Alliance of Kosovo won 78 per cent of the vote for the underground parliament; its leader, the writer Dr Ibrahim Rugova, was also elected president of Kosovo by more than 95 per cent of the votes cast. The Serbian government has not recognised any of the Kosovo Albanian political institutions or political parties.

Most Kosovo Albanians boycotted the first multiparty elections in Serbia, which were held in December 1990 and contested by more than

50 parties and a large number of independent candidates. The major opposition parties – including the Serbian Renewal Movement and the Democratic party – failed to form a united opposition until the second round of voting. As in Croatia, the first-past-the-post system (in two rounds) ensured that with 45.8 per cent of the vote, Milošević's (ex-communist) Socialist party gained 77.6 per cent of seats in the unicameral parliament (194 out of 250). The ex-communists were followed by the Serbian Renewal Movement with 19 seats and the Democratic party with 7 seats. The remaining seats went to 14 smaller parties. In direct elections for the president of Serbia, Milošević, once again, proved his personal popularity by gaining 65.35 per cent of the votes (among 32 candidates running for the office). Milošević's 'Serbia unite' rallies begun in early 1988 and crowned by the rally commemorating the six-hundredth anniversary of the Kosovo battle in June 1989, in retrospect, appear to have served as his prolonged election campaign. In addition to Milošević's personal popularity, his Socialist party's victory could be explained by its use of the already existing communist clientele networks, its almost total control of the electronic (but not the print) media, the fragmentation of the opposition parties and the Socialists' superior marketing. Their slogan 'With us there is no uncertainty' captured the Serbian – in particular provincial – electorate in the midst of a severe political and economic crisis. Moreover, Drašković's attempts to outbid Milošević's Socialists with his own nationalist programme badly backfired as the electorate came to regard the Socialists as the party of stability and moderation.

Milošević's supporters in Montenegro did not even trouble to change the name of the Communist party; they won 83 out of 125 seats in the parliament, under their old name of the League of Communists of Montenegro, while their leader won the presidency of this, the smallest Yugoslav republic with 42.2 per cent of the vote.

## THE OUTCOME OF THE ELECTIONS

The introduction of nationalist political moblisation in Yugoslav politics thus brought new elites and parties to power. The Communist party which pioneered this process – that of Serbia – was able to retain its power and its dominant position in the politics of its republic. The ex-communist parties which refused to transform themselves into single nation parties – such as the ex-communists of Bosnia–Hercegovina and of Croatia – were decisively defeated. Those communists who

embraced the national cause early, allowing them to show a good record in fighting for it – like the Slovene ones – were able retain a share
of power. Even those which came to embrace the national cause relatively late, such as the Macedonian communists, could – partly due to
the fragmentation of their opposition – retain substantial power.

The multiparty elections not only brought to or confirmed in power
the new political elites but they completed the process of the political
fragmentation of the Yugoslav federation commenced in the early
1960s. Instead of national communist elites, each of the republics by
late 1990 was ruled by non-communist (or no-longer-communist) national elites. The national communist elites in the past shared an all-
Yugoslav communist ideology as well as common political interests and
loyalties. These shared political interests and loyalties kept the highly
fragmented semiconfederation together as a common state. The new
non-communist national elites had neither an ideology nor political
interests (let alone loyalties) in common. On the contrary, they pro-
fessed separate national ideologies which were in conflict not only regarding the desirable constitutional structure for their respective
nations but also regarding their nation's territorial claims. Neither the
Yugoslav communist constitution of 1974 – which all of the major political parties rejected in one way or another – nor the separate national
ideologies which they espoused, offered any arbitration procedure or
guidance for the peaceful resolution of these conflicts. As we shall see,
the international organisations – such as the European Community
and the United Nations – also failed to provide any such framework or
arbitration procedure. Under such circumstances it should not have
been surprising that the political leaders of the national groups resorted to an armed resolution of their conflicts. Yet at the end of 1990
neither their electorates nor any outside powers expected the resolution
of by then quite obvious conflicts to take this turn. This misapprehen-
sion seems, in retrospect, to have been based on a profound misunder-
standing of how the political leaders, elected in the multiparty
elections, would calculate the potential costs and benefits of armed resolution of these, principally territorial, conflicts. The political leaders
of each side in the conflict appear to have calculated that the benefits
of military actions – such as an armed seizure of the contested territory
– would outweigh the costs in destruction and loss of human life (which
each of them initially believed would be very limited). Crudely put, the
political leaders of each side appeared to have calculated that a mere
show of force would suffice to subdue their opponents and to gain control of the desired territory. Each side, except the Slovenes, badly mis-

calculated but none, after committing their armed forces, would willingly admit to its miscalculation and seek a peaceful solution to the conflict. The international organisations had done little if anything to correct these faulty calculations of the Yugoslav political leaders and, once the fighting started, proved incapable of arranging for a peaceful resolution of the conflicting territorial claims.

# 9 On the Road to War 1990–1

## ON THE ROAD TO SECESSION: SLOVENIA AND CROATIA

The new Croatian and Slovenian governments were committed to extricating their republics from the Yugoslav federation either by transforming the federation into an alliance of sovereign states, or by unilaterally declaring independence. The ex-communist elites brought to power by Milošević in Serbia and Montenegro, the communist elites in the Yugoslav federal army and the new pan-Serb national movement and its elites in Croatia and Bosnia–Hercegovina strongly opposed these plans. All three groups were, in various degrees, ideologically committed to the existing Yugoslav state as their common homeland and as their protector from foreign domination. In addition, Milošević saw in Yugoslavia the possibility of extending his power even further; the new Serb elites in Croatia and Bosnia–Hercegovina found in Yugoslavia the protection from domination by the Croat or Muslim governments of their republics and a common state with other Serbs. The military elites saw in Yugoslavia the source of their pay and status as well as the legitimation of their role.

A unilateral declaration of independence by these two republics would have breached the territorial integrity of the Yugoslav state which the Yugoslav federal army was obliged, by the constitution of 1974, to defend. The Serb elites of the Krajina region in Croatia would have opposed by the force of arms – as they did later – any attempt to compel them to break their links with other Serbs in Yugoslavia. In April 1990 the new Slovenian and Croatian governments had no military forces capable of countering the opposition of either the army or, in the case of Croatia, an armed rebellion of the Serbs supported by the Yugoslav army. In consequence, the new Croatian and Slovenian governments proposed to negotiate with other republican leaders the transformation of Yugoslavia into a confederation of sovereign states while, at the same time, building up their own military forces for any future showdown with their opponents.

Before reopening negotiations with the other republican leaders, in May–July 1990 the Croatian and Slovenian parliaments adopted a series of declarations and constitutional amendments asserting the sovereignty of their republics and legally enabling their own governments to counter any move by Yugoslav federal organs. As expected, the leaders of the Serb Democratic party in Croatia rejected the Croatian constitutional amendments. Amidst increased unrest and violence in the Serb populated areas of Croatia, in October 1990 the Slovenian and Croatian governments submitted to the Yugoslav state presidency an official proposal for the restructuring of Yugoslavia entitled 'A Model of Confederation'. According to the proposal, the existing republics should constitute themselves as independent and sovereign states, based on the right of national self-determination, and, then, as independent states enter into a confederal agreement with other republics or federations which would be based on international law governing relations among independent states.[1] Confederation was thus conceived as an instrument for gaining recognition of independence for the Yugoslav republics. The counterproposal submitted by the Yugoslav state presidency a few weeks later, entitled 'A Concept for the Federal Organisation of Yugoslavia' would have established 'the federal republic' of Yugoslavia on the basis of the sovereignty of its individual citizens. No special rights were attributed to nations as collective entities, except for the declaration that the nations as well as federal units were in the new federal republic deemed to be equal.[2] According to the Slovenian and Croatian proposal, former federal units would become independent states while the Yugoslav state presidency proposal – almost identical to the Serbian and Montenegrin proposal submitted in February 1991 – regarded the federal units as separate but equal units in a single state administration.

The negotiations, started in January 1991 at the expanded sessions of the Yugoslav state presidency, were widely publicised in expectation that they would soon resolve the continuing constitutional crisis which was paralysing the functioning of the state. Neither side, however, showed any willingness to modify its constitutional proposal and the Yugoslav state presidency soon became deadlocked over the election of a Croat HDZ nominee as its next president.[3] On 25 March 1991 presidents Tudjman and Milošević met in Tito's old hunting lodge of Karadordevo ostensibly to discuss the constitutional impasse. According to rumours originating from various sources, they principally discussed a possible partition of Bosnia–Hercegovina between Serbia and Croatia.[4] Whatever the subject of their discussion, their talks brought no change in their previous positions. In April 1991 the negotiations on the future of Yugoslavia were transferred directly to the presidents[5] of the six republics who, in spite of meeting fortnightly until June, likewise failed to reach any agreement. Early in June 1991 the president of the

presidency of Bosnia–Hercegovina, Alija Izetbegović, and the president of Macedonia, Kiro Gligorov, submitted their 'Platform concerning the Future of the Yugoslav State' which avoided using either of the
terms 'confederal' or 'federal'. However, their 'Platform' attributed the
original state sovereignty to the republics and not to the citizens and
defined Yugoslavia as an 'alliance of republics'.[6] In this new alliance,
the republics could establish mutual relations of varying closeness;
some could form a federation while others would establish only confederal ties. Their proposal explicitly denied the right of national self-determination to the each of these nations as a whole which inhabited more
than one republic. According to this, the Serb nation would have its
right of self- determination restricted to its 'titular' homeland, Serbia.
In this way, the Izetbegović–Gligorov proposal attempted to prevent a
possible secession of the Serbs from Bosnia-Hercegovina and the republic's eventual fragmentation. A few weeks later Marković's federal
government endorsed a very similar concept of a 'community of sovereign republics'. In retrospect these compromise proposals look like belated attempts to stave off the disintegration of the Yugoslav state by
those who would lose most from it. Ante Marković would lose a state
of which he was the prime minister; the Macedonian president a state
which provided external security and financial support for his small,
land-locked and poor republic; and Alija Izetbegović a state which until then provided a common homeland both for the Serbs and Croats
of Bosnia–Hercegovina. With the disappearance of their common Yugoslav homeland, Bosnian Serbs and Croats could be expected to join
their newly created homeland states.

Although all the other presidents initially offered guarded support
for the proposal, the Slovenian and the Croatian governments were
not prepared to postpone their respective declarations of independence
which they jointly planned for late June 1991. In the May 1991 referendum on the future of Croatia (which Serbs from Krajina had boycotted), 94.7 per cent of voters (in an 83 per cent turn out) declared for
an independent and sovereign Croatia. After a year-long media campaign for an independent Croatia, in which any dissenting opinion had
been effectively excluded, no other result could have been expected. In
a similar plebiscite in December 1990 in Slovenia, 86 per cent voted
for a sovereign and independent Slovenia. The last-minute tripartite
talks between Tudjman, Milošević and Izetbegović on 12 June 1991
could not halt the planned declarations. Neither could they be halted
by a last-minute warning from the US Secretary of State, James Baker,
on 21 June 1990, that the US would not recognise unilateral acts of seces-

sion. The unanimous vote of the European Community representatives on 23 June that they would not recognise the unilateral secession of Slovenia and Croatia had no more impact either. On 25 June 1991 the Slovenian parliament declared Slovenia an independent state which was no longer a part of the Yugoslav federation while the Croatian Diet declared Croatia an independent and sovereign state which was beginning the process of 'disassociation' from Yugoslavia and of gaining international recognition.

The two governments clearly did not expect immediate international recognition. But as they had already secured support in the mainstream German and Austrian media as well as among German and Austrian politicians they could have reasonably expected to widen their support in time to include other Western European countries; this is probably one of the reasons why the last-minute warnings from foreign governments had no impact. The local media campaign the two governments had launched to demonstrate that, after the repeated failures of the Yugoslav top-level negotiations, the only way out was by unilateral proclamation of independence, had by June 1991 gathered so much momentum that any postponement might have appeared to their electorates as a backdown. Moreover, Slovenian and, to a lesser extent, Croatian military preparedness was, it now appears, deemed sufficient to deter – if not actually defeat – any attempt by the already highly fragmented Yugoslav federal army to oust the two governments from power.

But the secession of Croatia and Slovenia from Yugoslavia had been preceded by another secession – the secession of the Serb-held territories of Krajina and Slavonia from Croatia and their proclaimed 'unification' with Serbia.

## THE SERB INSURRECTION IN CROATIA

The Serbs formed an absolute majority in 11 municipalities (communes) of the Krajina region, bordering Bosnia–Hercegovina and substantial minorities – of close to 40 per cent of the inhabitants – in 14 municipalities in western and eastern Slavonia.[7] In consequence, in the municipal elections in 1990 the Serb Democratic party gained control of local governments in most Serb-majority municipalities. In June 1990 the Krajina Serb municipalities attempted to form a regional grouping which the Croatian government immediately declared illegal. Instead of the special administrative status and 'cultural autonomy' (including Serb electronic and print media) demanded by the Serb Democratic party, the Croatian government offered the Serbs in Serb-majority municipalities the right to form cultural organisations and to use the Cyrillic alphabet in education and official correspondence as well as having a Serb in one of the posts of deputy speaker of the Croatian Diet. The Serb party leaders deeply mistrusted the motives and intentions of the Croat HDZ leadership because of the latter's partial rehabilitation of the Croat Ustasha state and its state emblems. After the failure of talks between the Serb party leader Dr Rašković and president Tudjman in June 1990, the Croatian government, in a bid to undermine Dr Rašković's position in his constituency, released the secretly taped transcripts of the talks thus breaching the agreement to keep the talks confidential. This led to a complete breakdown in relations between the two parties.

In response to a series of Croatian constitutional changes passed by the Croatian Diet in July 1990, the Serb parties in Croatia called a general Serb assembly, formed the Serb National Council and passed a Declaration on the Sovereignty and Autonomy of the Serbs in Croatia. In August, four months before a similar Slovenian plebiscite, the newly formed Serb National Council organised a referendum of Serbs – but not of Croats or any other nationalities – in Croatia. According to its organisers, an overwhelming majority of the votes were cast in support of the proposition that the Serbs be granted cultural autonomy in Croatia and that if Croatia left the Yugoslav federation, the Serbs should be granted political autonomy.[8] The Croatian government proclaimed the referendum illegal, accusing Milošević and the Serbian leadership of instigating the referendum and the ensuing insurrection as part of their expansionist plans for a Greater Serbia which was to include parts of Croatia.

In response to the attempts of the Croatian police to gain control of Serb-held towns and police stations, in late August Serbs took over police stations and armouries in several Serb-populated municipalities, erecting barricades and check-points on the roads leading in to them. This was variously described as an insurrection (harking back to Serb insurrections against Ottoman rule) or a 'log revolution' in reference to the logs felled to barricade the roads. In January 1991, the Serb-controlled districts in Croatia formed the Serb Autonomous Region of Krajina, with its own police force independent of the Croatian government; to this the Croatian government responded by a full mobilisation of police reserves. Alarmed by the Croatian government's response, in early January the Yugoslav state presidency ordered the dissolution of all illegally formed and armed units in Yugoslavia. The Croatian and

Slovenian governments at first refused to carry out the order but, faced with continuing threats from the Yugoslav federal army, the Croatian government demobilised a part of its mobilised police force, refusing, however, to hand over any weapons to the army. While the Croatian government continued clandestinely to purchase arms abroad for its armed forces, Milošević's government continued to arm Serb insurgents. At the same time opposition parties from Serbia, including the revived Chetnik movement of Dr Šešelj, began dispatching volunteers to Krajina to be organised into various paramilitary formations.

On 28 February 1991 the Serb National Council in Krajina declared the 'disassociation' of Krajina region from Croatia and its intention of remaining within Yugoslavia. The Yugoslav state presidency also ordered the Yugoslav federal army to interpose itself between the Serb militias and the Croatian forces in Pakrac in western Slavonia. As the Yugoslav army's intervention blocked the Croatian government's attempt to establish its authority by force, the Croatian government saw this, as well as all previous such interventions, as hostile acts. As skirmishes between the Croat and Serb armed forces continued in mixed-population areas of Krajina and Slavonia, in May 1991 large demonstrations erupted in various Croatian cities against both the Serbs and Yugoslav federal army. Serb properties were destroyed and many Serbs forced to flee to Serbia and Serb-controlled areas; Yugoslav army conscripts also came under attack. The Croat inhabitants who remained in the Serb-controlled areas in spite of the earlier pressures to leave, were at that time also forced to flee to Croatia. As the Yugoslav state presidency's efforts at mediation through a joint Croat and Serb commission produced no results, the stage was set for a further escalation of fighting in July and August and the outbreak of war in Croatia in September 1991 (see Chapter 10).

Calling for a boycott of the referendum for the independence of Croatia scheduled for 19 May 1991 the Serb assembly of Krajina on 16 May unanimously voted for the unification of Krajina with Serbia. Although Milošević's government had from 1990 on aided the Serb authorities in Krajina in various ways, the Serbian parliament (which he controlled) never officially accepted the unification of Krajina with Serbia. Unlike the Croatian and Slovenian secessions, this act of Serb secession from Croatia, which mirrored the former,[9] has never been internationally recognised. A similar secession of Kosovo Albanians from Serbia, who, on 30 September 1991, in a clandestine referendum declared for a sovereign and independent state of Kosovo, also failed to gain international recognition. The principal reasons for the absence of recognition in these two cases was the view, adopted by the European Community and other Western countries (see Chapter 10), that only the former Yugoslav republics have the right of self-determination and not any single national group within Yugoslavia. This, of course, did not stop the leaders of these national groups from pursuing their secessionist claims. In both cases the leaders' ability to mobilise their respective electorates for secession was greatly facilitated by the refusal of the governments of Serbia and of Croatia to grant their demands for cultural and political autonomy and by the two governments' attempts to establish their authority through the use of force.

## THE FRAGMENTATION OF THE YUGOSLAV FEDERAL ARMY

From 1971 the Croat and Slovene dissident nationalists regarded the existence of a unified armed force in Yugoslavia, the Yugoslav People's Army, as the principal obstacle to the achievement of their goals – the sovereignty of their nations within or without a Yugoslav confederation. In contrast, some Serb nationalists regarded the army as the ultimate safeguard of Serb interests within Yugoslavia. According to the Yugoslav Communist party doctrine, the army, continuing the tradition of the communist-led Partisans, was an all-Yugoslav institution, defending the integrity of the country and the interests of all its nations. In the late 1980s, however, the rising nationalism among Slovene, Croat and Kosovo Albanian youth – as well as deteriorating pay and conditions of army officers – led to a virtual halt in the recruitment of cadet officers from these national groups. In keeping with its all-Yugoslav doctrine, the Yugoslav military authorities, in the words of one Western expert, 'bent its rules to try to maintain ethnic proportionality'[10] but to no effect. From 1986 the youth weekly *Mladina* in Slovenia systematically targeted the Yugoslav federal army as a corrupt and foreign body; the latter's arrest and trial of four Slovenes led to the formation of a mass movement demanding sovereignty for Slovenia (see Chapter 8). By 1989 the Yugoslav federal army was viewed in Slovenian official as well as youth media as a foreign – primarily Serb – force imposing a foreign, communist system on Slovenia. As an increasing number of young Slovenes had already refused to serve in the Yugoslav army, in March 1991 the Slovenian parliament proclaimed a moratorium on the dispatch of Slovene conscripts and in April it withdrew all Slovene conscripts from the Yugoslav army. In early 1990 for similar reasons the number of Croat and Muslim conscripts in the Yugoslav army significantly declined as well.

With the effective dissolution of the Yugoslav Communist party in January 1990, the army officer corps, left without the political and ideological guidance it had before, had to look for the legitimation and definition of their task elsewhere. In late 1990 the largest number of the army's High Command officers were Croats (38 per cent), followed by Serbs and Montenegrins (33 per cent), Slovenes (8.3 per cent), Macedonians (8.3 per cent) and Muslims (4.1 per cent).[11] Of the nine highest commanding officers of the Yugoslav federal army, four were Croats, there were two Slovenes, one Serb, one Macedonian and one – the Minister for Defence Veljko Kadijević – came from a mixed Croato-Serb marriage.[12] With the exception of a few who defected to the Slovenian and Croatian government forces (see below), most of the High Command officers remained aloof from politics and committed to a single Yugoslavia in one form or another. As only a few of them offered political support to Milošević,[13] they were ultimately dismissed from their posts either during the Croato-Serb war in 1991 or in the final purge of the Yugoslav federal army by Milošević in April 1992. The figures for officers of all ranks in the army (excluding the navy – which had a higher proportion of Croats – and air force) were Serbs (42.63 per cent of the officer corps; 36.5 per cent of the total population), followed by Croats (14.21 per cent; 19.7 per cent of the total population), self-declared Yugoslavs (10 per cent; 3 per cent of the total population), Montenegrins (9.45 per cent; 2.3 per cent of the total population), Slovenes (6.4 per cent; 7.5 per cent of the total population), Macedonians (6.3 per cent; 5.8 per cent of the total population), Muslims (5.6 per cent; 10 per cent of the total population), Albanians (3.15 per cent; 9.3 of the total population).[14] The most obvious disproportion, compared to the their percentage of the total population, was among Montenegrins and self-declared Yugoslavs (a larger number of officers than in the total population) and among Albanians, Muslims and Croats (a smaller number of officers than in the total population).

Already in late 1989 a number of Croat and Slovene officers found a new allegiance in the nationalist parties in Slovenia and Croatia. Thus the retired Yugoslav general Croat Martin Špegelj, the first HDZ minister of defence, organised separate Croatian armed forces. Following the public scandal in January 1991 in which he was exposed as the initiator of the Croatian purchase of arms in Hungary and elsewhere, the Yugoslav army authorities issued a warrant for his arrest which he, with the help of the Croatian government security service, successfully avoided. In August–September 1991, prior to the outbreak of the war in Croatia, several thousand Croat officers, including the commander-in-chief of the Yugoslav air force general Anton Tus and vice-admiral Pavle Grubišić, defected to the Croatian government forces.[15] Many of those who changed sides at that time probably did so not out of a newly found Croat patriotism but because they could foresee that the Yugoslav federal army, on the eve of the war against the Croatian government, would probably dismiss them in any case. According to the Slovene sources, a significant number of Slovene officers in the Yugoslav federal army worked for the Slovenian defence ministry even before the war broke out in Slovenia in June 1991. Many middle-ranking and non-commissioned Serb officers, who came from Bosnian Serb or Krajina Serb background, had aided the Bosnian Serb Democratic party as well as Krajina Serb authorities with arms, supplies and advice long before the outbreak of hostilities in these regions. At the outbreak of the hostilities several thousand proceeded to join the Serb military formed in Croatian Krajina and in Bosnia–Hercegovina. For example, colonel Ratko Mladić, as a commanding officer of the Knin garrison in 1991, helped the Krajina Serb authorities with arms and logistic support to organise their armed resistance against the Croatian government. Promoted to a major-general after the Croato-Serb war in 1991, he chose to remain in his native Bosnia and in May 1992 became the head of the High Command of the Bosnian Serb military.

In November 1990 a group of retired Serb and Croat generals together with Serb, Muslim, Macedonian and Croat communist politicians of pro-Yugoslav orientation resurrected the Yugoslav Communist party under the name of League of Communists – Movement for Yugoslavia. In spite of the support that the party got from Milošević (through his wife, Mirjana Marković, one of its founders) and a few serving generals, the majority of the High Command generals and the officers corps stood aloof from this or any other political party. However, the secession of Slovenia and Croatia as well as the outbreak of hostilities in Serb-populated regions of Croatia presented a severe test of allegiance for the politically uncommitted self-declared Yugoslav, Serb and Montenegrin officers. The Croatian and Slovenian secessions threatened to destroy their homeland, Yugoslavia, and the Croatian government's use of armed force to subdue the Serbs of Krajina were for many Serbs and Montenegrins – in particular the Serbs from outside Serbia proper – a re-enactment of the Croatian Ustashe policy of extermination of Serbs which was deeply embedded in their families' memories. While many of the officers had earlier shown no sympathy for Milošević's Serb nationalist rhetoric and mass mobilisation and rallies, in the period from 1990 to 1991 he was the only politician in Yugo-

slavia whose programme of preservation of Yugoslavia had any appeal
to them. This probably explains why the Belgrade garrison command
in March 1991, on Milošević's request, sent out tanks and soldiers into
the streets of Belgrade, after the violent opposition demonstrations
erupted against his government. In a way, Milošević's government won
the allegiance of these officers by default.

In contrast, many pro-Yugoslav army officers viewed the refusal of
the federal prime minister, Ante Marković, and his government to order any action against the Croatian and Slovenian governments' creation of their own armed forces and their clandestine import of arms,
as a betrayal of Yugoslavia. In addition, many officers viewed his policy
of severe budget cuts on army expenditure as part of the Slovene and
Croat conspiracy to emasculate the capacity of the Yugoslav federal
army to protect Yugoslavia.[16] While still accepting the authority of the
Yugoslav federal bodies at the time of Slovenia's and Croatia's declarations of independence in June 1991, the Yugoslav army's High Command no longer had any trust in Marković's government and in the
Croatian and Slovenian members of the Yugoslav state presidency.[17]

In June 1991 the High Command carried out the orders of the minister for defence and Marković's government to secure the border posts
in Slovenia, as well as orders of the Yugoslav state presidency, in July
1991, to evacuate from Slovenia. However, as the Croat armed forces
started to blockade and attack the Yugoslav federal army units in Croatia, Ante Marković demanded the resignation of his defence minister,
general Kadijević, and his deputy, the Slovene admiral Brovet, charging
them with conducting secret talks with their Soviet counterparts, in
March 1991, in Moscow. By refusing to resign and accusing the prime
minister of treason in September 1991, the High Command officers
finally repudiated the authority of Marković and his federal government.[18] The High Command, however, continued to accept the
authority of the Yugoslav state presidency, which was, in October 1991,
reduced to four members, the representatives of Serbia, Montenegro,
Vojvodina and Kosovo, all of whom were controlled by Milošević. It
was only at this point that the Yugoslav federal army came under Milošević's direct control. At that point it still retained a good number of
pro-Yugoslav officers who were not of Serb origin and a significant
number of conscripts of Hungarian, Macedonian, Albanian and Bosnian Muslim origin.

In retrospect, it is quite surprising for how long the Yugoslav federal
army recognised the authority of the constitutional federal bodies –
Marković's government and the Yugoslav state presidency – in the face of

both the progressive loss of Yugoslav federal authority in all parts of Yugoslavia and severe disagreements between the High Command and the prime minister and members of the Yugoslav state presidency.

# 10 Slovenia and Croatia at War 1991–2

## SLOVENIA'S LITTLE WAR WITH THE YUGOSLAV FEDERAL ARMY

Having gained control over all territorial defence units in Slovenia during 1990, the Slovenian ministry of defence proceeded to take over most of the territorial defence armouries and to import a substantial quantity of arms from abroad. The existing territorial defence units, commanded by Slovene reserve officers, were expanded with new recruits and transformed it into a lightly armed but well-organised force capable of fielding more than 100 000 soldiers. In parallel with these preparations for a showdown with the Yugoslav federal army, the Slovene defence ministry, through the Slovene officers serving in the Yugo-

*Map 3*    Yugoslavia in 1991
*Source*: J. Zametica, *The Yugoslav Conflict*, Adelphi Paper 270, London, 1992.

slav federal army's headquarters in Ljubljana and in Belgrade, gained information about the Yugoslav army's plans, deployment and strength as well as about its counter-intelligence operations in Slovenia.[1] The latter information enabled the Slovenian defence force to block the Yugoslav federal army's attempts to gain intelligence about the Slovenian defence preparations.

The Slovenian defence ministry, headed by the former pacifist activist Janez Janša, planned to expel the Yugoslav federal army from Slovenia by cutting its communications by a series of guerilla actions which would isolate its units and garrisons.[2] Since it had no chance of defeating the Yugoslav federal army in frontal battles, the Slovenian forces primarily aimed at incapacitating the opponent. As part of these plans, the Slovenian government was also preparing to mobilise public opinion in Western Europe, in particular the media and politicians of Austria and Germany, to exert pressure on the Yugoslav federal organs to order the withdrawal of its thus incapacitated army.

The Yugoslav federal army's plans – which the Slovenian defence ministry acquired through its informants – envisaged the capture and disarming of the Slovene territorial defence outposts and officers and the blocking of Slovene territorial defence mobilisation. While the army made preliminary preparations for this action, on 26 June 1991 the Yugoslav federal government proclaimed the Slovenian declaration of independence illegal and ordered the army only to capture and hold 136 outposts at or near the Yugoslav border with Austria and Italy, international airport crossings at Ljubljana and Maribor as well as the internal border outposts which the Slovenian government started to erect between Slovenia and Croatia. The aim of this operation was to prevent the Slovenian government from setting up internal border checkpoints and taking over international border crossings from the existing Yugoslav federal authorities. The army was ordered to fire only in self-defence; its conscript soldiers were not briefed on the nature and aims of the operation nor on potential Slovenian resistance. Lacking intelligence and not expecting armed resistance, most of the Yugoslav federal army units were ambushed; some were surrounded and forced to surrender while others were continually harassed and their communication with their bases cut. At a few points, the army units called for air support and at a number of crossing points, tanks were used to break through the Slovenian defence positions. In three days of fighting the Yugoslav army units, often under persistent fire, had by 28 June 1991 taken most of their targets. According to the Yugoslav army High Command, only 10 per cent of its effective troops in Slovenia (over 3000 men and officers) were used in this initial operation. The Slovenian government was able to mobilise a much greater number of soldiers, who surrounded and blockaded all Yugoslav army barracks and units in Slovenia. After a week of fighting, the Yugoslav state presidency rejected the Yugoslav army's plan for a full-scale invasion and occupation of Slovenia and, instead, proposed a cease-fire which the Slovenian government, fearing a full-scale war, accepted on 2 July 1991. In spite of this, sporadic fighting continued as the Slovene defence units maintained their blockade of all Yugoslav army units and barracks, refusing either to let army units return to the barracks or to lift the blockade of the barracks.[3] The final cease-fire was concluded only on 7 July 1991 through the mediation of the EC mission – the EC Troika – consisting of foreign ministers from three EC countries (see next section).

The Yugoslav federal army casualties included 45 conscripts killed (almost from all national groups in Yugoslavia) while the Slovene defence forces had 12 dead. Over 2000 Yugoslav federal army conscripts surrendered to the Slovene defence forces. The Yugoslav federal army intervention sparked off demonstrations in Belgrade on 2 July 1991 in which the Yugoslav army conscripts' parents invaded the Serbian parliament demanding the return of their sons from Slovenia. The operation showed how unprepared the Yugoslav federal army was for an armed conflict with the well-organised and highly motivated armed forces of the two secessionist republics. Not only did its command lack vital intelligence and failed to plan adequately for this confrontation, but conscripts and officers lacked the motivation and training to fight this type of war.

While the Slovenian armed forces did not stop the Yugoslav army from reaching most of its targets, their resistance enabled the Slovenian government to run a successful media campaign against the Yugoslav federal army and the Yugoslav federal bodies. While the Slovenian government press centre fed the foreign media highly exaggerated and false accounts of fighting and of death counts, the foreign journalists and inhabitants of the Slovenian capital Ljubljana were repeatedly warned of imminent aerial bombardment which never came (and, as the Slovenian government well knew, was never planned). In foreign television broadcasts, young, often blond, Slovenes in immaculate camouflage uniforms, preferably with sunglasses – speaking English and, at times, German – stood in sharp contrast to the sight of the Yugoslav army tanks brutally crushing civilian cars or firing at peaceful homes.[4] The Yugoslav federal army operation was portrayed as an all-out communist invasion – similar to but more violent than the Soviet invasions of Czechoslovakia in 1968 and Hungary in 1956 – of a small 'westward-leaning democracy'.

Well before the start of the hostilities, the Slovenian government was able to recruit various Austrian and German political parties as well as the Austrian government and its foreign minister, Alois Mock, to support its bid for independence. Already in March 1991, Mock urged the European governments to consider Slovenia's and Croatia's demands for independence and the Greens group in Austria's parliament tabled a resolution calling for the recognition of Slovenia's independence.[5] In early July 1991 the chairman of the ruling Christian Democratic party in Germany also appealed for the international recognition of Slovenia as well as Croatia. As the fighting in Slovenia continued after 2 July, Mock reiterated his proposals and called for European Community military intervention to stop the fighting. Instead of military intervention, the European Community foreign ministers had already sent, on 28 June, the foreign ministers of Italy, Luxembourg and the Netherlands – the Troika – to mediate in the conflict. Thus started the first mediation effort by the European Community in the Yugoslav conflict.

## THE EC: A SUCCESSFUL PEACEMAKER IN SLOVENIA

Slovenia's and Croatia's respective declarations of independence and the fighting in Slovenia did not immediately change the commitment of most European governments as well as the US government to the preservation of Yugoslavia in some form or another.[6] At the urging of the German government, the foreign ministers of the Western European Union[7] on 27 June requested the Conference for Security and Cooperation in Europe (CSCE), under its emergency procedures, to dispatch an investigating team to Yugoslavia. The CSCE agreed to let the European Community act on its behalf. The EC ministerial Troika's first apparent success was the agreement of all warring parties to a cease-fire on 2 July 1991 and Croatia's and Slovenia's acceptance of a three-month moratorium on their declarations of independence during which a negotiated overall settlement of the dispute should be reached. This was crowned by the installation of the Croat representative, Stipe Mesić, as the president of the Yugoslav state presidency, in the presence of the EC's Troika.[8] The idea behind this EC plan was to get the republican leaders to resume negotiations over the constitutional framework of Yugoslavia which had been going on since January 1991.

As the fighting continued after 2 July, the EC cut arms sales and economic aid to all Yugoslav republics and sent its Troika once again to negotiate. On 7 July 1991 the EC Troika at Tito's former private island of

Brioni issued a joint declaration which committed the European Community both to monitoring and to offering assistance in the negotiating process among the Yugoslav republics which had to start at the latest on 1 August. The declaration also envisaged the lifting of the blockade of the Yugoslav army units and barracks in Slovenia, the clearing of all roads and the deactivation of territorial defence units and their return to quarters. Finally, the declaration established an observer mission of unarmed military and civilian officials from the EC countries: these were nominally under CSCE control. The Yugoslav state presidency and the presidents of all six republics accepted the declaration and the Yugoslav army units began to return to their bases. Although the Slovene defence units were not deactivated, the Yugoslav state presidency, on 18 July 1991, decided unilaterally to withdraw all Yugoslav army units from Slovenia within three months. This decision, reached quite independently of the EC-sponsored negotiations, signalled the victory of the Slovenian government: with the withdrawal of the Yugoslav federal army, the last link with the Yugoslav federal government was severed and Slovenia had *de facto* seceded from the federation.

At the time this appeared to be an easily won victory which the political leaders in Croatia and Bosnia–Hercegovina probably thought could be copied in their republics. For a start it seemed sufficient to attack the Yugoslav federal army units so as to provoke their retaliation. The brutality of the retaliation, if sufficiently well publicised abroad, should in turn mobilise international public opinion and the European Community governments to negotiate a cease-fire, to send its observers to oversee the withdrawal of the Yugoslav army units and thus to ensure a peaceful transfer of power to the republican armed forces. This scenario of the internationalisation of Yugoslav conflicts presupposed not only the willingness but also the ability of the EC or some other international organisation to secure a cease-fire which it could then monitor. Unless this could be achieved in a fairly short time, the Yugoslav federal army could use its huge firepower to destroy both the military and civilian targets which it deemed to stand on its way. In their bid to achieve independence on a similar scenario of internationalisation, the Croatian and Bosnian Muslim political leaders not only overestimated the ability of the European Community and, later, the United Nations, to halt the Yugoslav federal army's advance but also ignored the possibility that, in the process, the army itself would change its personnel and its objectives.

The EC Troika's success in stopping the fighting and securing an EC-supervised cease-fire gave the impression that the EC's involvement was the principal catalyst in the peaceful resolution of the conflict in

Slovenia. In consequence, it appeared that the EC could fairly easily secure peace in Yugoslavia. In fact, the EC Troika's success did not signal
any recognition of the EC's peacemaking capabilities, but the willingness of the Yugoslav federal army High Command and the Serbian representatives in the Yugoslav state presidency to abandon Slovenia.
Once the two bodies had decided that Slovenia was not worth fighting
for, the EC's Brioni declaration and subsequent monitoring of the
cease-fire was a good way of not only saving face but also of securing
an orderly withdrawal of Yugoslav army troops and equipment needed
for its next operation, the defence and enlargement of the Serb-held territories in Croatia. The Slovenian government, on the other hand,
needed the presence of EC monitors in Slovenia not only to ensure
that the Yugoslav federal army would be effectively neutralised but also
to guarantee the *de facto* recognition of Slovenian independence. In
the conflict which flared up in Croatia a few months later, the EC and
its officials soon proved incapable of either securing a cease-fire or an
agreement among the warring parties to negotiate. The EC's success in
Slovenia was a one-off affair in which both the Slovenian government
and the Yugoslav federal army and its Serbian supporters used the EC
Troika's good offices for their own quite different ends.


THE WAR IN CROATIA: 1991

The armed clashes between the Croatian government forces and Serb
militias in the border areas of the Serb-held territories in Croatia (see
Chapter 9) culminated in an ambush, on 2 May 1991, by local Serb
militias and irregulars from Serbia of a large detachment of Croatian
police at Borovo Selo in eastern Slavonia which left twelve Croat policemen dead. After the clash the Croatian authorities showed photos
of the Croatian policemen's bodies to the foreign media, claiming that
some of the dead were tortured while others were savagely mutilated
by the Serbs. This clash, with the single largest death toll thus far, triggered a concentrated media campaign in Croatia and abroad against
the alleged Serb invasion and occupation of Croat territory. The media
campaign was followed by attacks on Yugoslav army conscripts and
barracks, notably in Split, in which one conscript was killed. The block-
ades of the Yugoslav army barracks were lifted after negotiations with
the Yugoslav state presidency and the army.
    During the war in Slovenia in late June 1991, the Croatian government
made no attempt to hinder the movement of Yugoslav army units. How-

*Map 4*     Serbs in the population of Croatia and Bosnia–Hercegovina, by Commune (1981)

*Source*: L. J. Cohen, *Broken Bonds* Boulder: Westview Press, 1995.

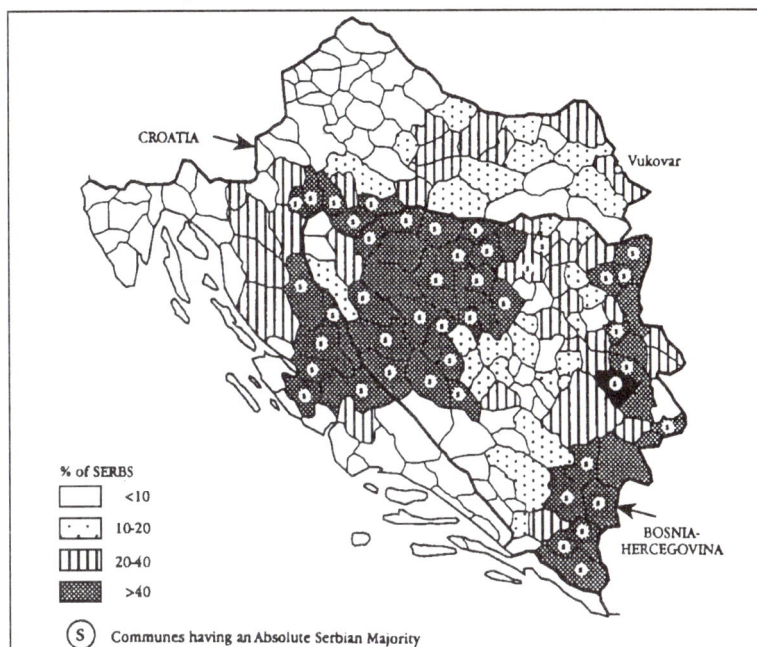

ever, fighting between the Croatian police and armed forces and Serb militias spread in late July to several mixed-population areas of the three regions – Krajina, eastern and western Slavonia – controlled by the Serbs. In response, the Yugoslav state presidency, presided over by its Croatian president, issued a declaration calling for a halt in hostilities in Croatia and appointed a commission to monitor the cease-fire. Disagreeing with the election of the Serbian representative to head this commission, the Croatian president of the presidency, Stipe Mesić walked out of the meeting. After his walk-out, the Croatian government publicly announced emergency measures to facilitate mobilisation of its newly created Croatian National Guard; at the same time, it tabled legislation in the Croatian Diet offering the Serbs in majority Serb areas in Croatia 'political and territorial autonomy' (without the right to secession) which until then it had refused to discuss with the Serb political representatives. None of these measures halted escalation of the fighting.

In late August 1991, the Croatian government openly accused the Yugoslav federal army of aiding the Serb insurgents and proclaimed the blockade of the Yugoslav army barracks throughout the republic. From 13 September the Croatian National Guard (later renamed the Croatian army) and police units closed access to over 100 barracks of the Yugoslav army in Croatia, cutting off their water, electricity and food supplies, and firing on the guards. The Yugoslav army High Command took this as a declaration of war and ordered its units first to resist and, later, to break out of the blockade, by force if necessary. At the same time it started to mobilise reservists in Montenengro and Serbia, amassing troops for an assault on Croatia. In late September 1991 the Yugoslav federal army units moved from Serbia and Montenegro into Croatia attacking Croatian communication lines and relieving some of the blockaded garrisons. No civilian authorities initially authorised these moves. On 18 September the federal prime minister, the Croat Ante Marković, opposed these moves[9] and demanded the resignation of his minister for defence and his Slovene deputy, while the Croat president of the Yugoslav state presidency, Stipe Mesić, refused to call a meeting of the presidency. Only in early October did the four remaining members of the Yugoslav state presidency who were controlled by Milošević (the other republics' representatives had left the presidency), proclaim an imminent danger of war and authorised the Yugoslav federal army to restore order.

The Yugoslav army originally planned to secure control over all the communication links in Croatia, including access to its capital Zagreb, and to isolate Croatia from the outside world through a naval and land blockade.[10] However, in the face of well-organised and stiff resistance from the Croatian army and various Croat paramilitary units, the Yugoslav federal army, severely depleted in manpower[11] and plagued by low morale and poor command and communications, quickly abandoned this plan and restricted itself to the following four areas of military action:

- a concentrated assault on western and eastern Slavonia and Baranja, including the cities of Vukovar and Osijek (with substantial Serb populations);[12]
- an assault on the seaside town of Dubrovnik and its hinterland;
- a naval blockade of the largest ports in Croatia and the extrication of the Yugoslav federal navy's equipment from those ports;
- the withdrawal of personnel and heavy weapons from its garrisons in Croatia, including the central garrison in Zagreb.

In its operations the Yugoslav army commanders appeared to be guided by geostrategic considerations as well as by a desire to enlarge the territories already controlled by Serb insurgents. For example, one of the army's main targets, the city of Vukovar – with a mixed Serb and Croat population of almost equal proportions – has one of the largest ports on the river Danube and is located on the border with Serbia. While the strategic importance of the seaside town of Dubrovnik is minimal, its mountainous hinterland (with a very small Serb population) controls the communication links to the main Yugoslav navy base at Kotor in Montenegro. In addition, the Yugoslav army supported the Serb militias from Krajina in their drive south to the Dalmatian coast which would cut the only land communication link between mainland Croatia and the Dalmatian littoral around the seaside cities of Zadar and Šibenik.

The Croatian forces – the Croatian army, police units, various paramilitary units as well as foreign mercenaries – probably mobilised over 120 000 men, who were commanded by former Yugoslav army officers of Croat origin as well as by emigré Croats who responded to the call for the defence of the homeland.[13] Unlike their Slovenian counterparts, they were equipped with heavy artillery and engaged the Yugoslav army in frontal battles in which their superior numbers and morale matched the Yugoslav army's superiority in armour and overall firepower. After almost three months of intensive artillery bombardment and fighting, in November 1991 the Yugoslav federal army took the ruins of the city of Vukovar which in the last few weeks of fighting was defended only by a small force of volunteer paramilitaries. All of its remaining Croat population – as well as the Croat population of the neighbouring towns and villages – was forced to leave (most Serbs in the Croat-held areas of eastern and western Slavonia had by that time also been forced to leave their homes). While the Yugoslav army occupied most of Dubrovnik's hinterland – exposing the latter to pillage by its Montenegrin reservists – it made no attempt to take the medieval city of Dubrovnik itself. However, the widely televised albeit sporadic shelling of the city by the Yugoslav army and navy was successfully presented abroad as a symbol of the barbarity of the Yugoslav federal army and of Croatia's will to resist it (see next section).

The Yugoslav army's major success was the retrieval of most of its equipment and personnel from its Croatian garrisons; only a few of its major garrisons were forced to surrender and hand over its weaponry. As in Slovenia, the Yugoslav army command initially left its units in Croatia stranded in their garrisons unprepared for the blockade and attack; it often took weeks (sometimes months) to organise their relief or withdrawal. Their withdrawal as well as the very limited territorial gains in eastern Slavonia[14] and the Dubrovnik area were extracted at a very heavy cost in terms of its own casualties as well as the casualties among civilians and the Croatian forces. The Yugoslav federal army had thousands of its conscripts and reservists killed and even a larger number wounded while the Croatian armed forces, exposed to the Yugoslav army's superior firepower, probably suffered an even larger rate of causalities.[15] It is estimated that well over 10 000 civilians and soldiers died during this war. Hundred of thousands of Croats, Serbs and members of other nationalities were forced to flee their homes and to become refugees. Whole areas which were previously of mixed population were cleared of their Croat or Serb inhabitants.

In spite of the gains of the Yugoslav federal army and Serb militias and the heavy casualties and destruction of property on the Croatian side, president Tudjman and his HDZ-dominated government could triumphantly proclaim Croatia to be the victor in the Homeland war (as it was named): its armed forces succeeded in defending most of its territory and in the process Croatia gained international recognition as an independent state. His government and his party thus took credit for both preparing for and waging a victorious war. In contrast, the war eroded the support of president Milošević in Serbia (but not among Serbs outside of Serbia). Not only did his government throughout the war pretend that Serbia itself was not at war but it also failed to explain why Serbian soldiers were dying in the fighting in Croatia or what the objectives of the Yugoslav federal army were. As a result, tens of thousands of conscripts and reservists from all social strata – both in Belgrade and in the provincial areas – avoided the call-up or abandoned their units.[16] Several opposition leaders – including the previously fierce nationalist Vuk Drašković – came out against the war claiming that it served only the interests of the communist generals and politicians as well as the Croatian ruling party and its leader.

The war finally demonstrated that the Yugoslav federal army – or what was left of it – and the Milošević regime lacked both the popular support and the military capability and manpower needed to rule over non-Serb areas of Yugoslavia. Likewise, the Croatian government, in spite of the defection of a large number of Yugoslav army officers and imports of foreign arms, had not acquired the military capability needed to defeat the Serb insurgent militias which were armed and supported by the Yugoslav federal army. The military capability of both sides was limited for similar reasons: soldiers of both the Serb militias in Croatia and of the Croatian defence forces were successfully indoctrinated with the belief that they were fighting for their respective homes and homeland. Among the Serb militias raised in their places of residence, the belief was often literally true: they fought near their homes and families against the Croat forces which, they believed, were intent on their destruction and elimination. For them the homeland meant the Serb-populated areas of Yugoslavia, primarily the local area from which they came; in a wider sense they regarded Yugoslavia and not Croatia as their homeland. Among the Croat soldiers both in the conscript army and in the volunteer paramilitary units, the homeland took a wider meaning of Croatia as home for all Croats (including, possibly, Croatian patriots of Serb origin or of Eastern Orthodox faith).[17] According to the widely accepted official doctrine, Croatia is not the homeland of the insurgent Serbs who are simply helping Belgrade Serbian rulers in their endeavour to subjugate Croatia to their rule. The two opposing beliefs about one's homeland and the resulting strong motivation to fight for it, had made these two groups into bitter and staunch enemies. The Yugoslav federal army conscripts and officers – Serbs from Serbia as well as members of other nationalities – not only lacked this type of patriotic motivation, but had no clear ideological conception of what they were fighting for. The Yugoslav federal army's High Command belatedly realised this when, in the midst of the war, it ordered the Partisan army red star insignia removed and replaced by a badge with no previous historical connotations. The removal of the old Partisan emblem symbolised the total failure of the old Partisan ideology to provide a legitimisation for the Yugoslav federal army's operations in Croatia.

Because of the limits of the military capabilities of each side in the conflict, in December 1991 the war reached a stalemate. The Croatian forces could not dislodge the Serb insurgents and the Yugoslav army from approximately one-third of the territory of the former Yugoslav republic of Croatia; the Yugoslav federal army could not defeat the Croatian forces nor take more territory than it had. Partly as a result of this stalemate, both sides agreed to the cessation of hostilities which the UN special envoy, former US Secretary of State Cyrus Vance negotiated in December 1991.

## MEDIA AT WAR: THE IMAGES OF REVERSED STEREOTYPES

The media preparation for this war could probably be traced back to early 1990. The Croat HDZ, even before its electoral victory, was branded in the Belgrade and Zagreb communist-controlled media, as pro-

Ustasha or 'ustašoid', on the ground that its leaders had rehabilitated the Ustasha state. As the fighting between the Croatian government forces and the Serb insurgents in Krajina broke out, both in the local Serb media in Krajina and in the Belgrade media, the Croatian government forces were routinely referred to as 'Ustashe', thus invoking the memory of the Ustashe wartime massacres.[18] This image of Croatian authorities and their armed force as Ustashe was naturally reinforced by the decision of the Croatian government to replace the communist red star insignia on police uniforms and the flag with the traditional Croat shield with chequered squares resembling the insignia used by the Ustashe during World War II. The fear of a re-enactment of Ustashe massacres among the Serbs of Croatia was further reinforced by regular references in all Serb media to Jasenovac – the principal Ustasha World War II death camp – and to *jame,* the pits into which Ustashe threw their Serb victims.[19] To reinforce the Ustasha image of the Croatian regime, the Serbian tabloid press, controlled by Milošević appointees since 1988, started in early 1991 to carry false reports of Croat killings of Serbs in Croatia. The usual pattern was to portray the actual fighting between Croatian police units and Serb insurgents as raiding parties by Croatian policemen intent on slaughtering barehanded Serbs.[20]

As the Croat HDZ took over control of the Croatian media after April 1990, stories of wartime massacres of Croats by Partisans and Chetniks were also given wide publicity.[21] These were often presented as cautionary tales with a clear reference to contemporary Serb and communist attitudes towards the Croats. At the outbreak of the war the newly coined term 'Serbo-communist' was officially prescribed for the use in the media as a common label for Serb forces and the Yugoslav federal army. Just as the Serb media used the term 'Ustasha' so from mid-1990 the HDZ-controlled media had started to use the term 'Chetnik'[22] to refer to Serb insurgents and politicians in the Serb-controlled regions of Croatia on the opposing side (often qualified by 'terrorists', 'aggressors', 'occupiers', 'criminals', 'barbarians', 'butchers', 'extremists').[23] The Croatian mass-circulation dailies at the same time regularly carried stories about violence and brutality by the Serb 'bandits' in the Serb-controlled territories which called for the intervention of Croatian police as well as cartoons in which the Serb side was regularly presented in the stereotyped Chetnik garb – the fur cap with Chetnik insignia, disorderly black uniform, a long knife (with its connotation of throat-cutting), a plum brandy flask and a bomb. The image of the Serb people was slowly merging with that of the Chetniks. In the first month of the war the Croatian government also issued a set of instructions, regulating the language, presentation and tone of reporting about the war. It prescribed the use of 'Serb terrorist' and 'Serbo-communist army of occupation' as the only admissible terms, prohibited the broadcasting of pictures of wounded Croatian soldiers and of the names of the Serbs whose houses were mined (blown-up) by Croats, and enjoined optimistic reporting of defeats.[24]

A new stage of the Croatian propaganda campaign came with the Borovo Selo massacre in May 1991 after which the Croatian ministry of information issued to foreign media photos of the allegedly mutilated and tortured Croatian soldiers. In the Croatian campaign aimed at Western – primarily German and Austrian – media, the Serb forces and the Yugoslav federal army were from then on presented as perpetrators of savage atrocities against civilians and captured soldiers. Thus a German network in 1991 showed Croatian film footage of the mutilated bodies of two young men who were described as victims of a massacre of Croats by Serbs in Gospić; the network later apologised as the bodies turned out to be Serbs killed by Croats.[25] Television footage shot by the Western media of Croatian villages and towns shelled by the Yugoslav federal army reinforced the image of a peaceful, Western country being invaded by savages in unkempt uniforms. The shelling of Dubrovnik, the well-known tourist destination, provided an excellent focus for a concentrated Croatian TV and radio campaign aimed at the international public. It promoted widespread protests and hurried visits of politicians and celebrities to the sight of an allegedly destroyed town. As it turned out, the Croatian army units deliberately provoked shelling by the Yugoslav army for the benefit of the Western media by using the old city ramparts as well as hotels housing foreign journalists as gun emplacements; in the process the old city received relatively limited damage.[26] Aided by the multinational public relations firm Rudder-Finn,[27] the Croatian government's media campaign proved to be very successful. Not only did the image of a peaceful 'Western' people invaded by brutal forces dominate the European and the US television and press coverage of the war, but the Western media often refused to run any stories which contradicted the dominant image in any way. During the war stories of the massacres of Serb civilians by Croat forces were frequently either 'spiked' or represented as massacres of Croats by the Serbs.[28] Only the atrocities by Bosnian Croat forces against another untouchable victim of the war – the Bosnian Muslims – in the village of Ahmići in Bosnia–Hercegovina in 1993, filmed by a British television crew and corroborated in the British UN forces, shattered this dominant image.

Like the Croatian government, the Serbian government also produced photos of mutilated bodies of Serb civilians, allegedly murdered
by Croatian forces as well as photos of destroyed Serb churches and
monuments. Presented as glossy photo brochures, resembling tourist
information guidebooks, these documents were never reproduced in the
Western media nor were the allegations made in them ever investigated
by foreign journalists. Faced with the almost universal hostility of the
Western media and denied the assistance of international public relations firms,[29] the Serbian government proved incapable of mounting a
public relations campaign through the Western media comparable to
that of the Croatian government. Instead, it concentrated on its home
media over which, like its Croatian counterpart, it had a high degree
of control.[30] At the outbreak of the war in September 1991, the mass cir-
culation dailies and the main television stations in Belgrade had already established the pattern of presenting the war as an assault by the
separatist Ustasha-like murderers and torturers against defenceless Serb
population of Croatia. The Yugoslav army and Serb fighters were always presented as acting in defence and the latter's destruction of
Croatian villages and towns was neither mentioned nor portrayed until
well after the cessation of hostilities. The image presented to Serb audiences outside and inside Serbia was thus the very reverse of the Croatian image of the war: defenceless Serbs were the victims of a savage
attack by Croats; only the timely intervention of the Yugoslav army in
defence of the Serbs prevented a complete re-enactment of the Ustasha
massacres of World War II.

As Igor Kotnik notes in his analysis, the aim of this overall extremely
negative presentation of each side was to 'achieve a mobilizing effect'
which, in his opinion, it often failed to do, at least among the Croats.[31]
Whatever their effect on mobilising the nation for war, the propaganda
campaign of each side certainly produced fear as well as hatred.


RESOLVING THE CONFLICT IN CROATIA: THE FAILURE OF
THE EC

Confronted with the escalation of fighting in Croatia, the EC tried the
same approach as it did in Slovenia: it negotiated cease-fires and sent unarmed EC monitors clad in white (and popularly called the 'ice-cream
men') to monitor them. The first cease-fire agreements signed in July
collapsed within hours or days and Serb authorities initially refused to
recognise the jurisdiction of the EC cease-fire monitors in Croatia. To

this the EC responded with a series of regular and extraordinary ministerial meetings. The first meeting in the series, on 6 August 1991 in the Hague, examined all the options which were to be repeatedly rehearsed in the months to come: a UN peace-keeping force (proposed by the French government); further mediation through an enlarged Troika; a EC or WEU military intervention; and an immediate recognition of Croatia's and Slovenia's independence (proposed by the German government).[32] The first meeting endorsed none of these options.

The EC ministerial meeting of 27 August (after the failed coup in Moscow), in its Declaration on Yugoslavia, threatened that, if the cease-fires were not kept and EC monitors not allowed to monitor them, further measures 'including international action' will be taken against the Serb side which was blamed for the collapse of the cease-fires.[33] The Declaration also announced the convening of an EC-sponsored Peace Conference on Yugoslavia which was supposed to find an overall settlement to the Yugoslav conflict and ensure a lasting peace. The Peace Conference on Yugoslavia, which opened on 7 September in the Hague, was solemnly greeted by another EC Declaration which stated that the 'outcome of [the Conference] must take into account the interests of all who live there' and that the EC is 'determined never to recognise changes of any borders which have not been brought about by peaceful means and by agreement'.[34] As it turned out, the outcome of the conference failed to take into account the interests of all who live there and the EC recognised the new borders of a few new states which were not brought about by agreement.

The conference had an old cast of characters – the Yugoslav state presidency, the Yugoslav federal government and the presidents of the six Yugoslav republics – plus the new add-ons, the EC officials and its chairman, the former British Foreign Secretary Lord Carrington. As the fighting in Croatia escalated during September and the series of cease-fires negotiated by Lord Carrington and other foreign dignitaries collapsed, the closed sessions of the Peace Conference produced no results. On 18 October 1991 Lord Carrington and the Dutch foreign minister offered a proposal for 'A General Settlement to the Yugoslav Crisis' which would have created a 'free association' of sovereign and independent republics within their previous internal borders. In addition, this proposal envisaged a 'special status (autonomy)' to a national or ethnic group forming a majority in an area of each of these republics. The special status would entail a separate legislative body, judiciary, educational system and the display of separate national emblems as well as international monitoring. The first draft of the proposal singled out 'the Serbs living in areas in Croatia where they form a majority' as recipients of this special status.[35] Apart from the provision of the special status for national minorities, this greatly resembled Slovenia's and Croatia's 'Model for a Confederation' put forward in October 1990 and rejected by the Serbian and Montenegrin governments during the lengthy negotiations in the first half of 1991. In his plan Lord Carrington was apparently trying to offer some security to the Serbs in Croatia while at the same time satisfying the demands of the Slovenian and Croatian governments. His attempt clearly came too late. On the expiry of the three-month moratorium on their independence on 8 October, Slovenia and Croatia reiterated their declarations of independence; and Milošević later rejected Lord Carrington's proposal saying that it would abolish Yugoslavia as a state which had existed for 70 years. Undaunted, Lord Carrington attempted to satisfy the demands of all parties to the conflict by producing further drafts of the proposal, which came to include a permanent demilitarisation of the special status areas and, in early November, the possibility of a common state of those republics which wished to stay in Yugoslavia (resembling the compromise Izetbegović–Gligorov proposal of June 1991). Thus most of the options previously rehearsed and rejected by the Yugoslav political leaders during their negotiations in the first half of 1991 (see Chapter 9) were rejected by them once again at the EC Peace Conference in its second half. It is unclear why the EC officials thought that at the EC conference any of the parties could be induced to change its position and to agree to any options which had already been rejected during their own negotiations.

While the conference was in progress, in September 1991 Macedonians voted in a referendum for independence from Yugoslavia while in October Muslim and Croat deputies of the Bosnian parliament (in spite of a walk-out by their Serb colleagues) voted to cut ties with Yugoslavia. Faced with the failure to reach an overall constitutional settlement in Yugoslavia, Lord Carrington in mid-November 1991 brought into action the Arbitration Commission of the Conference on Yugoslavia established by the EC declaration of 27 August. The Commission, headed by the French constitutional judge Richard Badinter and staffed by jurists appointed by the EC member states, was asked by Lord Carrington to pronounce their legal opinion on those very issues on which the representatives of the Yugoslav republics could not agree. Thus Lord Carrington appeared to call on the EC lawyers to resolve the differences which neither the Yugoslav politicians nor the EC negotiators could resolve. The Arbitration Commission, in its Opinion

No. 1, had already proclaimed Yugoslavia to be 'in the process of disso-lution' (a category previously unknown in legal literature) while it left it to the republics to form 'a new association endowed with the demo-cratic institutions of their choice' and to settle any legal issues of its suc-cession (which the Commission as a body of legal experts was asked to settle).[36] In Opinions No. 2 and No. 3, it pronounced that in the absence of any agreement to the contrary, internal borders acquire the status of international (state) borders on the basis of the principle of the respect for the territorial *status quo*. In defence of this principle, the Commis-sion, in Opinion No. 3, further proclaimed that the principle of *uti pos-sidetis juris,* used to settle disputes over the borders of former European colonies in America and Africa, is of a universal nature and thus applicable in cases of independence of non-colonial states such as the one involving the Yugoslav republics. To prove this, the Commis-sion – apparently without noting the irony – quoted a previous legal opinion stating that the principle's 'goal is to prevent the independence and the stability of the new states being endangered by fratricidal war....'[37] Finally, in Opinion No. 2 the Commission proclaimed the Serb populations of Bosnia-Hercegovina and Croatia minority groups which, by implication, have no right of self-determination. It also noted that although international law does not precisely define the conse-quences of the right of self-determination, self-determination 'must not involve changes to existing frontiers at the time of independence (*uti possidetis juris*)' unless the states concerned agree to such changes.[38] Thus the Commission in effect legalised the change of external or inter-national borders of a state 'in the process of dissolution' while at the same time proclaimed the internal borders of such a dissolving state legally sacrosanct.[39] This was done by inventing a new legal category of states 'in the process of dissolution' and applying to it a principle which has so far been used only in border disputes among former Eur-opean colonies. Whatever the value of this argument, the Commission unreservedly sided with Croatia and Slovenia by effectively legitimising their secession; it ruled against Serbia and Montenegro, declaring that the Yugoslav state, which their governments claimed to represent, had no legal existence.

The Commission's Opinions No. 2 and 3, hastily delivered on 7 De-cember 1991 in time for the EC summit at Maastricht, offered little if any arbitration of the disputes. Instead, they provided a legal justifica-tion for the EC decision to proceed to recognise the independence of individual republics of the dissolving Yugoslavia. Faced with continued fighting – in particular with the Yugoslav army bombardment of Du-

brovnik – and the repeated collapse of the EC-sponsored and monitored cease-fires, in late November the EC finally abandoned its role
of peacemaker in Yugoslavia. Instead of a peacemaker, the EC became
the grantor of independence to former Yugoslav republics; it had taken
this role reluctantly and under the threat of the German government's
unilateral recognition of the independence of Slovenia and Croatia.
Even before Slovenia's and Croatia's declarations of independence in
June 1991, the German media, citing the Germans' exercise of the right
to self-determination in 1989, promoted the right of these two nations
to do likewise. As German Chancellor Kohl was to say later 'How can
Germany, which has just succeeded in achieving unity on the principle
of self-determination, refuse it to others?'[40] German television, in particular Bavarian TV, greatly enhanced public sympathy for the plight of
the two nations through its daily broadcasts of destroyed Croatian villages and towns during the war in Croatia. Responding to public pressure, the German government from August 1991 repeatedly used the
threat of Germany's unilateral recognition of the two republics to influence EC policies (and to put pressure on the Serbian government).
The threat was backed by the argument that international recognition
of the two republics' independence would internationalise the Yugoslav
conflict; this, the German ministry of foreign affairs argued, would
either deter or halt the alleged Serbian aggression or, alternatively,
would legalise an international military intervention against the alleged aggressor. While the French and British governments continued
to doubt the validity of this argument,[41] the evident failure of Lord Carrington to reach an overall settlement, left them without any alternative
policy for the solution of the Yugoslav conflict. The German government's promotion of the cause of Slovenian and Croatian independence threatened to split the European Community into pro- and anti-
independence camps. By yielding to German pressure, the two governments prevented a split among the European Community members
which threatened to postpone the signing, on 11 December, of the
Maastricht treaty transforming the European Community into the European Union. The new unanimity of EC member states on the need
for recognition of the former Yugoslav republics was to symbolise the
common foreign and security policy of the newly established European
Union. The already badly fractured Yugoslav federation was thus sacrificed for the achievement of the lofty ideals of European unity.

Following the signing of the Maastricht treaty, the EC extraordinary
ministerial meeting on 17 December adopted the Guidelines on the Recognition of New States in Eastern Europe and the Soviet Union which

reiterated the earlier EC commitment to the inviolability of all frontiers and the rights of ethnic and national groups and minorities. At the same meeting, the EC set down separate conditions for the recognition of independence of the Yugoslav republics and invited their governments to submit by 23 December 1991 their requests for recognition. In response to the requests, the EC Arbitration Commission advised that Slovenia and Macedonia fully comply with the EC Guidelines as well as separate conditions for recognition. In relation to Croatia's request it noted that its constitutional law of 4 December 1991 did not completely cover all the provisions of the EC's Draft Agreement of the Conference on Yugoslavia, in particular, provisions on the special status of the national groups and advised its authorities to complete the constitutional law in accordance with these provisions. In regard to Bosnia-Hercegovina, the Commission, noted the Serb plebiscites in favour of remaining in Yugoslavia and the proclamation of the independence of the 'Serbian Republic of Bosnia–Herzegovina' on 9 January 1992. In view of this, it advised that 'the expression of the will of the peoples of Bosnia and Herzegovina to constitute the SRBH [the Socialist Republic of Bosnia and Herzegovina] as a sovereign and independent state cannot be held to have been fully established;' this could be assessed again, the Commission stated, once 'appropriate guarantees' are given by the republic 'possibly by means of a referendum of all the citizens of the SRBH without distinction, carried out under international supervision'.[42] The governments of Serbia and Montenegro refused to request recognition, noting that their independence was recognised at the Berlin Congress in 1878 and that the opinions of the Arbitration Commission in any case cannot be considered legally binding. Without waiting for the opinions of the EC Arbitration Commission and the EC, on 23 December 1991 the German government unilaterally recognised Croatia and Slovenia. The EC ministerial meeting of 15 January 1992 followed the German lead and within a few days more than 50 states formally recognised the independence of these two republics. In granting recognition to these two states, the EC unintentionally concurred with the Serbian government that the opinions of its Arbitration Commission were not legally binding. Against the opinion of its Arbitration Commission, it granted recognition to Croatia in spite of its failure to guarantee special status to its Serb population; it declined to grant recognition to Macedonia in spite of the recommendation of the Arbitration Commission, because the Greek government objected to this republic's name 'Macedonia' which is also the name of a northern province of Greece.

In order to preserve the appearance of unity, the EC followed the lead of the German government, disregarding, in the process, the opinions of its own Arbitration Commission, its own previous insistence on guarantees of ethnic and national group rights and, above all, the interests of many citizens of Yugoslavia who, partly as a result of the EC decision, were to lose their lives in the ensuing conflicts or were forced to abandon their homes. At the time of recognition, some EC officials openly warned that the recognition of these two states, outside an overall settlement on Yugoslavia, may widen the conflict to other parts of Yugoslavia.[43] This was obviously of no concern to the EC member states which had, by that time, given up on their search for a peaceful solution of the Yugoslav conflict. Already in November 1991 this task had been handed over to the United Nations.

## THE UN: THE PEACEKEEPER IN CROATIA

The United Nations' involvement in the Yugoslav conflict started on 25 September 1991 with the UN Security Council Resolution 713 imposing a 'general and complete embargo on all deliveries of weapons and military equipment to Yugoslavia' and supporting the EC Conference on Yugoslavia and the recent EC-brokered cease-fires. As the EC-brokered cease-fires collapsed, on 8 October the Secretary-General of the UN Perez de Cuellar appointed Cyrus Vance, former US Secretary of State, as his personal envoy to Yugoslavia. As the EC, under German pressure, prepared to recognise Croatia's and Slovenia's independence, the reduced four-member Yugoslav state presidency requested, on 9 November 1991, the deployment of UN peacekeeping troops in Yugoslavia. This helped Cyrus Vance to negotiate an implementing accord for the cease-fire which was signed on 2 January 1992 by the Croatian minister of defence and the Yugoslav army general in command in Croatia. In contrast to the previous 14 cease-fire agreements, all of which were sooner or later broken, this accord not only held but provided a basis for the deployment of the UN Protection Force in Croatia which the Security Council authorised on 24 February 1992 by resolution 743. The UN implementing accord, in contrast to the earlier EC-negotiated cease-fires, was an agreement to a complete cessation of hostilities and included detailed provisions for preventing possible violations and for their monitoring.[44] Unlike the previous EC-negotiated agreements which were often declaratory and signed by politicians seeking publicity, this accord was signed by the military from both sides in the conflict. The original mandate of the UN Protection Force (UNPROFOR) envisaged the deployment of around 14 000 military and civilian personnel in four United Nations Protected Areas (UNPAs) which were defined as areas 'in which Serbs constitute the majority or a substantial minority of the population and in which inter-communal tensions have led to armed conflict in the recent past'. These were eastern Slavonia, western Slavonia and south and north Krajina.[45]

The original UN mandate was twofold: first, to ensure that the UNPAs were demilitarised, through the withdrawal or disbandment of all armed forces in them. Second, to control access to UNPAs and to monitor the local police forces in order to protect human rights of all residents and to facilitate the return of displaced persons to their homes in UNPAs.[46] In carrying out the mandate, the UN forces were required to remain impartial and to use only minimum force, normally only in self-defence. All UN documents emphasised that these arrangements were of interim nature and in no way prejudicial to the final political settlement of the conflict which in 1991 and early 1992 the UN expected to be found within the framework of the EC Peace Conference on Yugoslavia. The UN forces successfully carried out the first part of the mandate: the hostilities ceased while the Yugoslav federal army withdrew from the UNPAs and a large amount of the remaining heavy weapons was stored in the arms depots. The UN was, however, unable to secure the cooperation of the Serb authorities for the return of displaced persons of Croat origin and for the reform of the local administration and police so as to reflect the 'national composition of the population which lived in the area concerned before the recent hostilities'.[47] The Serb authorities apparently held that the re-establishment of the previous national composition, if possible at all, should be part of the final political settlement of the Yugoslav conflict and should also include the previous mixed population areas under the control of the Croatian government.

The initial success of the UN mission in Croatia probably rested on the following three factors. First, the UN, unlike the EC (which to the Serb side appeared German-dominated and pro-Croat) was initially regarded by both sides as a neutral and impartial organisation with a restricted peacekeeping and no political mandate. Second, unlike the EC, the UN negotiated a detailed agreement for the implementation of the cessation of hostilities and had both the military personnel and expertise required to monitor it. Third, as mentioned above, the military conflict in Croatia reached a stalemate with neither side able to dislodge the other from the territory each held. Under these circumstances, the government of the now independent Croatia, could prepare for a military takeover of these areas by arming and training its army. For the Serb authorities the UN Protection Force offered at least a temporary respite from further Croatian attacks during which they could try to consolidate their rule over the areas. The respite lasted until January 1993 when the Croatian army overran several 'pink zones' under UN protection, adjacent to south Krajina. In May 1995 the Croatian army overran western Slavonia and in August it conquered both north and south Krajina. In August 1995, eastern Slavonia was the only UNPA zone (of the initial four UNPAs) which still had its Serb population; almost all Serbs from the other three UNPAs conquered by the Croatian army had been forced to leave. Thus in 1995 the UN mission in Croatia virtually came to an end through unilateral military actions of the Croatian government which were supported by the US (see Chapter 12).

# 11 War in Bosnia–
Hercegovina 1992–4

## FROM FRAGMENTATION TO CIVIL WAR

As war broke out in Croatia in September 1991, the three national parties in Bosnia–Hercegovina started arming, ostensibly in self-defence, their militant members and gun-running flourished under the patronage of the national parties' bosses.[1] After the first clashes between Serbs and Croats in Serb minority areas of western Hercegovina and northern Bosnia on the border with Croatia, the Yugoslav federal army was deployed in these areas as well as around major cities such as Mostar, Sarajevo and Tuzla. As in October 1991 the Croatian and Slovenian governments reiterated their declarations of independence, the Muslim and Croat parties in Bosnia–Hercegovina moved to disassociate the republic from the Yugoslav federation. Their 'Memorandum on the Sovereignty of Bosnia–Herzegovina' in effect cut the republic's ties with the Yugoslav federal bodies (which Slovenian, Croatian and Macedonian representatives were also leaving), proclaimed its neutrality in the war in Croatia as well as 'an aspiration' to demilitarise the republic.[2] On 14 October 1991 the Serbian Democratic party leader, Dr Karadžić, rejecting the Memorandum in the Bosnian parliament, warned that this may lead the republic into 'the hell of a war... in which the Muslim people could perhaps even disappear'.[3] The Muslim and Croat deputies rejected these warnings as blackmail and proceeded to adopt the Memorandum, in spite of the walk-out of all Serb Democratic party deputies. The Serb deputies responded by forming a parliament of the Serb nation and organising, on 9 November 1991, a Serb plebiscite in the municipalities under its control. As an overwhelming majority voted for the Serb territories to remain within Yugoslavia, in January 1992, the Republic of the Serb Nation in Bosnia–Hercegovina, consisting of Serb majority municipalities (around 45 per cent of the republic's territory), was proclaimed. Like their counterparts in Croatia in 1990, the Serb Democratic party leaders, responding to the Muslim and Croat disassociation from the Yugoslav federation, seceded the municipalities under their control from the government of Bosnia–Hercegovina.

The Bosnian Muslim and Croat leaders followed the example of the Croatian and Slovenian governments and, in response to the EC invitation, in December 1991 they requested recognition of the independence of the republic. Following the recommendations of the EC Arbitration Commission, on 28 February 1992 they also organised a referendum on the independence of the republic. As the Serb Democratic party called for a Serb boycott of the referendum, only about 64 per cent of the registered voters cast their vote, out of which, according to the organisers, around 99 per cent voted for independence. All these moves, in the view of the Serb Democratic party leaders, breached the principle of consensus between the three nations and their party representatives enshrined in the constitutional amendments of June 1990 (see Chapter 8). This breach, in their view, justified their secession from the republic.

The Muslim leadership, on the other hand, feared that by remaining in a truncated Yugoslav federation, dominated by Milošević's elites and their local Bosnian Serb supporters, they would be easily removed from power and their long-term project of creating an Islamic society thwarted. In disregarding the protests of Serb leaders, they probably held that with the support of the EC and the US as well their Croat HDZ allies they could, in time, prevail over the Serb opposition. Like the Croatian government, in early 1992 the Muslim and Croat leaders in the republic were probably prepared to trade a temporary loss of territory to the Serb Democratic party for the recognition of independence and international support. Aware of his own government's lack of a military force, Izetbegović in early February requested the deployment of EC observers and UN forces in the republic. Instead of the UN forces, the UN in February placed its headquarters of peace-keeping operations in Sarajevo and the EC sent around 50 monitors to Sarajevo and Banja Luka (both of which were later withdrawn).

During the referendum, the murder of a Serb at a wedding party in the old quarter of Sarajevo by unidentified gunmen resulted in the erection of Serb and Muslim barricades and checkpoints throughout the city. At the time the Serb and Muslim national leaders succeeded in calming the tensions. In early April, however, clashes broke out between Serb and Muslim militias in northeast Bosnia and between Serb and Croat militias in western Hercegovina and Bosnia. In response to this, tens of thousands of citizens of all nationalities demonstrated in Sarajevo and other Bosnian cities, demanding joint action of the national leaders to end the violence.[4] On 5 April snipers[5] broke up large demonstrations of citizens for peace in Sarajevo by killing 8 and wounding over 50 demonstrators.

After the US and EC recognition of the independence of Bosnia–
Hercegovina, on 7 April 1992, the Serb representatives left the presidency and the government and the Serb parliament proclaimed its
Serb Republic independent; from then on Bosnia–Hercegovina had no
government supported by the three principal national parties. On
3 April the presidency of Bosnia–Hercegovina, against the Serbian representatives' opposition, had already ordered the mobilisation of the
republic's territorial defence units. These lightly armed units, consisting
mainly of Muslim reservists and commanded by Muslim (and some
Serb) officers from the Yugoslav federal army, were later transformed
into the Bosnian army. As the Yugoslav federal army had already taken
control of most of the weapons depots, the territorial defence units
lacked weapons as well as lower-ranking officers. Together with the
Muslim party's militias, the 'Green berets', they formed the main military force of the Bosnian government which, from 7 April 1992, remained firmly in the hands of the Muslim party.

After 7 April fighting broke out in almost all regions of the republic.
In western Hercegovina, the Yugoslav federal army units engaged the
Bosnian Croat militias of the Croatian Defence Council (HVO) around
Mostar while the Bosnian Serb militias took over several Muslim-populated towns in eastern Hercegovina. Irregulars from Serbia, led by
the notorious criminal Željko Ražnjatović-Arkan seized a string of
towns on Bosnia's eastern border with Serbia, sending a stream of
Muslim refugees heading for central Bosnia. Yugoslav federal army
units and Serb militias also gained control of a vital corridor in northern Bosnia, along the river Sava, taking in the process several towns
with mixed populations. Several cities with Serb minority populations
– such as Mostar and Tuzla – were also besieged by the heavy artillery
units of the Yugoslav federal army. In Sarajevo, various criminal gangs
– as well as police forces and party militias – engaged in street fighting
for the control of city suburbs while the Yugoslav federal army remained in its barracks. During April the Serb forces consolidated their
grip on its outer suburbs expelling the Muslim population, and cutting
most of the city's links with its hinterland; the central parts of the city
remained under the control of the Muslim-dominated Bosnian government. In late May the Serb forces, using the former Yugoslav federal
army heavy artillery, already in position in the mountains around Sarajevo, subjected the city to a first large-scale bombardment; these bom-
bardments were to continue for the duration of the war. The actions of
various Serb forces and the Yugoslav federal army units appeared to
have been coordinated with the aim of securing strategic communica-

tion links throughout Bosnia–Hercegovina and of encircling Muslim and Croat territories.[6] As the Serb forces did not attempt to take over central Sarajevo or central Bosnian cities, their primary aim appeared to be the partition of the republic and not the overthrow of the Bosnian government.

Amidst the expanding war in Bosnia–Hercegovina, the Federal Republic of Yugoslavia, consisting of Montenegro and Serbia only, was proclaimed on 27 April 1992 and, on 4 May, its citizens serving in the Yugoslav federal army were recalled from Bosnia–Hercegovina. The recall did not affect those native to the republic, who, according to the official figures, numbered over 80 per cent of the Yugoslav army conscripts. In a prearranged move, the Bosnian Serb authorities took over the command of the remaining Yugoslav army units as well as their heavy weapons, and formed the Military of the Serb Republic. This force continued to receive supplies from Milošević's government until October 1994 when the latter imposed a blockade which considerably diminished the flow of supplies. In spite of continued supplies, the withdrawal of a significant number of Serbian officers and men as well as heavy weaponry and aircraft to Serbia in May 1992 significantly weakened the Bosnian Serb forces. As a result, in late May the Bosnian Croat forces supported by Croatian army units broke the siege of Mostar while the Muslim territorial defence forces captured a large quantity of weapons from a Yugoslav federal army convoy withdrawing from Tuzla and pushed back the Serb forces from the region. In June 1992 the whole of western Hercegovina fell to Bosnian Croat control, forcing the Serbs to leave the region.

A formal agreement on cooperation between the Croatian and Bosnian governments, signed in June 1992 by presidents Tudjman and Izetbegović, led to an increased Croatian supply of arms to the Muslim Bosnian army and to closer cooperation with the regular Croatian army operating in Bosnia–Hercegovina. In September the Croatian army and Bosnian Muslim forces engaged in a series of battles with the Serb forces in northern Bosnia along the Sava river, attempting, unsuccessfully, to cut off the main Serb supply corridor to western Bosnia. At the same time, Muslim forces intensified their attacks in the east Bosnian region around Srebrenica and Goražde which, without their Serb inhabitants, were under Muslim control; the break-out of the Bosnian army territorial units from Goražde at the time attested to the growing offensive capabilities of the Bosnian Muslim army. In spite of their increased capabilities and a huge superiority in numbers[7] the joint Muslim and Croat forces could not dislodge the Serb forces from most of the towns and territories the latter had taken during 1992. By the end of 1992 the Serb forces had mostly entrenched themselves on the high ground attempting to compensate for their smaller numbers by their superior artillery and armour; at the time they had come to control close to 70 per cent of the republic's territory. Thus the battlefield situation did not change much until March 1993 when war broke out between the Muslim and Croat forces in central Bosnia and western Hercegovina. The Bosnian Muslim government, faced early in the war with a large loss of territory and lacking the heavy weaponry its opponents possessed, was well aware that it could not defeat the Serb forces without foreign military aid. At the very beginning of the conflict it had requested UN military intervention and, as the request went unheeded, it attempted in various ways to provoke a military intervention against its Serb opponents who, as in the earlier war in Croatia, were generally perceived as the aggressors.[8] Although unsuccessful in securing military intervention, the wide publicity given in the Western media to the suffering of civilians in Sarajevo and elsewhere had, as we shall see, a significant impact on the foreign involvement in this conflict.

The outbreak of war had at the very beginning caused a massive movement of populations of all three nationalities. Even before April 1992, Serbs started to leave parts of western Hercegovina and Bosnia in which they were in a minority while Muslims started to leave Serb-majority areas. At the outbreak of war, both Serb and Muslim refugees fled the areas of protracted fighting in north and east Bosnia. In the first clashes, national party militias and criminal gangs engaged in large-scale plunder, wanton murder and rape of the members of opposing nationalities, causing the survivors to flee. Apart from plunder which motivated many already established criminals to head for the battlefront, revenge soon came to be one of the main motivating factors in atrocities and torture committed by all sides in the conflict. After the outbreak of fighting, the spiral of violence which characterised the civil war in the region during World War II was established once again, often in the very areas which suffered most in the years 1941–5. In addition, each side encouraged or organised forced eviction of hostile populations from the territory under its control (the infamous 'ethnic cleansing') for the following reasons. First, and probably most importantly, by removing the population of their opponent's nationality, the newly established authorities were denying their opponents a source of supply and recruits for any future military operations in the area. Second, in this way each side was consolidating its authority by removing any source of potential political opposition and civil disobedience from persons of an opposing nationality who were, in effect, considered to be citizens of a hostile state. Third, forced eviction of an opposing nationality enabled each side to settle, into the homes of the evicted, refugees of their own nationality who were expelled from enemy-controlled territory. Finally, by eliminating the population of another nationality, the new authorities were establishing their claim to the territory in any future settlement. In the process of removing populations, all sides established detention camps in which murder, torture and sexual abuse were often committed. During the war the Bosnian Serb authorities had initiated or condoned forced eviction of huge numbers – according to some estimates, hundreds of thousands – of Muslims from the Muslim-majority areas in eastern Bosnia as well as from areas of western Bosnia in which the Muslims were in a minority. Bosnian Croat authorities had encouraged the eviction of almost all Serbs from western Hercegovina, its capital Mostar (which had a 20 per cent Serb population before the war) and from western Bosnia under its control; in early 1993 the same fate befell the Muslims inhabiting this area. During the war over 150 000 citizens of Sarajevo – mostly Serbs but also Muslims, Croats and Jews – left the city for Serbia or for areas controlled by their national authorities. Bosnian Muslim-controlled cities of central Bosnia such as Tuzla and Zenica as well as the region's countryside had lost most of their Serb inhabitants.[9] All in all the demographic picture of Bosnia-Hercegovina drastically changed already during the first year of the war. Although no local national authority (except the Bosnian Croat one in western Hercegovina) in the first year of the war succeeded in removing all of the population of the opposing nationalities from its territory, all previous mixed population areas were rapidly becoming single nationality areas. This change was somewhat slowed down by the Muslim authorities' ban on Serb departures from the cities under their control. Principally through this ban these cities retained their, much reduced, Serb populations as a symbol of the Muslim-dominated Bosnian government's ostensible commitment to a multi-ethnic Bosnia–Hercegovina.[10]

## IN SEARCH OF PEACE: THE FAILURE OF THE FIRST EC PEACE PLAN

In view of the delicate balance of power among the national parties in Bosnia–Hercegovina, the EC invitation in December 1991 to all Yugoslav republics, including Bosnia–Hercegovina, to request recognition was an invitation to split this republic and its population: the Bosnian

Muslim and Croat leaders could not agree to remaining a powerless minority in a Serb-dominated Yugoslavia and the Bosnian Serb leaders could not likewise agree to the same status in an independent republic. Still believing that all such differences were to be resolved by international conferences – in spite of the dismal failure of its peace conference on Yugoslavia – the EC convened another conference, this time on Bosnia–Hercegovina. The EC plan, submitted at the conference, defined the republic as 'one state composed of three constituent units, based on national principles and taking into account economic, geographical and other criteria'.[11] While all three sides appeared to agree on these principles, the map of the constituent units and cantons, drawn by the EC experts, was rejected both by the Croat HDZ and by the Muslim party (but not by the Serb side). Although the map gave the Muslim side 44 per cent of the territory (more, as it turned out, than any other future international peace plan), on 31 March the Muslim leader Izetbegović rejected it as showing 'the complete absurdity of a strict division on national lines'.[12] The EC conference then formed a working group which was supposed to produce, by 15 May 1992, another map which would not be based on national division only. Disregarding the Bosnian Serb insistence that the republic's independence be recognised only after the agreed constitutional principles and boundaries are implemented, the EC Council of Ministers recommended on 6 April 1992 that recognition be granted immediately. As R. M. Hayden noted,[13] in April 1992 the republic hardly satisfied the conditions set by the EC Arbitration Commission for recognition of independence. With the virtual secession of a large part of its territory, it was obviously in as much of 'the process of dissolution' as the Yugoslav federation had been a few months earlier. Moreover, the EC Arbitration Commission in its Opinion no. 4 suggested that 'a referendum in which all of the citizens of Bosnia and Herzegovina' could possibly establish 'the will of the *peoples*' (emphasis added) of Bosnia–Hercegovina to constitute an independent state (see Chapter 10). As most Serbs refused to participate in the referendum organised by the Muslim and Croat parties in late February 1992, it could hardly have been deemed that the republic's 'peoples' agreed to its independence.

As it later transpired, in March 1992 the Muslim leader Izetbegović, had sought the advice of the then US ambassador to Yugoslavia Warren Zimmerman on the EC plan, before he finally rejected it. Although Zimmerman denies encouraging him to reject the plan,[14] it was clear at the time that the US government would continue its support for the Muslim party even if it rejected the plan. In fact, from the very start of

negotiations on a peace settlement, the US government supported the
Bosnian Muslim government's demand for a single state in which the
Bosnian Muslims, as the largest national group, would be politically
dominant; thus the Muslim leaders could count on continued US
support in spite of their rejection of any EC and/or UN peace plan
which did not suit them. This US policy of unconditional support for
the Muslim side was, probably, dictated by the US alliance with Islamic
countries, in particular Turkey, which had supported the Bosnian
Muslim party even before the outbreak of the war. In addition to this, it
appears that the US officials held, as Zimmerman did, that there is no
historical or moral ground for the demand that 'all Serbs live in one
state', that is, for the Serbs outside Serbia to choose the state in which
they want to live.[15] In denying the right of Serbs outside Serbia to form
their own state or to unite with Serbia, the US officials appeared to have
endorsed the Croat nationalist position on the Serb question (see Chapter
7) and had accordingly endeavoured to contain Serbia's presumed expansionism in Bosnia–Hercegovina and the rest of the Balkans.

Having failed to negotiate a constitutional settlement and a lasting
cease-fire, in May 1992 the EC was once again ready to hand over the
search for peace to the UN. However, in early May the UN Secretary-
General reported that because of the absence of any agreement between
the hostile parties, no peacekeeping operation of the UN appeared to be
possible. Both the EC and the UN were soon prompted to further action
by the explosion at the bread queue in the Vasa Miskina street in Sarajevo which killed 16 and wounded 144 people. As the Western TV crews
appeared at the scene only minutes after the bomb exploded, European
and world audiences were given the first in a series of instant TV broadcasts of the carnage of civilians in Sarajevo. In spite of the UN observers'
doubts of the Serb responsibility for this crime,[16] the EC permanent representatives imposed a wide-ranging trade embargo against Serbia
and Montenegro and urged the UN Security Council to do likewise.
The UN Security Council on 30 May in Resolution 757 imposed comprehensive mandatory sanctions, which excluded only the import of
food and medicine, against the Federal Republic of Yugoslavia while re-
iterating its earlier demand that the elements of the Croatian army be
withdrawn from Bosnia–Hercegovina. The sanctions had no effect on
the continuation of the fighting in Bosnia–Hercegovina nor did they
bring about a peaceful solution of the conflict as they were intended to.
The primary reason for their failure was the relative independence of the
Bosnian Serb armed forces from the Milošević government's control; in
his report to the UN Security Council at the time, the UN Secretary-

General already expressed his doubts about the extent of the Serbian government's control over these forces. As they were prove during late 1994 and in 1995, the Bosnian Serb forces were able to operate with little support from Milošević's government and in direct opposition to his proclaimed policies. While the sanctions had influenced Serbian president Milošević to cut his supplies to the Bosnian Serbs in October 1994, they had not caused Bosnian Serb leaders to change their position. Moreover, the sanctions – at least until mid-1995 – did not significantly affect the Bosnian Serb military capability. The UN sanctions, however, caused a huge decline of economic activity in Serbia and Montenegro, leading to an unemployment level of over 40 per cent and to the drastic impoverishment of the middle- and low-income strata.[17]

Although the sanctions qualified the Serbs as the main culprits in the conflict, the UN action fell short of the Bosnian Muslim government's request for UN military intervention against them. Instead of a military response, the UN Security Council in early June decided to deploy a small UN peacekeeping force to take over and protect the Sarajevo airport for the purposes of humanitarian aid to the city's inhabitants. The Serb forces handed the airport over to the UN force and, after a lightning visit by French president Mitterand to Sarajevo, the humanitarian aid airlift to the airport started on 30 June. Thus the UN mission in Bosnia–Hercegovina started not as a peacekeeping mission – since there was no peace to be kept – but as a mission aimed at protecting the transport of humanitarian aid (primarily food and medicine) for the civilians caught in the conflict. Of all sides involved in the conflict (including the EC and its members states), the UN and its agencies were the first to take effective action to alleviate their suffering.

The EC peace efforts in Bosnia–Hercegovina, followed the very same pattern as its efforts in Croatia: it first sponsored a conference which failed because of the unwillingness of the principal parties in the conflict to change their previous positions. After the failure of its peace conference, the EC, against the criteria of its own Arbitration Commission, recognised the independence of the republic. Then, unable to halt the fighting, the EC, as before, blamed the Serb side (in spite of the Bosnian Serbs' acceptance of the first EC peace plan) and handed over the search for peace to the UN.

## IN SEARCH OF PEACE: THE JOINT EC AND UN PEACE PLANS

Faced with the failure of the UN sanctions and Lord Carrington's on-going negotiating efforts to stop the fighting, the British government, which was then holding the EC presidency, convened on 26 August 1992 in London yet another international conference on Yugoslavia, this time under joint UN and EC auspices. This time, apart from the cast from the previous conferences, representatives of over 30 countries and organisations, including the largest minority groups in former Yugoslavia (such as Hungarians and Albanians) and the Islamic countries, also attended. The two co-chairmen of its Steering Committee were, for the EC, Lord Owen, a former British Foreign Secretary (Lord Carrington had by then resigned his post), and for the UN, the UN Secretary-General's personal envoy to Yugoslavia, Cyrus Vance. The only tangible result of their negotiating efforts were joint declarations in September and October 1992 by Croatian president Tudjman and the president of the new Yugoslavia, the Serbian novelist Dobrica Ćosić, which endorsed the deployment of the UN peacekeepers in the Dubrovnik hinterland to replace the Yugoslav military units as well as the establishment of quasi-consular bureaus of the two states.

After a long series of talks and consultations, Lord Owen and Cyrus Vance produced, on 4 January 1993, yet another set of constitutional principles for Bosnia–Hercegovina accompanied by a map of ten provinces or cantons, three for each side, with the Sarajevo province under joint control. This second international peace plan – called the Vance–Owen plan – envisaged a progressive demilitarisation of the whole republic, in which the central government would have responsibility only for foreign affairs, international trade and citizenship while all the other governmental functions would be either assigned to the provinces or to 'independent bodies'. In terms of territory, the Croat side gained most as its three provinces, directly adjacent to Croatia, could have been easily incorporated into that state. Some areas assigned in the first EC plan to the Muslim side, had now been transferred to the Croats and, to a lesser extent, the Serbs. The Serbs received about the same amount of the territory as in the first plan, but their provinces, unlike the Croat and to some extent Muslim ones, were not to adjacent to each other, thus bringing into question the viability of a separate Serb national unit.[18] After a series of talks in various world capitals, in late March a revised Vance–Owen plan, more favourable to the Muslim side, was accepted by both Bosnian Croat and Muslim leaders. Under intense pressure from the Greek and Russian governments as well as from presidents Milošević and Ćosić, the Bosnian Serb leader Dr Karadžić signed the plan on 2 May in Athens. However, the Bosnian Serb parliament, in spite of continued pressure from Milošević and Montenegrin president Bulatović, rejected the plan and in mid-May its Bosnian Serb electorate in a referendum followed suit.

As part of the campaign of pressure on the Serb side, the US government spokesmen had, since early 1993, repeatedly threatened air strikes against the Serb military, if the Serbs reject the plan. As these threats had no effect on the Bosnian Serb stance and the British and the French governments showed no support for US military involvement, the US dropped, at least for a time, any plans for military action in the region and left the negotiating initiative once again to its European allies.[19] In spite of the failure of the sanctions against Serbia and Montenegro to produce a change in the Bosnian Serb position, the UN Security Council, finding no other instrument at its disposal, in late April 1993 decided to tighten the already existing sanctions. Undaunted by the failure of his first plan, Lord Owen together with the new UN co-chairman of the Steering Committee, Thorvald Stoltenberg,[20] designed a new peace plan which was supposed to take into account the new situation arising from the outbreak of war between Bosnian Croats and Muslims (see next section) and the consolidation of the Bosnian Croat mini-state in western Hercegovina, Herceg-Bosna, which was first proclaimed in July 1992. The Owen–Stoltenberg peace plan, the third international plan of this kind, envisaged a union of three republics – one for each national group – with a common rotating presidency and premiership as well as a parliament, all operating on the principle of consensus.[21] The whole union would be demilitarised, with each republic having its own police force. The Muslim republic would comprise 33.56 per cent, the Croat republic 17.5 per cent, the cities of Mostar and Sarajevo would be put under international control and the Serbs would get the rest (slightly less than 50 per cent). This proposal clearly met Serb demands for a separate and viable state-unit. It was, as could be expected, rejected by the Muslim leaders on the ostensible ground that the Muslims would require certain areas in eastern, central and western Bosnia (less than 4 per cent of the total territory of the republic) to make their republic-unit economically viable.[22] The negotiations on this peace plan dragged on until February 1994, when a new US initiative, creating a Bosnian Croat–Muslim federation, made it finally obsolete.

The negotiations over these two peace plans revealed that no side in the conflict was prepared to abandon its initial position. In spite of continuing threats of Western military action and the continued UN sanctions against Serbia and Montenegro (and the consequent pressure of the Serbian government on them), the Bosnian Serb leaders persisted in their demand for the recognition of a national mini-state of their own based on what they considered to be a continuous, defensible and economically viable territory. As their acceptance of the third international peace plan – the Owen–Stoltenberg plan – indicated, for the achievement of that goal they were ready to abandon some of the territory they had conquered during the war (the plan envisaged reducing their hold on 70 per cent to less than 50 per cent of the territory). The Bosnian Croat leaders were also ready to accept any plan – either the Vance–Owen or the Owen–Stoltenberg one – which would give them control over the Croat-populated territories adjacent to Croatia and thus enable them to unite, in one way or another, with Croatia. The Bosnian Muslim leaders, in spite of the huge loss of territory and expulsion of large numbers of Muslims from Serb- and Croat-held territories, were essentially not prepared to accept any division of Bosnia and Hercegovina along national lines which would countenance a constitutional separation of Serb and Croat mini-states from an integral republic. This was the publicly stated reason for their rejection of the first EC plan in March 1992 and very likely the actual reason for their rejection of the Owen–Stoltenberg plan. Each side was in effect expecting the negotiators and the foreign powers backing them to impose its particular political conception on the other side(s). The Bosnian Serb side hoped, in vain, that Western pressure on the Bosnian Muslim leaders would induce them to abandon their unitary conception and accept a division of Bosnia–Hercegovina along national lines sufficiently favourable to the Serb leaders. After the Serb rejection of the Vance–Owen plan, it became obvious that in order to impose the Muslim conception of a unitary Bosnia–Hercegovina on the Serb side, one would need military action which would defeat or remove the Serb military forces from the territories they held. As the French and British governments appeared unwilling, during 1993 and 1994, to be involved in a military operation of this kind, the Muslim side had to continue to negotiate while at the same time try to elicit support, in any other available way, for military assistance for its cause. During this period, it faced two new enemies: the Bosnian Croat forces as well as the forces of the Muslim Fikret Abdić in northwest Bosnia.

## NEW ADVERSARIES AND BATTLEFRONTS

In response to the attacks of Muslim forces in eastern Bosnia, the Bosnian Serb forces in early March 1993 launched a counteroffensive, using aircraft and driving tens of thousands of Muslim villagers from this area to Goražde and Srebrenica which were still under Muslim control. As the aircraft bombing contravened the ban on military flights which the UN instituted in October 1992, the UN Secretary-General in April 1993 agreed to the enforcement of the extended ban on any unauthorised flights by using NATO aircraft operating from US aircraft carriers in the Adriatic and NATO bases in Italy. While NATO involvement was at first limited to monitoring and enforcing the ban on unauthorised flights, it was soon expanded to include air support to the UN forces in the protection of the UN safe areas from Serb attacks. Since the use of NATO airpower was aimed at Serb forces only, from the very start of its operations, the Serb forces regarded NATO as a new adversary supporting their Muslim enemies.

The influx of Muslim refugees into Srebrenica and Goražde, given wide publicity in the Western media, prompted the UN Security Council to proclaim, on 16 April 1993, Srebrenica the first 'safe area' – 'to be free from any armed attack or any other hostile act' – and to arrange an agreement between Serb and Muslim commanders for the demilitarisation of the town. In May Goražde and Žepa (in east Bosnia), Tuzla (in central Bosnia), Bihać (in northwest Bosnia) as well as Sarajevo were proclaimed safe areas and UN military observers were sent to these areas to monitor the humanitarian situation. The mandate of the UN forces in the republic was extended, in June 1993, to include the protection of these safe areas and the deterring of attacks on them; the UN contingent in Bosnia–Hercegovina was also increased, reaching in July 1995 the total of 22 500 military personnel.[23] Unlike the first safe zone in Srebrenica, the UN made no attempt to demilitarise Sarajevo, Tuzla and Bihać, all of which served as bases and headquarters for large contingents of the Muslim-dominated Bosnian army. During 1993 and 1994 the Muslim forces used all the non-demilitarised safe areas to attack the Serb forces in expectation of Serb retaliation; Serb attacks, whether retaliatory or not, were qualified as attacks on the civilians in the safe areas. As the UN forces were expected to repel such attacks, in their new role they in fact became yet another adversary of the Serb forces. As the UN commanders – in particular, the British general Sir Michael Rose – frequently pointed out, the UN peacekeeping forces on a humanitarian mission were not given the mandate nor equipped to wage war in this way. Partly because of the continued military action from the safe areas[24] and partly because of its insufficient manpower and equipment, the UN forces were unable to protect the civilian populations in the safe areas as effectively as originally expected. As the media on the spot were able to expose this quite easily, the US and other Western governments were, during 1994, putting increasing pressure on the UN 'to do something', that is to repel the Serb attacks. The UN was thus continually asked to become a combatant in spite of the absence of a mandate and the equipment for this role.

While the UN was attempting to restrict the Serb forces' ability to attack Muslim civilians, in late April 1993 war broke out between Bosnian Croat and Muslim forces in central Bosnia. In early April, the Bosnian Croat commanders requested their Muslim counterparts to withdraw Muslim forces from areas in central Bosnia – around Travnik, Gornji Vakuf and Fojnica – which the Vance–Owen plan assigned to the Croats. In this way, the leaders of the Croat mini-state Herceg-Bosna based on Hercegovina were trying to extend their control over the adjacent Croat-populated areas of central Bosnia. Upon the Muslim refusal to hand over control, the Bosnian Croat forces attacked the area, burning Muslim villages and massacring civilians (the widely publicised cases of Ahmići near Vitez and of Stupni Do). The Muslim Bosnian army, by moving its elite units from the area around Sarajevo, was able in late summer 1993 to launch a counteroffensive, taking a large area of central Bosnia from Bosnian Croat control. In the process, over 100 000 Bosnian Croats were forced to flee their homes from Fojnica and Travnik as well as other areas in central Bosnia.[25] As the familiar cycle of violence took hold, the Muslim troops also massacred Bosnian Croat civilians (for example, at Uzdol near Prozor and at Fojnica). In September large parts of the city of Mostar were destroyed in artillery exchanges, including its historic 16th century bridge, which the Bosnian Croat artillery finished off in November 1993; the level of destruction of Mostar surpassed that of Sarajevo or any other city in Bosnia–Hercegovina.[26] During the autumn, the Bosnian Croat troops forcibly evicted tens of thousands of Muslims from the city and its surroundings.

The Bosnian Serbs provided aid to the Croat refugees as well as ammunition and artillery support to Bosnian Croat forces. Moreover, the transfer of Muslim forces to new battlefields enabled Serb forces to take a number of strategic positions around Sarajevo and to enlarge their territory in the northern Bosnian corridor. In spite of this, the Bosnian Muslim forces made substantial territorial gains at the expense of Bosnian Croats. Thus the failed attempt by the Croat leadership in Hercegovina to expand its control over central Bosnian regions, in the expectation of the implementation of the Vance–Owen plan, led to yet another massive demographic change in the republic: the Croat populations of central Bosnia and the Muslim populations of western Hercegovina had been virtually removed from these two areas. As opposition to the war with the Bosnian Muslims grew both in his own party and the opposition (as well as among the Croat Roman Catholic bishops), president Tudjman removed certain Hercegovinian Croat leaders – the principal advocates of this policy – from power and in early 1994, with US assistance, restored the Croat–Muslim alliance.

In June 1993, Fikret Abdić, a member of the Bosnian republic's presidency and one of the key Bosnian Muslim leaders, accused the Muslim leader Izetbegović of trying to establish a military dictatorship and of obstructing peace negotiations.[27] After his final split with Izetbegović, Abdić proclaimed the Autonomous Region of Western Bosnia in his home base in northwest Bosnia around the city of Bihać which then seceded from the Bosnian Muslim government. In October the Bosnian Army's Fifth Corps, loyal to Izetbegović, attacked Abdić's local militia, thus opening yet another battlefield. At first Abdić was allied to both the Croatian and Serbian governments and their local supporters; as the Croats forged a new alliance with the Muslims, his main allies remained the Serb forces in the region. In late 1994 the reinforced Bosnian army succeeded in expelling Abdić's militia from his home town of Velika Kladuša, in the process sending tens of thousands Muslim refugees – Abdić's supporters – to the bordering Krajina region and to Croatia proper. With the help of Krajina and Bosnian Serb forces Abdić's militias retook the town and a large part of the region early in 1995 and continued fighting against Izetbegović's forces until the Croatian army offensive against the Krajina Serbs in August 1995 forced them to surrender.

In late 1993 the Muslim Bosnian army was thus fighting the Muslim militias around Bihać, the Bosnian Croat forces in western Hercegovina and the Bosnian Serb forces around Sarajevo as well as in eastern and northern Bosnia. The opening of the two further fronts – in particular the one with the Muslims of the Bihać region – showed that the origins of the war were hardly to be found in the oft-quoted historical interethnic hatred among the national groups in the region. These two battlefronts were opened as a result of attempts by political leaders to extend or consolidate political control over the territory they claimed for themselves. The initial fighting in April 1992 between the allied Muslim and Croat forces and the Serb military appears to have broken out for the very same reason.

## THE MEDIA: THE ULTIMATE WEAPON OF THE VICTIMS

At the outbreak of the war, as the Croatian media stereotypes were taken over by the Muslim media, the name and image of 'Chetnik' merged with that of any Serb opposing the Muslim-dominated government. The Bosnian Serb media were using the whole plethora of old and new pejoratives – 'Turks' (meaning Muslims), *'balije'*, as well as 'fundamentalists' and 'mujahedeen' – suggesting that the Muslims were foreigners and intruders or, alternatively, traitors to the Christian faith. In the way these stereotypes were used, the media war in Bosnia–Hercegovina was a continuation of the war in Croatia.[28]

The stereotyping used in the Muslim media campaign aimed at international audiences also followed the pattern already established in Croatia: the Serb forces were outside savages wantonly destroying the Bosnian cultural heritage, murdering innocent children and civilians and wrecking peaceful lives. The use of the same type of image as in the war in Croatia could be explained thus: by the similarity of Serb forces' heavy shelling of civilian areas; by the need of TV crews to film the same type of emotionally powerful scenes of war devastation; and by the Bosnian Muslim government's hiring of the same public relations firm, Ruder Finn, which had already waged a successful publicity campaign on behalf of the Croatian government. The methods used by the Croatian army in Dubrovnik and elsewhere to create the image of the wanton destructiveness of their enemies were used once again, with even greater effect, in Sarajevo: the Muslim artillery would fire on the Serb locations from which the Serbs were sure to respond with artillery barrages over the hotel 'Holiday Inn', housing foreign journalists.[29] In this way, the Muslim forces would make sure that the artillery barrages would reach, even if harmlessly, the foreign journalists.

As with all TV images, the image of besieged civilians in Sarajevo under brutal and murderous Serb shelling gave a very selective view of the war. The wider picture within which the shelling was often taking place – the artillery exchanges and fighting between the Muslim forces in the city and the Serb forces in its suburbs or in the hills – was usually missing.[30] In this selective TV image, the Bosnian government or Muslim side was presented in the way that the Bosnian government wanted it presented – as defenceless victims of a brutal, outside aggressor.

In addition to the image of a defenceless Sarajevo under siege, another highly selective but very potent TV image emerged in August 1992 – that of an emaciated Muslim prisoner in a Serb detention camp at Trnopolje first broadcast by the British ITN. In the first report, the camp was called 'a concentration camp', but the follow-up reports transformed it into 'a death camp' and explicitly likened it to Nazi camps. A new stereotype was quickly created – that of Nazi-like Serbs herding Jew-like Muslims into camps to be slaughtered. An examination of the footage, however, easily showed that not all prisoners pictured were starving and no evidence was ever produced of mass executions or mass starvation in the camp (in which the conditions were appalling enough).[31]

This stereotype was soon reinforced by that of Serbs as serial rapists. In late November 1992, the Bosnian Muslim government circulated the story of 50 000 raped Muslim women by Serb soldiers indicating that this was part of the planned Serb genocide of the Muslim population. The Western media gave it a worldwide publicity without making any attempts to verify it. The EC almost immediately dispatched a delegation which, without specifying its source, estimated the number of rapes at 20 000, a figure which was later rejected by the EC's Committee on Women's Rights as unsubstantiated. The UN Commission on Human Rights, in February 1993, while refraining from any official estimate, mentioned around 2300 rapes, most of which were of Muslim women (but also including Croat and Serb women).[32] In spite of this, neither the Bosnian Muslim government nor the media which ran the story ever retracted the original number.

The most potent TV image and media story of the war proved to be that of dozens of mangled and bloody bodies of dead and wounded civilians in Sarajevo, broadcast almost instantly after bomb explosions. In their immediacy, vividness and impact they surpassed any other TV image of civilian suffering, such as, for example, daily images of the wounded children and elderly rushed to the Sarajevo hospital. As the Serb artillery's shelling of Sarajevo had been causing civilian casualties almost every day, the media presented every civilian massacre as the work of Serb gunners. As a result, the two largest of such massacres – on Vasa Miskina street on 27 May 1992 and at the Markale Market on 5 February 1994 – served as catalysts for international intervention against the Serb side in the conflict.[33] After the Vasa Miskina massacre, the UN imposed mandatory sanctions against Serbia and Montenegro while the Markale market massacre was followed by the threat of NATO airstrikes against Serb artillery which, in turn, led to the creation of a UN monitored heavy weapons exclusion zone around Sarajevo and the withdrawal of Serb (as well as Muslim) heavy artillery from the area. Though the media at the time represented both as atrocities committed by the Serbs, the UN investigations could not establish

Serb culpability in either case.[34] The power of the TV images to influence the Western governments' policies became obvious quite early in
the war; this was the reason, in the opinion the first UN commander
in Sarajevo, general MacKenzie,[35] why the Muslim forces as well as
others appeared ready to target their own civilians for the benefit of
the Western TV crews.

Media reporting, however, was not only selective in the types of
image presented but also in the choice of the national group or side in
the conflict: there were no stories from those Muslim and Croat detention camps which were marked as places of maltreatment of Serb
prisoners; no TV images of dozens of wounded or dead Serb civilians
or of continual shelling of Mostar civilians either by the Croat or by
the Muslim forces. This selectiveness led, quite naturally, to the charges
that foreign journalists, like native ones, became combatants as well,
fighting on the side of those whom they saw as the war's principal
victims – the Bosnian Muslims.[36] In their hands, the media in this war
became their victims' most potent weapon.

## BOSNIA'S HUMANITARIAN DISASTER: THE UN IN ACTION

Through all the failed peace-negotiations and spreading war, the UN
agencies as well as other nongovernmental humanitarian agencies have
consistently supplied humanitarian aid – food, clothing and medicine
– to all groups in the war. As the UN forces' principal mandate, until
mid-1995 at least, remained the protection of the humanitarian aid supplies, these forces as well as the civilian aid workers had been, in the
course of their duties, attacked by forces of all three sides in the conflict
and the delivery of humanitarian aid obstructed in various ways.[37] By
March 1993, the UN High Commissioner for Refugees reported that
2.28 million people in Bosnia–Hercegovina (out of 3.8 million recipients in the whole of former Yugoslavia) were receiving humanitarian
aid from the UN agencies. This was approximately half of the population of the republic before the war started in 1992. By 1994 this number
had increased by a further half a million persons and in 1995, with the
influx of over 150 000 Serb refugees from the former Krajina region in
Croatia, the number of people assisted by the UN in the region would
probably exceed 3 million.

Apart from providing humanitarian aid, the UN launched systematic investigations of human rights abuses in the whole of former Yugoslavia. In August 1992 the UN Commission on Human Rights

appointed the former Polish prime minister Tadeusz Mazowiecki as Special Rapporteur on Human Rights. The Special Rapporteur set up field offices in Zagreb, Sarajevo and Skopje and visited areas in Bosnia–Hercegovina under the control of the Bosnian Muslim government. The Bosnian Serb authorities refused to co-operate with the Special Rapporteur while the government of the new Yugoslavia (Serbia and Montenegro) offered only limited cooperation. Mazowiecki's sources – his field staff, various governmental agencies (such as those of the Bosnian Muslims), nongovernmental organisations and international agencies – provided very detailed accounts of a variety of human rights abuses, including massacres, torture, sexual abuse, murder and the disappearance of civilians, maltreatment of prisoners, unlawful detention and various forms of ethnic discrimination. In particular, detailed information was provided of the forced displacement of non-Serbs from the areas held by Serb forces as well as civilian casualties of Bosnian Serb shelling and sniper fire in the UN safe areas. Already in one of his early reports, Mazowiecki noted that the Muslims in Bosnia–Hercegovina felt that they were threatened with extermination.[38] Apart from statistical information – apparently provided by governmental and international agencies' sources – the reports also detailed individual cases of human rights abuses in these areas, describing various forms of harassment to which non-Serbs were exposed. When dealing with abuses against Serb civilians by Bosnian Muslims and Croats, the reports principally detailed individual cases which Mazowiecki took up with the relevant authorities, attempting – mostly in vain – to seek redress and judicial inquiries. No information on the civilian casualties on the Serb side (although military activity against Serb civilians was mentioned) nor any statistical information on the displacement of Serb civilians from the areas held by Bosnian Croat and Muslim forces was offered.[39] After investigating human rights abuses against Bosnian Muslim civilians, following the Bosnian Serb forces' conquest of the UN safe areas of Srebrenica and Žepa in July 1995, Mazowiecki called for NATO airstrikes against the Serb forces in this area. As his call – as well as similar others – went unheeded, he resigned his post in protest.

Apart from the Special Rapporteur and a Commission of Experts (which concluded its work on the violations of humanitarian law in April 1994), the UN Security Council on 25 May 1994 established an International Tribunal, consisting of two trial and one appeal chamber with eleven judges in all, and charged with prosecuting those responsible for serious violations of international humanitarian law committed in

former Yugoslavia, as of 1 January 1991. The Tribunal, inaugurated in
November 1994 in the Hague, had to enact its own rules of procedure
and evidence and began working under a statute approved by the UN
Security Council. The Tribunal was empowered to take over the cases
of suspects from other states' legal jurisdictions and to pass only prison
sentences. The Bosnian Serb and Yugoslav authorities refused to recognise the jurisdiction of the Tribunal from its very inception, suggesting
that the Tribunal was biased against the Serb side.

Until August 1995, only one person, a Bosnian Serb, arrested in Ger-
many, had been brought to trial by the Tribunal; by this time his trial was
in its early stages. In July 1995 the Tribunal also indicted a group of 23
Serbs from Bosnia and Croatia including the Bosnian Serb leaders Dr
Karadžić and general Mladić and, later, a group of Bosnian Croat leaders and officers. No such actions have been planned against Bosnian
Muslim leaders in spite of the evidence of atrocities committed by
Bosnian Muslim forces. In a newspaper interview, the president of the
Tribunal, Antonio Casesse, made it clear that he already considered
Dr Karadžić guilty and noted that the Tribunal's indictment should
preclude the Bosnian Serb leaders from participating in any peace
negotiations.[40] The role of the International Tribunal, at least in
the opinion of its presiding judge, thus appears to go well beyond the
search for justice in former Yugoslavia.

While there had been no comprehensive assessment of the impact
the UN investigations had on the protection of civilians, from the UN
reports themselves, it appears that thus far their impact was quite limited. None of the warring parties was ready to try to punish members
of its own national group for human rights abuses which were documented by the UN. In this context, the initial focus of the International
Tribunal in the Hague on prosecuting Serbs alone was not likely to increase respect for or improve protection of human rights by the warring parties.


## TO IMPOSE A SETTLEMENT: THE CONTACT GROUP PLAN

As the Muslim side in late 1993 rejected the Owen–Stoltenberg peace
plan, the US initiated the creation of a new constitutional entity in Bosnia–Hercegovina, a Federation consisting of the areas with Croat and
Bosniac (formerly called 'Muslims') majorities. According to its framework agreement, the Federation would be made up of cantons each of
which would have a majority of either Muslims (Bosniacs) or Croats.

The office of president with a one-year term would be held by a Croat and a Muslim alternately; one-third of ministerial portfolios would go to the Croats and all decisions of vital interest to either of the two constituent peoples should be reached by consensus (there is no provision for the participation of Serbs or any other nationalities in the executive). The federal government would be in charge of foreign affairs, national defence (with a joint Muslim–Croat army), economic policy, currency and customs, while police, education and public services would be relegated to the cantons. This Federation was to enter into a confederation with the Republic of Croatia, the scope and nature of which was left open. The Federation's legal and political relation to the Muslim-dominated presidency and the government of Bosnia–Hercegovina – which continued to operate as before – were also left unclarified.[41] After the Muslim–Croat talks held in Washington, presidents Izetbegović and Tudjman signed the Federation and confederation agreements on 18 March 1994 at a ceremony presided over by president Clinton. The new state entity, however shaky its foundations might have appeared, significantly strengthened the Muslim position as the Muslim forces, in spite of the nominal UN embargo, could now be supplied with arms through Croatia and their troops trained by US officers (see Chapter 12).

The benefits which this new US-sponsored entity brought to the Muslim side became obvious in the next – fourth – international peace proposal unveiled in May 1994 by the Contact group on Yugoslavia, a new negotiating group formed in early May of representatives from the governments of the US, Russia, Germany, France and Britain. Its peace plan gave 51 per cent of the republic's territory to the Muslim–Croat Federation and 49 per cent to the Serbs. Unlike the earlier plans, the Contact group plan had no constitutional proposals to make (thus leaving the constitutional status of the Serb territories undefined) and was initially presented to the warring parties on a 'take-it-or-leave-it' basis. The map the Contact group presented in July 1994 assigned most urban centres as well as industrial and energy resources to the Muslim–Croat Federation and, like the Vance–Owen plan, cut the territorial link between western and eastern Serb territories. Not surprisingly, the Bosnian Serb leaders, after failing to renegotiate its terms, rejected it; in September 1994 their electorate, in a referendum, confirmed their rejection.

However, in October 1994 their erstwhile patron, president Milošević, accepted the plan and, in return for temporary easing of the UN sanctions against Yugoslavia (Serbia and Montenegro), imposed a blockade on the border between Bosnian Serb territories and Yugoslavia allowing the UN civilian observers to monitor it from the Yugoslav side. As the split between the Bosnian Serb leaders and Milošević deepened, the Milošević-controlled media in Serbia attacked the former with a venom previously reserved for national enemies. This marked a momentous split in the pan-Serb national movement which Milošević himself initiated in 1988. In October 1994 the movement, whose initial but rather vague aim was the creation of a single state of all Serb-populated lands in effect divided into a Milošević faction which appeared ready to seek accommodation with the Western powers, in particular the US, and a Karadžić faction, based in Bosnia–Hercegovina, which opposed this course.[42]

It was the new negotiating tactics, initiated by the US, which proved to be a catalyst for the split and which, as a consequence, brought about a major realignment of the forces in the region. Instead of searching further for an agreement among the warring parties – a search which had proved fruitless – the US government opted for supporting the Muslim–Croat Federation and its demands while at the same time offering Milošević inducements – the temporary easing of UN sanctions – in return for his abandonment of the Bosnian Serb leaders. The resulting split in the pan-Serb movement not only weakened the Bosnian Serb military by blocking its only source of support, Serbia and Montenegro, but probably disoriented and demoralised the Bosnian Serb – as well as Krajina Serb – populace, weakening the resolve of both to oppose the Muslim–Croat forces; this in turn would enable the latter to prove its superiority on the battlefield. In its strategy aiming at the isolation of the Bosnian Serb leaders – which was further aided by their indictment by the UN International Tribunal in July 1995 – the US government and its allies were, in effect, seeking to impose a settlement on the Bosnian Serb leadership or, failing that, to create conditions for a Bosnian Serb military defeat.

# 12 A US Enforced Peace?

In early December 1994 the Croatian government and Krajina Serb authorities signed an agreement, mediated by the US and Russian ambassadors to Croatia, which reopened for traffic a stretch of the Zagreb–Belgrade highway and an oil pipeline. This agreement was expected to lead to further agreements on economic cooperation between the two parties, in the hope that through the economic reintegration of the region a satisfactory political settlement on the status of Krajina could also be reached. In late December, the former US president Jimmy Carter negotiated an agreement for the cessation of hostilities in Bosnia–Hercegovina for four months (starting on 1 January 1995) with the possibility of an extension. As this was the first agreement for a cessation of hostilities in the Bosnian war, the UN negotiators hoped that, during this period, either an extension of this truce or a more comprehensive peace settlement could be reached. For this purpose in early December a slightly modified Contact group plan (see Chapter 11) was offered to the warring parties, this time only as a basis for further negotiations.

However, in November 1994 the US government, under increased pressure from Republican members of the Congress, proclaimed that it would no longer enforce the UN arms embargo against the Bosnian Muslim government. At the same time the US and Croatian governments signed a military cooperation agreement in Washington which provided for the training of Croatian officers by the US military both in the US and in Croatia. Possibly as a result of these two moves, an increased activity of US military was reported both among the Bosnian Muslim troops and in Croatia.[1] Early in 1995 the Bosnian Muslim armed forces, according to Western newspaper reports, started to receive arms and equipment directly by air from NATO members (possibly Turkey).[2] Until then most of the military aid to the Bosnian Muslims appears to have come via Croatia from Islamic countries such as Iran and Saudi Arabia (from where also came the Islamic mujahedeen fighters).[3] In retrospect, these reports had pointed to a major build-up of the Croatian and Bosnian Muslim forces as well as their training by US military personnel, in preparation for their offensives against the Bosnian and Krajina Serb forces which started in March 1995.

## THE TRUCE BROKEN: BOSNIAN MUSLIM, CROATIAN AND NATO FORCES ON THE OFFENSIVE

An early sign of the new policy direction of the Croatian and Bosnian Muslim governments was the Croatian government's refusal, in January 1995, to renew the UN peacekeeping mandate in Croatia. After intensive negotiations, in return for extending the mandate to a reduced UN force under a changed name, in March 1995 the Croatian government received a public pledge from the US Vice-President to support its bid to gain control over the Serb-held areas of Croatia. At the same time the Bosnian Muslim government refused to renegotiate any provisions of the Contact group plan and, in early March 1995, before the expiry of the four-month truce, its forces launched the first in a series of offensives; in this offensive they gained only a small patch of territory and a strategically important TV and communications tower in northern Bosnia.

Next to go into action was the Croatian army: in a lightning 48-hour strike in May 1995 it conquered the whole of western Slavonia. In this new display of military tactics (similar to the one used by the US in the Gulf war in 1991), the Serb forces were overwhelmed by a concentrated attack of a Croatian army thrice its strength. In the assault the UN peacekeepers were brushed aside and an unknown number of fleeing Serb civilians killed. During the attack, the Krajina Serb forces fired unguided Soviet-made missiles on Zagreb causing damage and civilian casualties and shelled various Croatian towns. In the aftermath of the attack almost the entire Serb civilian population – around 15 000 persons – left the area, in some cases in the UN organised convoys. The US administration condemned only the Serb missile attack on Zagreb and the shelling of Croatian towns.

In late May the Bosnian Muslim army's attempt at a break-out from Sarajevo was met with new rounds of Serb artillery bombardment of the city. While the Bosnian Muslim request for NATO airstrikes was refused by the UN command, the Serb units took, by force, some of their heavy weapons from the UN guarded weapons depots set up in 1994 in the Sarajevo 20-kilometres exclusion zone. In response, in its eighth action since the beginning of the war, NATO aircraft bombed Serb ammunition depots near Sarajevo. The Bosnian Serb authorities then took more than 300 UN personnel hostage, hand-cuffing some of them to the outbuildings of the ammunition and weapons depots, as human shields against further NATO strikes. After prolonged negotiations, the UN personnel were handed over, unharmed, to the Serbian government in Belgrade for release.

The hostage crisis prompted the UN to set up, in June, a 12 000 strong Rapid Reaction Force, whose declared aim was to offer effective artillery and airpower protection to the UN forces. While the preparations were made for the landing of these forces in Dalmatia, the Bosnian Muslim forces launched a massive three-pronged offensive aimed at relieving Sarajevo and breaking the Serb semi-encirclement of the centre of the city. Using a new tactic of simultaneous and coordinated pincer attacks on a series of Serb positions around Sarajevo, the Muslim forces broke Serb defence lines at several points, threatening their vital communication links; but, after several weeks of bitter fighting, the attacking forces were pushed back to their starting positions.

In July the Bosnian Serb forces launched attacks against the Muslim forces in Srebrenica and Žepa, two of the UN safe areas in east Bosnia. After taking the towns, tens of thousands of Muslim civilians were expelled amidst allegations of looting, rape and widespread massacres of civilians and of captured Bosnian Muslim soldiers; this proved to be the last in the series of expulsions of the Muslim population from east Bosnia which the Bosnian Serb authorities started in April 1992. The UN humanitarian agencies, long after the capture of the two zones, claimed that around 6000 men – mainly male adults, but including some adolescents – were still unaccounted for; it was suspected that they were massacred by the Serb forces. Having taken these two areas, the Bosnian and Krajina Serb forces then shifted their attacks to the Muslim forces in the Bihać safe area in the northwest of the republic. At the same time the Croatian army and Bosnian Croat forces conquered the southwest Bosnian approach to Krajina, the Grahovo-Glamoč area, forcing the entire Serb population to flee.

Having secured the southwest approach to Krajina from Bosnia, on 4 August the Croatian army launched its operation 'Storm' – the largest single military operation in the Yugoslav conflict – against the Serb-held area of Krajina in Croatia. Well over 100 000 Croatian troops with hundreds of artillery pieces and armour, attacked, from Bosnia and from Croatia, the Serb forces of around 50 000 men. Under heavy bombardment and faced with a superior force, the commanding Serb officers (from the Yugoslav military in Belgrade) ordered their troops to abandon their positions and to evacuate their families to Serb-held areas in Bosnia. In four days most of the Serb-held territory was taken over by the Croatian army, while the Serb population left with the Croatian police and the UN, in some cases, providing escorts for Serb refugee convoys (under attack by Croat mobs) through Croatian territory. In less than a week between 150 000 and 200 000 Serbs left their homes, prompting the new European Union negotiator Carl Bildt[4] to describe it as one of the largest ethnic cleansing operations in the former Yugoslavia.[5] According to the Western news reports and UN officials, after the conquest Croatian soldiers started killing the remaining Serb civilians, looting and burning the abandoned Serb villages and houses.[6] As almost the entire Serb community had left Croatia, the 'scorched earth' policy appears to have aimed at ensuring that no Serbs return to Croatia; this appeared to be the final solution to the 'Serb problem' in Croatia. As before, the US administration refrained from condemning this policy.

Trained by retired US army generals and equipped by NATO,[7] in mid-1995 the Croatian army proved to be superior to Serb militias both in its training and equipment; together with the Bosnian Muslim and Bosnian Croat forces, in mid-1995 it also outnumbered the demoralised Bosnian Serb military by 5 to 1. The conquest of the Krajina region in Croatia opened the way to the Croatian army for its assault on adjacent Serb-held west Bosnia.

On 27 August the US chief negotiator in former Yugoslavia, Assistant Secretary of State Richard Holbrooke, warned of an imminent 'more active NATO air' involvement against the Bosnian Serb forces. On 28 August a mortar shell landed on a Sarajevo market place, leaving 38 people dead; a hastily conducted UN inquiry held the Bosnian Serb forces responsible.[8] On 30 August NATO launched its operation 'Deliberate Force' which it had been planning from early 1995 and which the UN command had approved in early August. The first wave of air strikes, carried out by NATO aircraft flying from bases in Italy and an US aircraft carrier in the Adriatic, targeted Bosnian Serb command and communication centres, troop barracks, ammunition depots and weapons factories around Sarajevo and other UN safe areas, while the UN Rapid Reaction Force artillery, in place around Sarajevo, kept up a steady bombardment of Bosnian Serb depots as well as artillery positions. The avowed aim of these air and ground attacks was to induce the Bosnian Serb command to comply with the UN demands to withdraw its heavy weapons from the 20-kilometeres exclusion zone around Sarajevo and other UN safe areas, to cease attacks on these areas and to allow unimpeded access to the Sarajevo airport and the roads leading to the city. The air strikes were suspended twice – on 1 and 5 September 1995 – to allow for negotiations for the withdrawal of the Serb heavy weapons and for the verification of the withdrawals. As the latter did not satisfy the NATO commanders, the air strikes were continued until 14 September when the UN brokered a 'framework agreement' for a ceasefire with the Bosnian Serb military, in accordance with which the latter withdrew its heavy weapons from the Sarajevo exclusion zone and NATO ceased its offensive operations.

In addition to the Bosnian Serb military communications and command centres, artillery and air defence emplacements, ammunition depots and military maintenance facilities, in the later stages of the operation NATO aircraft targeted bridges and civilian communication installations on almost the whole of Bosnian Serb territory. In addition to a variety of high technology weapons used by the aircraft, the US forces also fired Tomahawk cruise missiles against air defence installations in northern Bosnia. During the operation aircraft from eight NATO countries (US, UK, Germany, Italy, France, Netherlands, Spain and Turkey) flew 3515 sorties and dropped 1026 bombs.[9] While the Serb air defences brought down a French Mirage in the first day of the airstrikes, for the whole duration of the operation the Bosnian Serb artillery did not return fire at the UN Rapid Reaction ground forces, possibly in order to avoid more damage to its artillery positions. As relatively few Bosnian Serb artillery positions around Sarajevo were targeted at all,[10] it appears that the principal goal of the NATO airstrikes was to destroy the communication facilities and ammunition storage of the Bosnian Serb military and thus cripple both its mobility and firepower in the face of the impending offensives by the Croatian army and its Bosnian Muslim allies.

As the NATO aircraft pounded targets all over Serb-held territory, in mid-September the Croatian army jointly with Bosnian Muslim forces surged into the northwest and west Bosnia, taking in quick succession Donji Vakuf, Drvar, Jajce and Prijedor with a total of around 3900 square kilometres of land.[11] As in the assault on Krajina a month earlier, Serb units were often ordered to withdraw without fighting, followed or preceded by a huge number of Serb refugees. As Bosnian Serb chief of staff, general Mladić, was in Belgrade (officially in hospital for medical treatment), it appears that, as in Krajina a month before, the withdrawal orders came from the Yugoslav military command in Belgrade.[12] The principal resistance to the Croat–Bosnian Muslim attack seems to have come from the units under the direct command of Dr Karadžić or from various paramilitaries. By the end of September, the Croatian army and Bosnian Muslim forces were ready to assault central Bosnia and its capital Banja Luka. At this point, apparently under pressure from the US chief negotiator Richard Holbrooke,[13] the Croatian army halted its offensive; left without the support of the Croatian artillery and logistics, the Bosnian Muslim military followed suit. This lightning offensive led to an influx of the entire Serb population – over 150 000 people – of west and northwest Bosnia into Serb-held central Bosnia where they were stranded under appalling conditions. But it also reduced the Bosnian Serb control of territory to roughly 49 per cent of Bosnia–Hercegovina, the very percentage which the Contact group plan had set for the Bosnian Serbs.

In the face of this defeat, the Contact group division of territory must have appeared to the Bosnian Serb leaders a more acceptable option than the further loss of land. However, their prolonged defiance in the face of NATO air attacks indicated that they expected the Russian as well as Serbian government to intervene in their support. While the Russian government criticised the airstrikes from the very start and later branded them as a 'genocide of the Serb people', it was clearly not inclined to offer military support to the Bosnian Serb forces; Milošević's government in Belgrade took an even more guarded stance. In the eyes of Bosnian Serb politicians, their defeat was attributable solely to the intervention of the most powerful military organisation in the world, which, because of the lack of support from Russia and Serbia, they were unable to resist. The Bosnian Muslim leaders, on the other hand, could blame the US and NATO for failing to support their conquest of the whole of Bosnia–Hercegovina and the expulsion of most of its Serb population. Thus both sides could conveniently blame foreigners for their failure to achieve their ultimate goals.

## THE FIRST PEACE AGREEMENT IN BOSNIA–HERCEGOVINA: US DIPLOMACY ON THE OFFENSIVE

Parallel with the preparation for the NATO airstrikes against the Bosnian Serbs, the US chief negotiator Richard Holbrooke started, in early August 1995, a round of intensive negotiations in Zagreb, Sarajevo and Belgrade, aiming at a comprehensive peace settlement based on the Contact group plan of division. Prior to the NATO attack, on 29 August 1995 he secured the agreement of Milošević to represent Bosnian Serbs in further negotiations (to which the government of the Serb Republic in Bosnia–Hercegovina formally agreed). This made the governments of Bosnia–Hercegovina, Yugoslavia (Serbia and Montenegro)[14] and Croatia the only negotiating parties. While the NATO airstrikes against Bosnian Serb positions were in full swing, on 8 September in Geneva Holbrooke got the three negotiating parties to agree to the 'Basic Principles' (followed by 'Further Agreed Basic Principles' on 28 September), which reaffirmed the Contact group's 49:51 per cent division between the two 'constituent entities' of Bosnia–Hercegovina – Republika Srpska (the Serb Republic) and the Federation of Bosnia and Herzegovina (the Muslim–Croat federation formed in Washington in March 1994, see Chapter 11). The recognition of the Serb Republic as a constituent entity of the country was, however, a major change from the original Contact group plan, which had no such provision.

Having halted the Croatian/Bosnian Muslim offensive in late September, Holbrooke was then able to get the Bosnian Muslims and Bosnian Serbs to sign, on 8 October 1995, a general cease-fire in Bosnia–Hercegovina and to start, on 26 October, peace talks between the three negotiating parties at a US Air Force base in Dayton, Ohio. Helped once again by high technology (the use of computer-simulated images of the terrain), Holbrooke and his US team (the representatives of the other four Contact group governments and of the European Union acted only as observers) got the three negotiating parties to initial, on 21 November 1995, a comprehensive settlement, including a new constitution of Bosnia–Hercegovina and separate agreements for its internal division and for the deployment of a NATO-commanded peacekeeping force; this 'General Framework Agreement for Peace in Bosnia and Herzegovina' was signed in Paris on 14 December by Milošević, Izetbegović, and Tudjman as well as the heads of state or government of the five Contact group countries and a European Union representative.

The new constitution of the state renamed 'Bosnia and Herzegovina' (instead of the 'Republic of Bosnia and Herzegovina') envisaged a two-chamber parliament; in both two-thirds of its delegates would come from the Muslim–Croat Federation and one-third from the Serb Republic (the three constituent nations, Bosniacs [Bosnian Muslims], Croats and Serbs would delegate five members each to the smaller chamber, House of Peoples). For any legislation to be passed at least one-third of delegates from each entity would have to vote in favour of it (Art. IV, 3 (e)) and a majority of Bosniac or Croat or Serb delegates could declare a proposed decision of the parliament 'destructive of a vital interest' of their respective peoples; if the issue could not be resolved by a Joint Commission of the House of Peoples, it was to be decided by the Constitutional Court, one-third of whose members were to be foreign jurists appointed by the president of the European Court of Human Rights (Art. IV, 3 (f)). Foreign policy, foreign trade, customs, immigration and refugee policies as well common communications and air traffic control would be the responsibility of the central institutions of Bosnia–Hercegovina; all other matters, including defence and intra-entity law enforcement, would be responsibilities of each of the two entities. Each entity would also have the right to grant its own citizenship (which is automatically the citizenship of the whole country), to issue passports of Bosnia–Hercegovina as well as the right to establish a special parallel relationship with a neighbouring state (Art. III, 2 (a)). A three-person presidency (in which each member would take up the post of president for a year), the ministerial council, and the parliament[15] would, according to the Dayton agreements, be the only central institutions of Bosnia–Hercegovina which would have no foreign members appointed by international bodies. The central bank, the provisional electoral commission and the commissions on human rights, for displaced persons and refugees, for the preservation of national monuments and for public corporations would be chaired during a transition period (of six years or less) by an appointee of an international organisation who is not a citizen of Bosnia–Hercegovina. In addition, the UN Security Council was given the right to appoint a High Representative to supervise the civilian aspects of the implementation of the Dayton agreements and the international civil administration of the country. The international organisations appointing office-holders to all these institutions (including the constitutional court) were, in effect, taking on the supervision of the principal legal, economic and humanitarian aspects of civilian life in Bosnia–Hercegovina.

All military forces in the country, during the transition period of approximately one year (starting January 1996) would be come under the supervision of the Implementation Force (IFOR) consisting of 60 000 men from 32 countries, including a 20 000 strong US contingent, under NATO command. IFOR's mandate was to enforce the zones of separation between opposing sides, the withdrawal of their troops and weaponry to the barracks, the demobilisation of excess troops and the overall cessation of hostilities. As IFOR was given the right to use force to ensure compliance with its orders – which no other authority in Bosnia–Hercegovina could countermand – the IFOR commanding officer (a US general) was effectively in control of all military forces in the country.

The Dayton peace agreements thus left Bosnia–Hercegovina with a confederal arrangement between the two national 'entities,' each retaining significant sovereign powers including the right of self-defence, with international supervision of the most important aspects of its civilian life and a US officer in effective command of all military forces.[16] As it has been pointed out,[17] a *de jure* partition of the republic among its three constituent nations (similar to the partition of the former Yugoslavia), providing the Bosnian Muslims (Bosniacs) with a viable and real state, would have represented not only a much less costly but probably more stable constitutional arrangement. As the Dayton agreements were negotiated and signed by politicians who were not elected by the citizens of Bosnia–Hercegovina[18] and their ratification by elected bodies or through a referendum was neither planned nor required, it is in any case unclear whether they command the support of the majority of the citizens of any one of its three constituent nations.

## THE PROSPECTS FOR PEACE IN BOSNIA–HERCEGOVINA

The Dayton Agreement on Inter-Entity Boundary Line and Related Issues, (Art. V) left the status of the north Bosnian corridor around the

*Map 5*  Dayton Agreements division of Bosnia–Hercegovina
*Source*: US Department of Defense, Washington, DC.

town of Brčko, a vital Bosnian Serb supply route, to international arbitration and required the transfer of the Serb-held suburbs of Sarajevo to the Muslim–Croat federation; the Dayton agreements also created a special corridor within Bosnian Serb territory to the Muslim enclave of Goražde in east Bosnia. In terms of the division of territory, the Dayton agreements made the Bosnian Serbs, in Richard Holbrooke's own words, the 'big losers'.[19] In the only referendum ever held on the Dayton agreements, the Serb inhabitants of the Sarajevo suburbs, as expected, in December 1996 rejected the transfer to the Muslim–Croat federation and, as the referendum had no effect, started to leave the suburbs *en masse*, taking the remains of their dead with them. As in January 1996 the Muslim and Bosnian Croat militias clashed in the capital of their Federation, Mostar (under the EU administration), the UN High Representative, Carl Bildt, called for a programme of reconciliation of all three sides in the conflict, a programme which was not envisaged by the Dayton peace agreements. The Bosnian Croat mob's attempt to lynch the EU-appointed administrator of Mostar in early February 1996 amid continued violent protests against the unification of Muslim and Croat parts of Mostar, indicated not only how fragile the Muslim–Croat Federation was, but also how far from reconciliation Bosnian Muslims and Croats were.

In spite of the quick separation of their military forces, under IFOR supervision, in early 1996 the political leaders of all three sides appeared committed not to any sort of reconciliation but to their previous irreconcilable political goals. The Bosnian Serb leaders (those who were not indicted by the Hague Tribunal) were as committed as ever to maintaining the sovereignty of their entity as well as their power; possibly as a result of the severe defeats and demoralisation of their armed forces, they showed no intention of seeking to recover the territory they lost, let alone conquering any new territory. In contrast, the Bosnian Muslim leader, Alija Izetbegović, was committed to gaining control over the 'territory under Chetnik control' as he called the Serb Republic; in his view, its status as a separate, constituent entity of Bosnia–Hercegovina was only temporary.[20] In fact, the Muslim leaders could attempt to wrest control from the present Serb leaders in the Serb Republic by relying on the support of the returning Bosnian Muslim refugees and of those Serb politicians who are ready to acknowledge the Muslim supremacy in Bosnia–Hercegovina. As the Serb population in the Serb Republic has been seriously depleted by the continued Serb emigration to Serbia and elsewhere, Muslim refugees returning, under the provisions of the Dayton peace agreements, to their homes in the Serb Republic could form a strong constituency for Izetbegović's Party of Democratic Action or any other Muslim-led party. Further, the Muslim leaders could also attempt to attract Serb politicians and political groups dissatisfied with the present Bosnian Serb leaders by promising them positions in a future central government. So far the Muslim leaders have the support of only one small Serb political group, the Serb Civic Council, committed to a multiethnic democracy and made up exclusively of middle-class inhabitants of Sarajevo. To broaden their appeal the Muslim leaders would probably have to abandon the Islamic exclusiveness to which Izetbegović still firmly adheres.[21] In an attempt at creating such a broader electoral base, in January 1996 the former Muslim prime minister, Haris Silajdžić, publicly renounced his ties with Izetbegović's SDA and adopted a non-sectarian pan-national stance.[22]

The gradual Muslim takeover of the Serb Republic would be effectively thwarted were the Serbian president Slobodan Milošević to succeed in replacing the present Bosnian Serb leaders with his appointees. Once in control of this entity, his supporters could then invoke the 'special parallel relationship' article of the constitution to form a confederation with Yugoslavia parallel to the confederation between the Muslim–Croat Federation and the Republic of Croatia created in Washington in March 1994. As the Croatian government has already control over the Bosnian Croat cantons of the Muslim–Croat Federation (through its ruling party HDZ and the deputies elected from these cantons to the Croatian Diet in Zagreb), a confederation of the Serb Republic and Yugoslavia would effectively partition Bosnia–Hercegovina between Croatia and Yugoslavia, leaving the Bosnian Muslim leaders only with the landlocked Muslim cantons of the Federation.

Faced with any option which would deny them control of the Serb Republic, the Bosnian Muslim leaders may be ready to use their military force to conquer the Serb Republic and thus pre-empt any 'special parallel relationship' with Yugoslavia. As the US administration has publicly pledged to train and equip the Bosnian Muslim army, the Bosnian Serb military – demoralised and depleted of manpower and equipment – could offer no effective resistance to such a force without substantial aid from Yugoslavia.[23] Of course, a Bosnian Muslim attack on the Serb Republic would contravene the Dayton peace agreements and would cause an even larger exodus of the Serb population than the Croatian attack on Krajina. In spite of this, the US administration may support a future Bosnian Muslim attack on the Serb Republic as it did the Croatian attack on Krajina in 1995.

In view of the conflicting political goals of the leaders of the three national groups, the elaborate framework of institutions under international supervision created by the Dayton agreements can offer no guarantee for the maintenance of peace in Bosnia–Hercegovina. The lack of consistency in US policy in the region would not be of much help in maintaining the peace either. Until September 1995 the US administration refused to support any European Union and United Nations peace plans which denied the Bosnian Muslim claim for the whole of Bosnia–Hercegovina by recognising a separate Serb 'entity;' for this reason the US refused to give full support to the EC's first peace plan in 1992 and the Owen-Stoltenberg plan in 1993, both of which were accepted by the Bosnian Serb leaders. In September 1995 the US administration apparently changed this policy, recognised a Serb 'entity' in Bosnia–Hercegovina and proceeded to negotiate a settlement whose constitutional framework resembled the Owen-Stoltenberg plan. The US administration had thus withheld support from any settlement which was not negotiated by its own officials and over whose implementation it had no direct control. The US-led peace negotiations in Dayton were seen as a proof of US leadership in world affairs[24] and their successful completion as a proof of president Clinton's leadership in foreign policy (who, in 1996, was to run for re-election).[25]

In view of this, it is an open question, first, whether the US administration is really committed to preserving a Serb entity in Bosnia–Hercegovina, as provided by the Dayton peace agreements and, second, whether it will preserve its interest in maintaining peace in the region, once US involvement in the region is no longer required as a proof of its world leadership. If the answer to either or both questions is negative, the US-brokered peace in Bosnia–Hercegovina is not likely to survive for long.

# Epilogue: Why the Fragmentation?

The fragmentation of Yugoslavia could be viewed as a culmination of the process of creation of nation states in the region which started early in the nineteenth century. As in other parts of Eastern Europe, state building was at that time carried out within the framework of national ideologies which served as primary instruments of mass mobilisation. In the early twentieth century separate national ideologies – of Serbs, Croats and Slovenes – were subsumed under a pan-national ideology of Yugoslav national unity which provided the ideological framework and impetus for the creation, in 1918, of a new state – the Kingdom of Serbs, Croats and Slovenes, later renamed the Kingdom of Yugoslavia. The ideology of Yugoslav national unity did not, however, provide an effective legitimation of the new state and its constitutional foundations had been questioned by various national elites of Yugoslavia long before the country's dismemberment by the Axis in 1941. However, the Yugoslav communists, who emerged victorious from the civil war in 1945, reconstructed the Yugoslav state as a federation of six republics based on a supranational Yugoslavism which promoted a 'unity and brotherhood' of equal nations of Yugoslavia. As separate national communist elites consolidated their grip on power in the six republics, in the early 1970s Yugoslavia was transformed into a semiconfederation of semisovereign republics. The Yugoslav 'equal nations' ideology was also increasingly challenged, from the early 1970s, by re-emerging separate national ideologies each of which was asserting the dominance of its target nation on a particular territory. In multiparty elections in 1990 new national elites, promoting the national ideologies of this 'dominant nation' type, came to power in each of the six republics. The primary goal of most of the new elites was the creation of separate nation states, a process which was interrupted in the early twentieth century by the emergence of pan-national Yugoslavism as a state-building ideology.

Already in the late nineteenth century it was clear that the separate national ideologies of Serbs and Croats (as well as emerging national ideologies of Bosnian Muslims, Albanians and Macedonians) were in

189

conflict over their respective territorial claims. As the separate national ideologies became ideologies of the political elites in power in 1990, the conflict between Serb, Croat and Bosnian Muslim national ideologies and their national elites over their respective territorial claims resulted in wars in Croatia and Bosnia–Hercegovina. Each national elite attempted, by force of arms, to assert its claim over territories in which Serbs and Croats or Serbs, Croats and Muslims all lived intermixed. Since each of the national elites had earlier politically mobilised its target population in support for its own separate state-project, through this mobilisation members of each national group in effect became citizens of separate states even before such states and their borders had been fully established. In consequence, members of any opposing national group were, in the eyes of the newly established state authorities, citizens of a hostile state who endangered the new authority and should thus be expelled from their 'state'.

The reaction of the governments of European Community member states and of the US to the creation of new nation states radically shifted over a short period of time. Until September 1991 the Western governments – with the exception of the German and Austrian governments – did not support the creation of fully independent national states in the region but preferred a common constitutional framework for all of them. Then, as the war erupted in Croatia in September 1991, their overriding interest became a peaceful overall settlement which would, if necessary, allow for a high degree of independence of at least some of the former republics. Finally, in December 1991 having failed to find an overall settlement of the dispute through its peace conference, the European Community decided to recognise formally the independence of separate nation states within the internal borders of the federal units of former Yugoslavia outside any overall settlement or agreement among the parties in conflict. In accepting the former internal borders as state borders, the European Community backed the territorial claims of the Slovene, Croat and Bosnian Muslim national ideologies while denying the claim of the ruling Serb national ideology to the Serb-populated areas outside the republic of Serbia.

Having formally sanctioned the establishment of nation states, the newly constructed European Union and the US administration were not prepared to commit their armed forces to enforce the newly recognised states' borders and to quell the insurrections of the Serb populations – supported by the government of Serbia and the remnants of the Yugoslav federal army – against the newly recognised governments. Instead, the European Union together with the UN attempted to negotiate a peaceful settlement between the Serb political leaders and the newly recognised governments. As the search for a peaceful settlement appeared increasingly fruitless, the US administration began to equip and train the Croatian and Bosnian Muslim armies so as to enable their elites to assert their territorial claims against the Serb side by force of arms. This policy enabled the Croat political elites to expel, in 1995, most of the Serb population from Croatia and conquer formerly Serb-held areas in Croatia; together with its Bosnian Muslim allies, the Croatian army further conquered large areas of western Bosnia, expelling its Serb inhabitants as well. Following these military operations, the US negotiated a settlement creating a confederal state of Bosnia-Hercegovina, consisting of two national 'entities' whose borders roughly reflected the territorial division resulting from the previous military actions. The settlement was guaranteed by the country's two neighbours, Croatia and Yugoslavia, the five 'great' powers of the Contact group and the European Union, and administered by an international military force, commanded by US officers, as well as by international police and civil service personnel.

Thus the territorial claims originating in nineteenth and early twentieth century national ideologies, are, in the late twentieth century, being settled as they were in the nineteenth century: as in 1878 when the major European powers at the Congress of Berlin granted independence to new nation states in the Balkans and established their new state borders, so in 1991 the EC and then in 1995 the five-member Contact group did the same. As in the wake of a bloody rebellion of the Serb and Croat inhabitants against Muslim rule in Bosnia–Hercegovina in 1878 the major European powers authorised Austria–Hungary to occupy, pacify and administer this province of the Ottoman empire, so in 1995 the five-power Contact group and the United Nations Security Council authorised NATO forces first to attack the Bosnian Serb rebels and later to enter and to pacify the whole country. The UN Security Council, through its High Representative, in December 1995 took over the supervision of an international civilian administration of the country.

The settlement imposed by the European powers in 1878 in the Balkans was dependent on the continuing support and agreement of the major European powers; when this was withdrawn in 1914 the settlement of 1878 unravelled and new states emerged in 1918–20. In spite of the expulsion of opposing nationalities from the newly formed nation states in the Balkans, the settlement being imposed in the region in 1996 may still prove to be dependent on the continued support of the major power(s) which imposed it in the first place. In this case, the principal peacemaker, the US, would need to continue its military support of the Bosnian Muslim and Croatian armies, while at the same time continuing to restrain their political elites' drive for further territorial expansion. If at any time in the future, the US fails to do either or both, the settlement reached at Dayton in 1995 could quickly unravel, resulting in new states and borders with the attendant large-scale expulsions of populations. Moreover, the US will probably be called on to settle the outstanding territorial claims in the Balkans, in particular those of the Albanians in Kosovo and in western Macedonia, who are demanding a separate state of their own or unification with Albania. Thus at the end of the twentieth century, the outside powers are still being called upon to draw and maintain international or intrastate borders in the Balkans and help to enforce them by their own military force.

While outside powers could now (as they could in the past) use their overwhelming military superiority to enforce any borders they prefer, once their military forces are withdrawn they are unable to prevent a recurrence of armed conflict over contested territories, in spite of the large-scale expulsion of various national groups from them. The possible recurrence of armed conflict over contested territories in the future is primarily due to the persistence of national liberation ideologies as the principal instruments of political mobilisation in the Balkans. The liberation or recovery of lost territory from foreign occupiers – as well as defence of the homeland from barbarous Southerners – has provided and probably will continue to provide the most effective foci for mass mobilisation of various national groups in the Balkans. If peace among the new nation states in the Balkans is to be achieved, these instruments of mass mobilisation need to be abandoned. But territorial settlements imposed by the force of arms only help to perpetuate the perception that these territories were conquered by foreigners who then need to be expelled by force; this is the perception which stands at the core of the national liberation ideologies. In consequence, national ideologies as instruments of mass moblisation are unlikely to be abandoned as long as the territorial settlements in the region continue to be imposed by the force of arms with or without the help of outside powers.

Yet how could the US and its allies have settled the conflicting territorial claims in Bosnia–Hercegovina and in Croatia but by enabling the Croats and Bosnian Muslims to defeat the Serb armed takeover of their territory? This question is obviously raised within the framework of Bosnian Muslim and Croat national (liberation) ideologies which assert their respective nations' right to the territory 'taken over' by the Serbs. Posed in such a context, the question is obviously rhetorical: if the territory is conquered by foreign intruders, its rightful owners are obviously entitled to any help needed to recover it. But who are the 'rightful owners' of territories with nationally mixed populations (including the Serbs)? In order to understand the conflicting territorial claims in former Yugoslavia one needs, I think, to stand outside the framework of any such national ideology; perhaps the same approach was necessary in order to have prevented the war in the region.

The governments of the EC member states and the US could have refused to endorse any one of the national ideologies in the Balkans or to countenance any one territorial claim originating from such national ideologies. To do so they needed to realise first that the initial problem which confronted them was not the creation of a new constitutional framework for Yugoslavia but the creation of new nation states out of Yugoslavia. The creation of new nation states in nationally mixed population areas should, I think, have been carried out in such a way as to cause minimal transfer or exchange of populations. If this was the desideratum, then outside powers – for instance, the European Community in 1991 – should have attempted to ensure that the borders of the new states be drawn so as to require the minimum disruptive movement of populations. To achieve this, one should have left it to the nationally mixed populations of the potentially contested areas to decide – through internationally supervised plebiscites – which nation state they would want to join. Such plebiscites were used to establish a few borders of several new nation states (as well as those of the Kingdom of Serbs, Croats and Slovenes) created from disintegrating multinational empires after World War I; there is no reason why they should not have been tried in disintegrating multinational Yugoslavia, before the outbreak of war in Croatia in September 1991. As this method has neither been tried nor even proposed, the price which the inhabitants of former Yugoslavia were made to pay for the creation of new nation states in nationally mixed regions has been – and is likely to continue to be – horrendous.

# Further Reading

The most comprehenisive collection of legal documents in English relating to Yugoslav history and the dissolution of the country is found in S. Trifunovska (ed), *Yugoslavia Through Documents: From its creation to its dissolution* (Dordrecht: Martinus Nijhoff, 1994).

## Pre-1918 period

W. D. Behschnitt, *Nationalismus bei Serben und Croaten 1830–1914: Analyse und Typologie der nationalen Ideologie* (Munich: R. Oldernbourg, 1980).

S. Clissold (ed.), *A Short History of Yugoslavia* (Cambridge: Cambridge University Press, 1966).

D. Djordjevic and S. Fischer-Galati, *The Balkan Revolutionary Tradition* (New York: Columbia University Press, 1981).

B. Jelavich and C. Jelavich, *The Establishment of the Balkan National States, 1894–1920*, History of East Central Europe, vol. 8 (Seattle: University of Washington Press, 1977).

M. B. Petrovich, *A History of Modern Serbia, Vols 1 and 2* (London: Harcourt Brace Jovanovich, 1975).

## 1918–41 period

J. B. Hoptner, *Yugoslavia in Crisis, 1934–41* (New York: Columbia University Press, 1962).

J. Rothschild, *East Central Europe between Two World Wars*, History of East Central Europe, vol. 9 (Seattle: University of Washington Press, 1974), chapter 5: Yugoslavia.

## World War II

L. Kuchmar, *Draža Mihailović and the Rise of the Chetnik Movement 1941–2, Vols 1 and 2* (London: Garland Publishing, 1987).

P. Shoup, 'The Yugoslav Revolution: The First of a New Type,' *Studies on the Soviet Union*, vol. 11, no. 4 (1971) pp. 215–43.

M. Wheeler, 'Pariahs to partisans to power: the Communist Party of Yugoslavia,' in T. Judt (ed.), *Resistance and Revolution in Mediterranean Europe 1939–1948* (London: Routledge, 1989) pp. 110–56.

## 1945–90 period

L. J. Cohen, *The Socialist Pyramid: Elites and Power in Yugoslavia* (Oakville: Mosaic Press, 1989).

H. Lydall, *Yugoslavia in Crisis'* (Oxford: Clarendon Press, 1989).

S. K. Pavlowitch, *Tito: Yugoslavia's Great Dictator – A Reassessment* (London: C. Hurst, 1992).

D. Rusinow, *The Yugoslav Experiment, 1948–74* (London: C. Hurst, 1977).

P. Shoup, *Communism and the Yugoslav National Question* (New York: Columbia University Press, 1968).

## 1990–the present

Susan L. Woodward, *Balkan Tragedy. Chaos and Dissolution after the Cold War*, (Washington: The Brookings Institution, 1995). (The most comprehensive account published so far of the latest dissolution of Yugoslavia.)

J. Eyal, *Europe and Yugoslavia: Lessons from a Failure* (London: Royal United Services Institute for Defence Studies, 1993).

M. Glenny, *The Fall of Yugoslavia: The Third Balkan War*, revised edn, (Harmondsworth: Penguin, 1994). (A vivid account of the rise of nationalism and the ensuing wars.)

V. Gligorov, *Why do Countries Break Up? The Case of Yugoslavia* (Uppsala: Acta Universitatis Uppsaliensis – Uppsala Studies on Eastern Europe, vol. 2, 1994). (A theoretical explanation of the break-up of Yugoslavia by a liberal political theorist from Belgrade.)

J. Udovički and J. Ridgeway (eds), *Yugoslavia's Ethnic Nightmare: The Inside Story of Europe's Unfolding Ordeal* (Chicago: Lawrence Hill, 1995). (These politically correct and anti-nationalist essays by Yugoslav authors do offer a rare inside story.)

# Notes and References

## 1 Yugoslavia at the Crossroads of Competing National Myths

1. Not related to Ante Pavelić, the later Ustashe leader.
2. M. B. Petrovich, *A History of Modern Serbia*, vol. 2 (London: Harcourt Brace Jovanovich, 1975) p. 682.
3. In 1994 the Bosnian Muslim leaders started using the term 'Bosniac' to refer to Bosnian Muslims who were in the Yugoslav censa and terminology referred to as 'Muslims' (*Muslimani*). Since at the present the term is not widely known (and it is still unclear whether it will become widely accepted), I shall continue using 'Bosnian Muslim' to refer to this national group. My doing so indicates no preference for any particular view put forward on the nature of the Bosnian Muslim or Bosniacs' nationhood and national origins.
4. From the epic poem 'Musić Stevan'; translated by Radmila Gorup.
5. Pavao Ritter Vitezović (1652–1713) in his *Croatia rediviva: egnante Leopoldo Magno Caesare* (Agram, 1700).
6. See I. Banac, *The National Question in Yugoslavia: Origins, History, Politics* (London: Cornell University Press, 1985) pp. 72–3.
7. Ibid, pp. 87–8
8. See P. N. Hehn, 'The Origins of Modern Pan-Serbism – The 1844 *Načertanije* of Ilija Garašanin: Analysis and Translation', *East European Quarterly*, vol. 9 (1975) 153–71.
9. Eastern Orthodox populations, speaking various dialects, including štokavian, had resided in the Habsburg lands well before the Great Migration of Serbs. Many of them (already identified as Serbs) migrated to these lands prior to the Ottoman conquest of the last remnants of the Serbian kingdom in 1452.
10. For the politics of the period see N. J. Miller, *Between Great Serbianism and Yugoslavism: Serbian Politics in Croatia* (Ann Arbor: UMI, 1991, doctoral dissertation, Indiana University 1991).
11. Although they remained mutually fully comprehensible, the two literary standards developed in divergent ways: the Croat standard expanded its vocabulary through the construction of Slav calques while the Serbian resorted to direct foreign borrowings, mainly from French.
12. See W. D. Behschnitt, *Nationalismus bei Serben und Croaten 1830–1914: Analyse und Typologie der nationalen Ideologie* (Munich: R. Oldernbourg, 1980) pp. 206–7.
13. Due to a very high tax qualification for the right to vote, the Croatian electorate was a very small proportion of the total population. The electoral law of May 1910 increased the number of enfranchised males from 50 000 to 190 000 in a province which had around 2 500 000

inhabitants. See F. Šišić, *Pregled povjesti Hrvatskog naroda* (Zagreb: Matica Hrvatska, 1962) p. 468.

14.  See W. D. Behschnitt, op. cit. pp. 106–7.
15.  D. Djordjevic and S. Fischer-Galati, *The Balkan Revolutionary Tradition* (New York: Columbia University Press, 1981) p. 150. In 1991 the Bosnian Serbs and Croats proclaimed their respective autonomous states in the very same regions in which they rose in arms against the Ottomans in 1875. These were the regions in which Bosnian Serbs and Bosnian Croats, respectively, form majority populations.
16.  Ibid., pp. 92–3 and 118–9.
17.  The Austro-Hungarian occupation was resisted by Bosnian Muslim leaders who took over command of the native Ottoman regiments and recruited irregulars. In some areas the Bosnian Muslims were joined by Serb fighters. The Croat population and Roman Catholic clergy in general welcomed the Austrian takeover. In autumn 1878 the Austrian army, at its peak strength of 268 000 men, crushed the much smaller and ill-equipped Bosnian Muslim forces. R. J. Donia and J. V. A. Fine, Jr, *Bosnia–Hercegovina: A Tradition Betrayed* (New York: Columbia University Press, 1994) p. 94.
18.  This weekly was started in 1911 as an unofficial organ of the secret organisation 'Unity or Death', popularly known as the 'Black Hand', which was committed to Serb unification by armed force.
19.  See W. D. Behschnitt, op. cit., pp. 118–24
20.  See S. Skendi, *The Albanian National Awakening 1878–1912* (Princeton: Princeton University Press, 1967) pp. 36–9
21.  For a concise account of the policies and actions of the Balkan socialist parties see L. S. Stavrianos, *Balkan Federation: A History of the Movement toward Balkan Unity in Modern Times* (Hamden: Archon Books, 1964, originally published 1942) pp. 182–202.
22.  The extent to which the Serbian government and its premier Nikola Pašić knew of the assassination plot is still debated among historians. See W. D. Behschnitt, op. cit., note 346, pp. 307–9. See also M. B. Petrovich, op. cit., pp. 618–20 and M. Cornwall, 'Serbia' in K. Wilson (ed.), *Decisions for War, 1914* (London: University of California Press, 1995) pp. 56–60. In reviewing recent literature on the subject, John W. Langdon writes:

> The Serbian government did not inspire the plot and made well-intentioned but ineffective efforts to forestall it. The argument that governments are responsible for terrorist actions launched from their jurisdictions is technically correct but hopelessly abstract... Serbia bears responsibility, in the limited sense just outlined, for the Sarajevo crime. It does not bear responsibility for the outbreak of a general war, for which the murder of Franz Ferdinand was only a pretext.

J. W. Langdon, *July 1914: The Long Debate 1918–90* (New York: Berg, 1991) p. 176.
23.  See M. B. Petrovich, op. cit., pp. 613–8.
24.  D. Janković, 'O Niškoj deklaraciji 1914' in *Naučni Skup u povodu 50-godišnjice raspada Austro-Ugarske monarhije i stvaranja jugoslavenske države* (Zagreb: Jugoslavenska akademija znanosti i umjetnosti, 1969) p. 133.

25. They rejected the declaration on the grounds that there was no public debate on it. The Serbian Social Democrats opposed the war as an imperialist war and advocated a democratic Balkan federation of equal peoples. Ibid., p. 139.
26. See M. B. Petrovich, op.cit., pp. 644–5 and S. Trifunovska (ed.), *Yugoslavia Through Documents: From its Creation to its Dissolution* (Dordrecht: Martinus Nijhoff, 1994) pp. 141–2.
27. For the text of the speech see I. Mužić, *Hrvatska politika i jugoslavenska ideja* (Split: author's edition, 1969) pp. 135–44.
28. For the list of terms see M. B. Petrovich, op. cit. pp. 676–7 and S. Trifunovska (ed.) op. cit. pp. 151–2.
29. On 5 December 1918 a group of Croat non-commissioned officers and soldiers from a former Austro-Hungarian regiment took to the streets of Zagreb in armed protest against the union. A volunteer force under the orders of the National Council, armed with machine-guns, quickly dispersed the demonstrators (13 people, mainly soldiers from the Austro-Hungarian regiment, were killed). This demonstration entered the Croat nationalist mythology as an armed rebellion against the Serb hegemony. See F. Čulinović, *Jugoslavija između dva rata*, Vol. 1 (Zagreb: Izdavački zavod JAZU, 1961) pp. 160–9.

## 2   The First Yugoslavia

1. See J. Tomasevich, *Peasants, Politics and Economic Change in Yugoslavia* (Stanford: Stanford University Press, 1955) pp. 170–4. B. Petranović, *Istorija Jugoslavije* (Beograd: Nolit, 1988) p. 56.
2. W. E. Moore, *Economic Demography of Eastern and Southeastern Europe* (Geneva: League of Nations, 1945) pp. 63–4.
3. A. N. Dragnich, *The First Yugoslavia: Search for a Viable Political System* (Stanford: Hoover Institution Press, 1983) pp. 21–2.
4. Ibid., p. 24. This is the *Vidovdan* constitution, promulgated on St Vitius's day (*Vidovdan*), 28 June 1921, the anniversary of the Kosovo battle.
5. See F. Čulinović, *Jugoslavija i zmedju dva rata*, Vol. 2., pp. 519–31.
6. In the political jargon of the time, this was called the 'amputation'.
7. As the Croatian *banovina* was set up by a royal (regency) decree, its constitutionality was questioned at the time. Its model appeared to be the agreement (*Ausgleich*) of 1867 between the Habsburg and Hungarian governments on the dualist constitutional arrangement in Austria–Hungary. See A. Djilas, *The Contested Country: Yugoslav Unity and the Communist Revolution 1919–1953* (London: Harvard University Press, 1991) pp. 216–7, note 27 and A. N. Dragnich, op. cit., p. 123.

## 3   World War II

1. L. Kuchmar, *Draža Mihailović and the Rise of the Chetnik Movement 1941–2*, Vol. 2, (London: Garland Publishing, 1987) pp. 272–5.
2. In addition to these principal forces, in Serbia the military formations of the pro-fascist organisation *Zbor*, the Chetniks of the renegade Kosta

Pečanac and the forces of the German-installed quisling government all fought both Partisans and Mihailović's Chetniks. In Slovenia, the German-trained quisling forces and in Kosovo Italian-supported quisling Albanian militias were also fighting the Partisans.

3. With Serbs forming the majority of its rank-and-file and officer corps.

4. Some of the Ustashe officers and officials claimed to be of Serb origin. This was used by the Ustashe authorities in attempts to pacify the Serb population after 1942.

5. Whom the Ustashe interned because he refused to participate in their government.

6. Some Muslim notables and religious leaders rejected the Ustasha ideology and publicly protested against the massacres of Serbs.

7. L. Kuchmar, op. cit. vol. 2, pp. 602–5.

8. AVNOJ is the acronym for Anti-fašističko Veće Narodnog Oslobodjenja Jugoslavije – the Anti-fascist Council of National Liberation of Yugoslavia.

9. P. Shoup, *Communism and the Yugoslav National Question* (New York: Columbia University Press, 1968) pp. 144–5.

10. The effects of the Partisan emancipation of the peasantry are most visible in the families of split Chetnik and Partisan loyalties. Almost invariably, those members who joined the Partisans early on (for example, in the period from 1941 to 1943) were commissioned as officers and rapidly promoted while those who joined the Chetniks remained in the ranks.

11. This operation is known in Partisan historiography as the battle on the river Sutjeska.

12. The role of this British officer, Major Klugmann, and his circle is the topic of continuing controversy. See M. Lees, *The Rape of Serbia: The British Role in Tito's Grab for Power 1943–1944* (London: Harcourt Brace Jovanovich, 1990) and D. Martin, *The Web of Disinformation: Churchill's Yugoslav Blunder* (London: Harcourt Brace Jovanovich, 1990) chapters 12, 13 and 18.

13. As only a few Serb politicians would agree to enter a coalition government with the communist usurper Tito, the British government selected Ivan Šubašić, a Croat Peasant party leader and the last *ban* of the autonomous province of Croatia, to negotiate with Tito. Thus two Croats, Tito and Šubašić, formed a government of a country in which not only the largest nation but also the great majority of the resistance fighters were Serbs.

14. Many scholars have argued that in view of Tito's and the Partisans' popularity, the communist Popular Front would have won, albeit with a smaller majority, even in a free and fair election. See A. Djilas, op. cit., p. 159 and S. Clissold (ed.), *A Short History of Yugoslavia* (Cambridge: Cambridge University Press, 1966) p. 238. However, had the parties opposing the communists been allowed to campaign freely, probably the communists would not have won free elections either in Serbia or in Croatia (let alone Kosovo) where they had only limited popular support.

15. The total number of Muslim victims in World War II was calculated to be around 86 000 or 7.9 per cent of their population in 1941; after the Jews, Gipsies, Montenegrins and Serbs, the Muslims suffered the largest

demographic loss in the war of all peoples in Yugoslavia. See B. Kočović, *Žrtve drugog svetskog rata u Jugoslaviji* (London: Naše Delo, 1985) p. 126. Although it is difficult to estimate the total number of Muslims who were victims of Chetnik massacres, it would probably be safe to assume that most of the Muslim victims in World War II died in these massacres.

16. As a result neither has the number of the civilian victims of massacres by any side been ascertained with sufficient accuracy nor were comprehensive lists of the victims' names and burial sites ever collated under the communist regime.

## 4 Second Yugoslavia

1. See P. Shoup, *Communism and the Yugoslav National Question* (New York: Columbia University Press, 1968) pp. 115–16.
2. *Borba*, 22 May 1945, p. 1. Quoted in ibid., p. 116.
3. It is somewhat ironic that this revolutionary communist regime, intent on creating a new state and a new society, chose in 1946 to use the borders of the two empires which had disintegrated at the end of World War I.
4. The northern part of Istria with a Slovene-speaking population was assigned to Slovenia.
5. In fact, the only substantial modification to the historical borders of Bosnia–Hercegovina were made to give the republic nominal access to the Adriatic in the tiny strip of land around the small town of Neum.
6. Serbia was also the only republic which had an autonomous province or an autonomous region.
7. P. Shoup, op. cit., p. 120. He argues that the federal structure '... helped satisfy important psychological needs of the Yugoslav peoples for recognition of their national individuality... and it gave each nationality the assurance, for the first time, of enjoying a truly equal status with the other national groups.' P. Shoup, op. cit., p. 119. As noted above, this assurance must have been largely symbolic.
8. B. Petranović, *Istorija Jugoslavije 1918–78*, 2nd edn (Beograd: Nolit, 1981) p. 414. Every time it faced a Soviet military threat, the Yugoslav Party proceeded to recruit as many new members as possible. Thus its recruitment drive of 1948 was repeated in 1968 after the Soviet invasion of Czechoslovakia.
9. P. Shoup, op. cit., pp. 120–2 and pp. 269–70.
10. *Odeljenje za zaštitu naroda*, Department for the Protection of the People. The acronym proved suitable for various instructive rhymes such as 'OZNA sve dozna' – 'OZNA gets to know everything'.
11. At their 1955 value. D. Rusinow, *The Yugoslav Experiment, 1948–1974* (London: C. Hurst & Co, 1977) p. 46. The total aid coming from the USA. appears to have been much larger-totalling close to 2200 million US dollars. See S. K. Pavlowitch, *Yugoslavia* (London: Ernest Benn, 1971) p. 224, note 2.

12. Lj. Madžar, 'The Economy of Yugoslavia' in J. B. Allcock, J. J. Horton and M. Milivojevic (eds), *Yugoslavia in Transition* (New York: Berg, 1992) p. 84.
13. *Savez komunista Jugoslavije.* I shall retain the earlier name of the Communist party or, shortened, 'the Party' throughout the monograph.
14. Three years later he was gaoled for his dissident views and became one of the first and most famous ex-communist dissidents.
15. See A. Z. Rubinstein, *Yugoslavia and the Nonaligned World* (Princeton: Princeton University Press, 1970).
16. According to the US estimates, by 1990 Yugoslav defence industries were providing 80 per cent of Yugoslav military equipment. *Army Area Handbooks: Yugoslavia* (Washington: US Department of the Army, 1993) Chapter 5.06 'Defense and National Economy' (electronic distribution).
17. See J. Gow, *Legitimacy and the Military: The Yugoslav Crisis* (New York: St Martin's Press, 1992) pp. 45–9.

## 5  From a Centralised State to a Semiconfederation

1. D. Rusinow, *The Yugoslav Experiment, 1948–1974* (London: C. Hurst Co., 1977)
2. P. Shoup, *Communism and the Yugoslav National Question* (New York: Columbia University Press, 1968) p. 192.
3. Ibid., p. 197.
4. Ibid., p. 200.
5. For recent histories of the Yugoslav idea see J. R. Lampe, 'The Failure of the Yugoslav National Idea', *Studies in East European Thought*, vol. 46 (1994) 69–89; A. Pavković, 'The Yugoslav Idea: A Short History of a Failure', in J. Perkins and J. Tampke (eds), *Europe: Retrospects and Prospects* (Manly: Southern Highlands, 1996).
6. This was one of the reasons why the proportion of Serb, Montenegrin and (self-declared) Yugoslav middle-ranking and non-commissioned officers in the Yugoslav People's Army was allowed to exceed the proportion these groups had in the population of the country (see Chapter 9).
7. D. Rusinow, op. cit., p. 187.
8. His funeral in Belgrade in 1983, which was not announced in the press, drew a huge number of mourners (reports range from 30 000 to 100 000). The funeral thus became a political manifestation of loyalty to a Serb politician.
9. S. L. Burg, *Conflict and Cohesion in Socialist Yugoslavia: Political Decision Making Since 1966* (Princeton: Princeton University Press, 1983) p. 71.
10. For an account of Muslim nation-building in this period see W. Hopken, 'Yugoslavia's Communists and the Bosnian Muslims' in A. Kappeler, G. Simon, G. Brunner and E. Allworth (eds), *Muslim Communities Reemerge* (London: Duke University Press, 1994) pp. 214–50.
11. Small Albanian demonstrations were staged in 1974 and in 1975. During the 1970s the police claimed to have discovered several clandestine

groups of Albanians working for the overthrow of the regime. See A. J. Day (ed.), *Border and Territorial Disputes* (London: Longman, 1982) p. 9.
12.   D. Rusinow, op. cit., pp. 277–9.
13.   In only one year from 1970 to 1971, this organisation increased from 2300 to 41 000 members. S. L. Burg, op. cit., p. 121.
14.   D. Rusinow, op. cit., p. 305.
15.   The potentially most dangerous Party meetings were held at his 'royal' residences. The 1966 meeting ousting Ranković was held at Brioni and the meeting dismissing the Croatian Party leaders in 1971 was held at Karađorđevo, a hunting residence of the Karađorđević dynasty outside Belgrade.
16.   Indeed, one could argue that Tito was one of the world celebrities who attracted favourable publicity in Western media. This helped to create an image of a benign ruler and an elder statesman which he had cultivated since the late 1950s.
17.   M. Đurić, 'Smišljanje smutnje,' *Anali Pravnog fakulteta u Beogradu*, vol. 19, no. 3 (1972) 230–3, quoted in A. H. Budding, 'Dilemmas of Decentralization: The Serbian National Question 1966–72' (presented at Contemporary History Workshop, History Department, Harvard University, 12 February 1995).
18.   *The Constitution of the Socialist Federal Republic of Yugoslavia*, Introductory Part, Basic Principles I (Belgrade, 1974) p. 53.
19.   Article 1 states that Yugoslavia is '. . . a federal state having the form of a state community of voluntarily united nations and their Socialist Republics, and of the Socialist Autonomous Provinces of Vojvodina and Kosovo. . .'. *The Constitution of the Socialist Federal Republic of Yugoslavia* (Belgrade, 1974) p. 79.

## 6   The Loss of Legitimacy 1980–9

1.   H. Lydall, *Yugoslavia in Crisis* (Oxford: Clarendon Press, 1989) p. 198.
2.   The republican governments often spent the federal funds on status-enhancing projects such as large public buildings instead of on commercially viable industrial projects. Ibid., pp. 192–4.
3.   S. P. Ramet, *Nationalism and Federalism in Yugoslavia 1962–91*, 2nd edn (Bloomington: Indiana University Press, 1992) p. 196.
4.   H. Lydall, op. cit., pp. 40–8.
5.   According to one estimate, less than one-third of these loans was used for productive purposes, that is, invested in industry or infrastructure. Ibid., p. 53.
6.   Ibid., p. 81.
7.   V. Goati, *Jugoslavija na prekretnici: od monizma do građanskog rata* (Beograd: Jugoslovenski institut za novinarstvo, 1991) p. 23.
8.   In late 1990 Abdić brought over this large constituency to the main Muslim party, the Party of Democratic Action led by Alija Izetbegović with whom he parted in 1993, thus provoking the first Muslim–Muslim conflict in the civil war (see Chapter 11). Abdić's personal popularity and his well-organised network of supporters thus survived not only his arrest

and trial but two major shifts in his political affiliation. His ability to maintain so firm a grip on his constituency is without parallel in the countries of former Yugoslavia. After the surrender of his militia to the Croatian army in August 1995, he was reported to be residing in Zagreb.

9.  From 483 000 in 1948 to 1 226 736 in 1981.
10. S. P. Ramet, op. cit., p. 147. Ramet presents a whole range of statistics on the problem of underdevelopment.
11. Prishtine in Albanian. The geographical names used in the book are given in their official form at the time of writing. Hence the use of Serbian spelling for this city and the whole province which in 1995 was more than 90 per cent Albanian.
12. From 8000 to 47 000. This was later downgraded to only a fivefold increase. L. J. Cohen, *The Socialist Pyramid: Elites and Power in Yugoslavia* (Oakville: Mosaic Press, 1989) p. 361.
13. L. J. Cohen, op. cit., p. 350. This time, however, there was no attempt at the 'colonisation' of Serbs and Montenegrins and the pre-war Serb and Montenegrin colonists were effectively prevented from returning to their properties.
14. E. Biberaj, *Albania: A Socialist Maverick* (Boulder: Westview Press, 1990) p. 124. In this sympathetic account, the riots are called 'a popular uprising'.
15. S. P. Ramet, op. cit., p. 196.
16. As in 1968, the demonstrations of Albanians spread to the Albanian-populated towns of Macedonia. As the Albanian population of Macedonia, had reached around 20 per cent of the total population, the Macedonian leaders were particularly anxious to halt the spread of Albanian nationalism to Macedonia.
17. In October 1986 Fadil Hoxha, one of the top Kosovo Albanian communist leaders, at a lunch with reserve officers said that, given the Albanian women's refusal to work as prostitutes, Serb and other women should be allowed to do the work; this, he implied, would reduce the number of Serb women raped by Albanians. This statement, widely publicised in September 1987, was used to whip up Serb protest demonstrations, demanding his punishment. The whole incident and its political ramifications are discussed in some detail in D. Hudelist, *Kosovo: bitka bez iluzija* (Zagreb: Centar za informacije i publicitet, 1989) pp. 41–55.
18. Ibid., pp. 35–45.
19. Nebojša Popov, a sociologist and a politician strongly opposed to Milošević, argued that this movement was, after 1987, taken over by the secret police. N. Popov, 'Srpski populizam: od marginalne do dominante pojave', *Vreme*, No. 135 (24 May 1993) p. 20.
20. This unease is evident in the memoirs of Dragiša Pavlović, the first Serbian communist official from the Stambolić faction to be ritually dismissed by Milošević (see Chapter 8). D. Pavlović, *Olako obećana brzina* (Zagreb: Globus, 1988) pp. 90–3.
21. Born in 1941 in Požarevac, Serbia. Both of his parents were teachers (his father migrated from Montenegro to Serbia) and both, separately, committed suicide. He started his Party career in the 1960s at Belgrade University's Law Faculty where he completed a law degree and met his future

patron Ivan Stambolić. As one of the Ivan Stambolić's closest friends, Milošević rapidly advanced in his career, serving as the director of the largest state bank in Serbia and the head of the Belgrade Party Committee. In the late 1970s he also spent some time in the USA ostensibly studying the US financial system. In 1986 he replaced Stambolić as the president of the presidency of the Communist Party of Serbia and in 1987 he purged the Serbian Party of Stambolić's supporters (see Chapter 8). Even before the first multiparty elections in December 1990 – in which he was elected president of Serbia – he established himself as the undisputed ruler of Serbia and leader of a loosely organised pan-Serb movement in the Yugoslav federation. As in October 1994 he broke with the leaders of the Bosnian Serbs and imposed an internationally monitored blockade on the Bosnian Serb territory, he split the pan-Serb movement he had himself initiated in the late 1980s (see Chapter 12).

22. In Serbo-Croatian 'Niko ne sme da vas bije, vas niko ne sme da bije' has the tone of a paternal prohibition and assurance. As Slavoljub Đukić notes in his political biography of Milošević, *Između slave i anateme: politička biografija Slobodana Miloševića* (Beograd: Filip Višnjić, 1994) p. 51, this is exactly what the demonstrators yearned to hear.

23. The pattern of division of power is well documented in L. J. Cohen, op. cit., pp. 369–75.

## 7 The Rise of Nationalism: From Dissidence to Power 1980–90

1. For an outline of dissidence in Serbia see A. Pavković, 'Intellectual dissidence and the Serb national question' in A. Pavković' H. Koscharsky, A. Czarnota (eds), *Nationalism and Postcommunism: A Collection of Essays* (Aldershot: Dartmouth, 1995) pp. 121–8.

2. As a result of the fragmentation of secret police apparatus (see Chapter 5), the punishment differed from one republic to other. In Slovenia intellectual dissidents had to fear, at most, dismissal from their jobs (also the favourite punishment in Serbia). In the 1980s in Serbia a few lesser known dissidents were also sentenced to prison terms. In Croatia and Bosnia–Hercegovina, however, nationalist dissidence was punished with longer prison terms; especially severe prison sentences were meted out to renegade ex-communists such as Dr Tudjman or recidivists such Alija Izetbegović (see below).

3. For an array of similar arguments see S. S. Juka, *Kosova: The Albanians in Yugoslavia in Light of Historical Documents* (New York: Waldon Press, 1984).

4. The infamous term 'ethnic cleansing' (*etničko čišćenje* in Serbo-Croatian) was first used in the Yugoslav communist-controlled press to describe the forced emigration of Kosovo Serbs from Kosovo.

5. This draft was leaked in 1986 to the Belgrade Party-controlled press which proceeded to attack it as a counter- revolutionary and nationalist document. An authorised version was first published in 1995 in K. Mihailović and V. Krestić, *'Memorandum SANU' odgovori na kritike* (Beograd: SANU, 1995); the English translation in K. Mihailović and V. Krestić

*Memorandum of the Serbian Academy of Sciences and Arts, Answers to Criticisms* (Beograd, Serbian Academy of Sciences and Arts, 1995). For a discussion of the document see A. Pavković, op. cit., pp. 128–31.

6.  S. Naumović, 'Upotreba tradicije: politička tranzicija i promena odnosa prema nacionalnim vrednostima u Srbiji 1987–90' in M. Prošić-Dvornić (ed.), *Kulture u tranziciji* (Beograd: Plato, 1994) pp. 95–120.

7.  See A. Pavković, op. cit., pp. 133–4.

8.  For example, I. Urbančič, 'Jugoslavanska "nacionalistička kriza" in Slovenci v perspektivi konca nacija', p. 56, and F. Bučar, 'Pravni ureditev položaja Slovencev kot naroda', p. 159 in *Nova Revija* (1987).

9.  Born in 1922 in Veliko Trgovišće in Croatia, Tudjman joined the Partisans in 1941 where, as a political commissar, rose to the rank of major. In 1961, with the rank of major-general, he retired from the army to become the director of a history institute in Zagreb. In 1964, with a Party reprimand for 'bourgeois-nationalist deviation' his reputation as a nationalist historian was firmly established; in 1965 he earned his doctorate in history at the University of Zadar. In the late 1960s he became one of the leaders of the nationalist organisation *Matica Hrvatska*, and in the purges of nationalist leaders in 1972 was sentenced to two years in prison. For his continued dissident activity including interviews to foreign journalists, he was arrested in 1981 and sentenced to three years in prison. During his extensive travels in the USA, Canada and Europe in 1987, he established contacts in the Croat emigre communities and organisations. In 1989 he founded the first postwar Croatian opposition party – the Croat Democratic Union – and after its electoral victory in 1990, was elected president of Croatia (see Chapter 8). He was re-elected, in direct presidential elections, in 1992 and in 1995 was proclaimed 'vrhovnik' (generalissimo) of the Croatian armed forces.

10. In his *Nacionalno pitanje u suvremenoj Europi*, originally published in English in 1981, Dr Tudjman claimed that Bosnia–Hercegovina constitutes 'geographically... an economic and transport whole with south and southwestern Croatia' and is also 'linked with [Croatia] historically as well as by an ethnic and linguistic sameness'. *Izabrana djela Franje Tuđmana*, Vol. 2 (Zagreb: Matica Hrvatska, 1990) p. 164. By his criteria this provides good grounds for the incorporation of at least a part of Bosnia–Hercegovina into the future sovereign Croatia.

11. F. Tudjman, *Bespuća povijesne zbiljnosti* (first published in 1989), in *Izabrana djela Franje Tuđmana* (Zagreb: Matica Hrvatska, 1990) Vol. 3, pp. 158–62.

12. F. Tudjman, op. cit., p. 160.

13. For an example of this kind see F. Tudjman, op. cit., p. 118.

14. A. Purivatra, 'On the National Phenomenon of the Moslems of Bosnia–Herzegovina' in *Nations and Nationalities of Yugoslavia* (Belgrade: Medjunarodna Politika, 1974) p. 311.

15. See X. Bougarel, 'Le Parti de l'Action Democratique: De la Marginalité à la Hegemonie' (Paris: unpublished thesis, 1993) pp. 24–5.

16. Born in 1925 in Bosanski Šamac in Bosnia–Hercegovina, he joined the Young Muslims during World War II. In 1946 he was sentenced to three years in prison for his participation in this nationalist movement. After

his release from prison, he completed a law degree and worked as a lawyer for state firms. In 1983 he was arrested for nationalist dissident activity (including the writing of his *Islamic Declaration*) and with a group of fellow Muslims sentenced, on appeal, to six years in prison (of which he served four). His *Islam between East and West*, 2nd edn (Indianopolis: American Trust, 1989) was originally published in Serbo-Croatian in Belgrade in 1984. In 1989 he founded the first opposition party in Bosnia–Hercegovina, the Party of Democratic Action, and in 1990 was elected president of the presidency of Bosnia–Hercegovina.

17.  In Serbo-Croatian: *Islamska deklaracija: Jedan program islamizacije Muslimana i muslimanskih naroda*, 2nd edn (Sarajevo: Bosna, 1990).
18.  Ibid., p. 29.
19.  Ibid., p. 43.
20.  Ibid., p. 30. These are some of the social ills which the Muslim Party of Democratic Action, in its programme of 1990 pledged to eliminate. See Chapter 8.
21.  Ibid., p. 22.
22.  Ibid., p. 37.
23.  In 1971 and 1981 Muslims formed around 39.5 per cent of the population of the republic while in 1991 their share increased to 43.5 per cent. In this period the proportion of Serbs dropped from 32 to 31.3 per cent and the proportion of Croats from 18.4 to 17.5 per cent. The figures are from the official Yugoslav censa in S. Bogisavljević, V. Goati, Z. Grebo, J. Hasanbegović, D. Janjić, B. Jojić, Z. Slavujević and P. Shoup, (eds), *Bosna i Hercegovina između rata i mira* (Beograd: Institut društvenih nauka, 1992) p. 34. This rate of growth and the decrease in the proportion of Serbs and Croats, visible already in the early 1980s, could have resulted, by the end of the century, in a Muslim majority.
24.  In Serbo-Croatian: 'preuzimanje vlasti'. This was an explicitly set goal in the Muslim party's 'Resolution on Internal Policies, Justice and Administration' ('Rezolucija o unutrašnjoj politici, pravosuđu i upravi'), *Bilten 'Kongres' 1991* (Sarajevo: Stranka demokratske akcije, 1991) p. 51.
25.  Izetbegović's treatise and his public statements, prior to October 1991 when the Serb political leaders opposed the Memorandum of Sovereignty proposed by his party (see Chapter 12), did not target any nation as an enemy of the Muslims.

## 8   The Rise of New National Elites 1987–90

1.  Later the leader of the Slovene Liberal party and the prime minister of the independent Republic of Slovenia 1994–.
2.  M. Crnobrnja, *The Yugoslav Drama* (Montreal and Kingston: McGill-Queens University Press, 1994) p. 149.
3.  In an all-Yugoslav poll almost 49 per cent expressed *complete* and 36 per cent *partial* agreement with his policies while only 3 per cent *disagreed* (the rest having no opinion). Lj. Bašević et al., *Jugoslavija na kriznoj prekretnici* (Beograd: Institut društvenih nauka, 1991) pp. 58–9. The lowest level of support for his policies was recorded in Slovenia and in Kosovo.

4. Ibid. The researchers warned, however, that there were no large differences between supporters and critics of Marković's policies in terms of their social status.
5. 'Savez reformskih snaga Jugoslavije,' *Stranke u Jugoslaviji* (Beograd: Novinska agencija TANJUG, 1990) p. 24.
6. V. Goati, *Jugoslavija na prekretnici* (Beograd: Jugoslovenski institut za novinarstvo, 1991) p. 92 and p. 94. Apart from these two republics, Marković's party failed to win a seat anywhere else.
7. On Marković's deteriorating relations with the Yugoslav federal army's High Command see Chapter 9. On Marković's policies see also M. Crnobrnja, op. cit., p. 150 and P. Simić, 'Civil War in Yugoslavia and the Roots of Disintegration', in M. van den Heuvel and J. G. Siccama (eds), *The Disintegration of Yugoslavia* (Amsterdam: Rodopi, 1992) p. 92.
8. S. Đukić, *Između slave i anateme: politička biografija Slobodana Miloševića* (Beograd: Filip Višnjić, 1994) p. 51.
9. The liberal dissidents, who rejected Milošević's rule from its outset, were not given access to the popular media.
10. All official figures of rally attendance were brought into doubt by Milošević's opponents who implied, for example, that the crowning rally did not gather more than 300 000 people. See N. Popov, 'Srpski populizam: od marginale do dominantne pojave', *Vreme*, no. 135 (24 May 1993) p. 20. Even if the latter figure is correct, these numbers outstrip the turnout at rallies during Tito's era.
11. Later president of the independent Republic of Slovenia, 1990–.
12. Vllasi was acquitted and released in 1990, apparently in exchange for the release of a jailed Serb activist from Croatia.
13. L. J. Cohen, *Broken Bonds: Yugoslavia's Disintegration and Balkan Politics in Transition*, 2nd edn (Boulder: Westview, 1995) pp. 55–9.
14. And, as many non-Serbs pointed out, potential dominance over other nations in Yugoslavia.
15. A. Bibič, 'The Emergence of Pluralism in Slovenia,' *Communist and Post-Communist Studies*, vol. 26, no. 4 (1993) 370–1.
16. See M. Bakić-Hayden and R. M. Hayden, 'Orientalist Variations on the Theme "Balkans": Symbolic Geography in Recent Yugoslav Cultural Politics', *Slavic Review*, vol. 51, no. 1 (1992) 1–16.
17. See A. H. Budding, 'End of Dialogue: Serbs, Slovenes, and the Collapse of the League of Writers of Yugoslavia,' unpublished paper, Harvard University.
18. The future defence minister of Slovenia. See Chapter 10.
19. J. Janša, *The Making of the Slovenian State 1988–92: The Collapse of Yugoslavia* (Ljubljana: Založba Mladinska knjiga, 1994) p. 26.
20. T. Mastnak, 'Civil Society in Slovenia: From Opposition to Power,' *Studies in Comparative Communism*, vol. 23, 3/4 (1990) p. 305–17.
21. S. P. Ramet, *Nationalism and Federalism in Yugoslavia, 1962–1991*, 2nd edn (Bloomington: Indiana University Press, 1992) p. 211.
22. T. Mastnak, op. cit., p. 312.
23. S. P. Ramet, op. cit., p. 211.
24. These amendments as well as constitutional changes by Serbia and other republics were subsequently declared unconstitutional by the

Yugoslav Constitutional Court (whose jurisdiction the Slovenian government refused to recognise in this case). R. M. Hayden, *The Beginning of the End of Federal Yugoslavia: The Slovenian Amendment Crisis of 1989* (Pittsburgh: The Centre for Russian and East European Studies, The Carl Beck Papers No. 1001, 1992) pp. 11–20.

25.   The official translation of Hrvatska demokratska zajednica is 'Croatian Democratic Union'. Partly to avoid confusion with various translations, I shall be using its widely used Croatian acronym 'HDZ'.

26.   *Hrvatska demokratska zajednica: Bilten za članstvo br. 1* (Zagreb, 1989) pp. 108–10.

27.   Including the nineteenth-century 'father of the Croatian nation' Ante Starčević. On Starčević see Chapter 1.

28.   Ibid., p. 6.

29.   See V. Radovic, 'Croatia Orders Inquiry into Rising Nationalist Party', *Reuters* (27 February 1990).

30.   L. J. Cohen, op. cit., p. 98

31.   The obvious similarities with Milošević's image among his followers were noted by many commentators as well as political rivals.

32.   *Stranke u Jugoslaviji* (Beograd: Tanjug, 1990) pp. 40–1. For the parallel with Izetbegović's *Islamic Declaration*, see Chapter 7.

33.   'Građanska republika ili građanski rat' in *Izbori '90: Stranke, programi, ličnosti* (Sarajevo: Oslobođenje, 1990) p. 21.

34.   Ibid.

35.   Called the 'Muslim Bosniac Organisation'. Zulfikarpašić has argued for decades (while living in exile in Switzerland) that 'Bosniac' is a correct appellation for Bosnian Muslims (Izetbegović's government adopted this term only in 1994).

36.   *Izbori '90: Stranke, programi, ličnosti*, op. cit. p. 74.

37.   *Stranke u Jugoslaviji*, op. cit., p. 45

38.   Ibid., p. 33.

39.   This procedure was enshrined in Amendment LXX, clause 10 to the Constitution of the Republic which envisaged the creation of a Council for issues relating to the equality of nations and nationalities of the republic. The Council had the power to recommend legislation concerning such issues to be adopted by a special procedure of the parliament requiring a two-thirds majority. *Službeni list Socijalističke Republike Bosne i Hercegovine*, vol. 46, no. 21 (31 July 1990).

40.   *Stranke u Jugoslaviji*, op. cit., p. 203–4.

41.   Some Albanian leaders in Macedonia claimed the figure to be around 40 per cent.

42.   H. Poulton, *Who are the Macedonians?* (London: Hurst, 1995) p. 172.

43.   The bearded and long-haired Drašković was formerly a minor communist apparatchik who in the early 1980s came to prominence with his novels about the wartime Croat and Muslim Ustashe terror over the Serbs. The founders of the Democratic party were also dissidents but their primary orientation was not nationalist. See A. Pavković, 'Intellectual dissidence and the Serb national question' in Pavković *et al.* (eds), *Nationalism and Postcommunism: A Collection of Essays* (Aldershot: Dartmouth, 1995) pp. 122–8.

44. See K. Čavoški, 'Nationalism and Constitutionality: the National and the Universal in the Constitutions of Serbia and Croatia', University of Belgrade, Faculty of Law, unpublished manuscript.

## 9   On the Road to War 1990–1

1. 'Model konfederacije,' *Vjesnik*, Zagreb, 6 October 1990.
2. 'Koncept federativnog uredenja Jugoslavije,' *Borba*, Beograd, 18 October 1990.
3. From March to May 1990 Milošević unsuccessfully attempted to pressure the Yugoslav state presidency into military action against the Slovenian and Croatian governments. First, in March he engineered the resignation of the Serb president of the presidency and, then in May 1990, with the four representatives in the presidency which he controlled, he blocked the election of the Croatian representative, a HDZ leader Stipe Mesić, to the rotating office of the president of the presidency. Yielding to pressure from the European Community and West European governments after the war in Slovenia, Milošević in July 1991 agreed to the election of Mesić (see Chapter 10).
4. For the rumour originating from the British politician Paddy Ashdown see M. Evans, 'Tudjman unveils plan for land carve-up,' *The Times*, 8 August 1995, reproduced in *The Australian* 8 August 1995, 10. This rumour comes with a map, allegedly drawn by Tudjman, allotting a larger portion of Bosnia–Hercegovina to Croatia. See also L. J. Cohen, *Broken Bonds: Yugoslavia's Disintegration and Balkan Politics in Transition*, 2nd edn (Boulder: Westview, 1995) p. 207–9.
5. These were: Milan Kučan (ex-communist, Slovenia), Franjo Tudjman (ex-communist and ex-dissident, Croatia), Miomir Bulatović (communist, Montenegro), Kiro Gligorov (ex-communist, Macedonia), Slobodan Milošević (ex-communist, Serbia), Alija Izetbegović (ex-dissident, Bosnia–Hercegovina).
6. *Borba*, Beograd, 4 June 1991. Partial translation into English in *Focus*, Special Issue (1992) 82–7.
7. See Map 4, p. 139.
8. As there were no outside observers of this referendum, the claims of the organisers could not verified.
9. The procedure of the Serbs in Krajina closely mirrored the actions of the Slovenian and Croatian governments: first, the declaration of sovereignty of the Serb nation within Croatia; second, the referendum on the issue of autonomy; third, the creation of its own police and militia enabling them to resist police actions of the Croatian government; and, finally, in March 1991, the decision to 'disassociate' from Croatia.
10. J. Gow, *Legitimacy and the Military: The Yugoslav Crisis* (New York: St Martin's Press, 1992) p. 110.
11. J. Gow, 'The Yugoslav Crisis and the Role of the Military: In Search for Authority,' *South Slav Journal*, vol. 13, 1–2 (1990) 54–9.
12. The Croats were Commander of the Third Military Area (Bosnia and Hercegovina) general A. Luketić; Commander of the Navy, admiral

S. Letica; Commander of the Maritime Area, admiral P. Grubišić; and Commander of the Yugoslav Air Force, general A. Tus. The Slovenes were: Commander of the Fifth Military Area (Croatia and Slovenia), general K. Kolšek and Federal Deputy Defence Minister admiral Stane Brovet. The Commander of the First Military Area (Serbia) was a Macedonian general A. Spirovski; the Chief of the General Staff was a Serb from Croatian Krajina, general Blagoje Adžić and the Minister of Defence (the highest position of all) was general Veljko Kadijević who was of a mixed Croato-Serb parentage.

13. The much criticised speech of the minister of defence, general Kadijević, on the eve of Serbian elections in December 1990, was a call to support socialism – and thus Milošević's ex-communist Socialist party – rather than Milošević himself.

14. The figures concerning the Yugoslav federal army were taken from J. Gow, op. cit., p. 59. The percentages of the total population are based on the 1991 census, see Table 1.

15. J. Zametica, *The Yugoslav Conflict*, Adelphi Paper 270, International Institute of Strategic Studies (London: Brassey's, 1992) p. 43.

16. Marković's minister of defence also accused him of betraying state secrets to foreign diplomats. V. Kadijević, *Moje viđenje raspada* (Beograd: Politika, 1993) p. 109.

17. Ibid., p. 118–20.

18. Marković later accused Kadijević of trying to murder him when, in October 1991, the office of Croatian president Tudjman was bombed while Marković was in conference with Tudjman. The Yugoslav federal army denied bombing the office; the government-controlled press in Belgrade suggested that Marković, a Croat, was receiving instructions from Tudjman. Marković resigned his office only in December 1991 in protest against the high allocation of the federal budget for the Yugoslav federal army. His antagonism towards the Yugoslav army's High Command obviously fuelled the generals' suspicions that he was covertly working for their opponents in Slovenia and Croatia.

## 10  Slovenia and Croatia at War 1991–2

1. J. Janša, *The Making of the Slovenian State 1988–92* (Ljubljana: Mladinska knjiga, 1994) p. 61.

2. Ibid., p. 102.

3. J. Gow and J. D. D. Smith, *Peace-making, Peace-keeping: European Security and the Yugoslav Wars* (London: Centre For Defence Studies, 1992) p. 10.

4. See S. Poggioli, 'Scouts Without Compasses: War in the Balkans is Forcing Correspondents to Rewrite Their Guidelines', *Nieman Reports*, vol. 47, no. 3 (1993) 16–19.

5. J. Eyal, *Europe and Yugoslavia: Lessons from a Failure* (London: Royal United Services Institute for Defence Studies, 1993) p. 6.

6. Ibid., p. 23–4.

7. A pan-European defence organisation established in 1948, the Western European Union (WEU) in 1991 had nine members. Under the Maastricht

treaty provisions adopted in 1992, the WEU, now joined by all member states of the European Union, is regarded as the main defence arm of the European Union.

8. His election was stalled since April 1991 by Milošević's government (see Chapter 9).

9. He also alleged, on the basis of secretly taped telephone conversations he had acquired, that the Yugoslav federal army generals together with Milošević and Serb politicians outside Serbia had prepared a plan, code-named *RAM* ('frame' in Serbo-Croatian), of military operations leading to the creation of a new Yugoslavia or greater Serbia which would incorporate all Serb-populated areas. This allegation, denied by the Yugoslav army generals, was widely publicised by the Belgrade weekly *Vreme*, vol. 2, 49 (30 September 1991). At the time *Vreme* enthusiastically supported Ante Marković's policies and has since continued to offer support for US, and, at times, EC policies in former Yugoslavia.

10. V. Kadijević, *Moje viđenje raspada* (Beqgrad: Politika, 1993) p. 135.

11. No official figures are available on the strength of the Yugoslav army units deployed in these operations. General Špegelj who was then the Croatian minister of defence estimated that the total strength of the Yugoslav federal army in Slovenia, Croatia and parts of Bosnia–Hercegovina (the Fifth Army Area and parts of the First Army Area) were 44 000 men and officers, out of which only 16 000 were fully trained; according to his estimates, 50 per cent of the conscripts were of non-Serb origin (D. Hudelist, 'Plan obrane – lipanj 1991', *Globus*, no. 242 (28 July 1995), (electronic distribution: bit.listserv.hrvatska). In addition, no more than 20 000 (probably less) troops were moved to Croatia from Serbia and Montenegro in September and early October 1991.

12. See P. Shoup, 'The Future of Croatia's Border Regions,' *Report on Eastern Europe*, vol. 2, 48 (1991) 26–33.

13. For an estimate of their total strength as well as an account of all military formations in the war see J. Gow, 'Military-Political Affiliations in the Yugoslav Conflict,' *RFE/RL Research Report*, vol. 1, 20 (1992) 16–25.

14. The Yugoslav federal army failed to expand the areas held by the Serb insurgents in western Slavonia.

15. Both sides probably underreported its military casualties. The official Yugoslav army casualties were set at 1279 killed and the Croatian army at 1448 killed and over 10 000 wounded (N. Cigar, 'The Serbo-Croatian War, 1991: Political and Military Dimensions', *The Journal of Strategic Studies*, vol. 16, 3 (1993), 297–338.

16. Some estimates, by opposition and anti-war groups, go up to 100 000 reservists and new recruits.

17. The Croat defence forces also conscripted Croatian Serbs living outside the Serb-held territories.

18. See I. Kotnik, 'Characterization of the Opposing Sides in the War in Croatia' in M. Malešić (ed.), *The Role of Mass Media in the Serbian-Croatian Conflict* (Stockholm: Psykologiskt Forsvar, 1993) p. 78.

19. See M. Košuta, 'Media and the War in Croatia,' *Medicine and War*, vol. 9 (1993) 134–40. In fact, many of these pits in Croatia and Bosnia–Herce-

govina, sealed by the communist authorities after 1945, were, re-opened in 1990 in order to allow the remains of the victims to be properly buried for the first time. This was widely reported in all Serb media.

20. M. Košuta, op. cit., p. 142.

21. For the media presentation of the main themes of Serb and Croat nationalism see D. Trickovic, 'Yugoslavia and the Rise of *Volkgeist*' in H. G. De Soto and D. G. Anderson (eds), *The Curtain Rises: Rethinking Culture, Ideology, and the State in Eastern Europe* (New Jersey: Humanities Press, 1993) pp. 150–81.

22. For these two movements, the Ustashe and the Chetniks, see Chapter 3.

23. I. Kotnik, op. cit., p. 76.

24. The translation of the full text is in M. Malešić (ed.), op. cit., p. 34–5. An adapted text is in M. Thompson, *Forging War: The Media in Serbia, Croatia and Bosnia–Hercegovina* (London: Article 19, 1994) pp. 161–2.

25. S. Poggioli, op. cit., pp. 16–9.

26. Ibid. See also M. Glenny, *The Fall of Yugoslavia: The Third Balkan War,* (Harmondsworth: Penguin, 1992) p. 136. P. Knightley, 'Women In The War Zone', *The Independent Monthly,* (October 1993) pp. 10–6.

27. J. Merlino, *Les vérités Yougoslaves ne sont pas toutes bonnes à dire* (Paris: Albin Michel, 1993) pp. 125–6.

28. Misha Glenny on BBC's 'spiking' of the story of the massacre of Serb civilians at Gospić in P. Knightley, op. cit., p. 16. For a similar dominant image in the war in Bosnia–Hercegovina, see N. Gowing, 'Instant TV and foreign policy', *The World Today,* vol. 50, 10 (October 1994) 189.

29. The economic sanctions imposed against Serbia in December 1991 made it also impossible for the Serbian government to hire Western public relations firms.

30. See M. Thompson, op. cit., pp. 50–63.

31. I. Kotnik, op. cit., p. 77.

32. J. Eyal, op. cit., p. 34.

33. Milošević and the Yugoslav state presidency had let the EC monitors in but the cease-fires continue to breakdown as before.

34. S. Trifunovska (ed.), *Yugoslavia Through Documents: From its creation to its dissolution* (Dordrecht: Martinus Nijhoff, 1994) p. 343.

35. Ibid., p. 359.

36. Ibid., pp. 416–7.

37. Ibid., p. 480. The effect of the application of the principle of *uti possidetis juris* to the case of Yugoslavia, one could have noted, was exactly the opposite: the old internal borders, which were now to be preserved, had undermined the stability of the new states by giving rise to fratricidal wars.

38. Ibid., p. 474.

39. See P. Radan, 'Secessionist Self-Determination: The Cases of Slovenia and Croatia' in A. Pavković *et al.* (eds), *Nationalism and Postcommunism: A Collection of Essays* (Aldershot: Dartmouth, 1995) p. 139.

40. On the role of the German media see F. Lewis, 'Bavarian TV and the Balkan War,' *New Perspectives Quarterly,* vol. 11, 3 (1994) 44–7.

41. See H. Stark, 'Dissonance franco-allemandes sur fond de guerre serbo-croate,' *Politique Étrangère* (1992) no. 2, 339–47.

# Notes and References

213

42. S. Trifunovska (ed.), op. cit., p. 488.
43. For example, Ed Koestal, the spokesman for the EC Monitors' Mission in Croatia who was dismissed from his post after his warning. See J. Eyal, op. cit., p. 47.
44. J. Gow and J. D. D. Smith, *Peace-Making, Peace-Keeping: European Security and the Yugoslav Wars* (London: Centre for Defence Studies, 1992) p. 39.
45. *The United Nations and the Situation in the Former Yugoslavia* (New York: UN Department for Public Information, 15 March, 1994) p. 3.
46. Ibid.
47. Ibid., p. 43.

## 11 War in Bosnia–Hercegovina 1992–4

1. For gun-running see E. Štitkovac and J. Udovički, 'Bosnia–Hercegovina: The Second War' in J. Udovički and J. Ridgeway (eds), *Yugoslavia's Ethnic Nightmare: The Inside Story of Europe's Unfolding Ordeal* (Chicago: Lawrence Hill, 1995) pp. 175–7.
2. *Focus*, Special Issue (1992) pp. 182–3.
3. *Oslobođenje*, Evropsko nedjeljno izdanje (13–20 October 1994) p. 17.
4. E. Štitkovac and J. Udovički, op. cit., p. 174.
5. Like the gunmen who attacked the Serb wedding party in March, these snipers were unidentified. The accusation that they belonged to the Serb Democratic party was, naturally, strongly denied by its leaders.
6. J. Gow, 'One Year of War in Bosnia and Herzegovina,' *RFE/RL Research Report*, vol. 2, 23 (1993) pp. 1–13.
7. According to J. Gow's estimates, the Muslim-dominated Bosnian army in 1993 had between 80 000 and 100 000 troops, the Bosnian Croat forces totalled around 45 000 men while Bosnian Serb forces had only 60 000 men. Ibid., p. 11. In 1995 the Bosnian army was estimated to have increased to 200 000 men and officers.
8. Major-General MacKenzie, the first commander of the UN forces in Bosnia, was one of the first to expose these attempts of the Muslim government (which, in return, branded him a war criminal). L. MacKenzie, *Peacekeeper: The Road to Sarajevo* (Vancouver: Douglas & McIntyre, 1993) pp. 230, 310–11.
9. According to some estimates, in 1995 there were no more than 100 000 Serbs left in the Muslim-controlled areas of the republic. F. Curta, 'Alija's Serbs – those who stayed behind,' *Agence France Press* (17 April 1995).
10. During 1992 larger Serb-controlled cities and towns such as Banja Luka and Bjeljina also retained reduced Croat and Muslim populations. These populations were further reduced by expulsion during 1993–5.
11. R. M. Hayden, 'The Partition of Bosnia and Herzegovina, 1990–3,' *RFE/RL Research Report*, vol. 2, 22 (28 May 1993) pp. 1–15.
12. Ibid., p. 7.
13. Ibid.
14. Lj. Smajlović, 'Intervju: Voren Zimerman: Moja uloga u Bosni,' *Vreme*, no. 144 (27 June 1994) pp. 16–8.
15. Ibid., p. 16.

16. J. Eyal, op. cit., p. 67. L. Doyle, 'Muslims Slaughter Their Own People', *The Independent* (22 August 1992) 1; A. Borowiec, 'Bosnians Stage Sacrifices, Peackeeper Alleges,' *Washington Times*, (21 February 1995) (electronic distribution).
17. D. Dyker and V. Bojicic, 'The Impact of Sanctions on the Serbian Economy,' *RFE/RL Research Report*, vol. 2, 21 (21 May 1993) pp. 50–4.
18. R. M. Hayden, op. cit., pp. 9–11.
19. For the adverse effects of this stop-go approach to peace negotiation see L. J. Cohen, op. cit., pp. 282–5.
20. Cyrus Vance resigned the post on 5 May 1993.
21. The striking resemblance of these arrangements to the Yugoslav constitution of 1974 was probably not intentional.
22. *The United Nations and the Situation in Former Yugoslavia* (New York: UN Department for Public Information, 15 March, 1994 p. 30–3.
23. The largest contingents coming from Britain and France. *The Economist*, vol. 335, 7917 (3 June 1995) p. 46.
24. See excepts from UN Secretary-General report in 'Black and grey,' *The Economist*, vol. 336, 7926 (5 August 1995) p. 46.
25. P. Moore, 'A New Stage in the Bosnian Conflict,' *RFE/RL Research Report*, vol. 3, 9 (4 March 1994) pp. 33–6.
26. N. Gowing, 'The One-Eyed King of Real-Time Coverage', *New Perspectives Quarterly*, vol. 11, 3 (Fall 1994) 45–55.
27. On Abdić see Chapter 6 and M. Glenny 'The Godfather of Bihac', *The New York Review of Books*, 12 August 1993, 18–9.
28. For an insider's view of the media wars see N. Pejic, 'Media and Responsibility in the War,' *Peuples Méditeranéens*, no. 61 (October–December 1992) 35–45.
29. N. Gowing, 'Instant Pictures, Instant Policy,' *Independent on Sunday* (3 July 1994) (electronic distribution).
30. Ibid.
31. While there was some evidence of murder and torture of prisoners within the camp, the British journalists who broke the story later rejected the 'death camp' comparison. P. Knightley, 'Women in the War Zone', *The Independent Monthly* (October 1993) pp. 11–2.
32. P. Brock, 'Dateline Yugoslavia: The Partisan Press,' *Foreign Policy*, No. 93 (Winter 1993/94) pp. 151–72. As the article attacked the integrity of several well-known journalists supporting the Muslim cause, it caused a considerable controversy, see 'Editor's Note', *Foreign Policy*, No. 97 (Winter 1994/95) (electronic distribution).
33. N. Gowing, op. cit., (electronic distribution).
34. For the second massacre which killed around 68 people see D. Binder, 'Anatomy of a Massacre,' *Foreign Policy*, no. 97 (Winter 1994/5) 70–8.
35. L. MacKenzie, op. cit., p. 308.
36. See P. Brock, op. cit., p. 172 and N. Gowing, 'Instant TV and foreign policy,' *The World Today*, vol. 50, 10 (October 1994) 187–90 (in particular, p. 189); R. Thornton, 'A Conflict of Views: The Press and the Soldier in Bosnia', *South Slav Journal*, vol. 15, 3–4 (1994) pp. 10–7.
37. *The United Nations and the Situation in the Former Yugoslavia*, op. cit., pp. 36–7.

38.  Ibid., p. 40.
39.  For details of war crimes and human rights abuses see *War Crimes in Bosnia–Herzegovina*, vols 1 and 2 (New York: Human Rights Watch, 1992–3).
40.  He is quoted as saying 'What is the sense of a peace treaty which does not respect the rights of people, one which, reached with Karadzic, would mean whitewashing horrendous crimes?', 'Karadzic a pariah, says war crimes tribunal chief,' *Reuter*, (26 July 1995) (electronic distribution).
41.  *Framework Agreement establishing a Federation in the areas of the Republic of Bosnia and Herzegovina . . .* (Washington: Embassy of the Republic of Croatia, March 1994).
42.  Although the Krajina Serb leadership also split into these two factions, Milošević was able to retain control over Krajina Serbs and to place, in 1995, Yugoslav military officers, loyal to him, in command of the Krajina Serb forces.

## 12  A US Enforced Peace?

1.  A. Krushelnycky and I. Mather, 'America "has joined war" in Bosnia', *European*, (18–24 November 1994) (electronic distribution); A. Krushelnycky, 'How the CIA helps Bosnia fight back', *European*, (26 November – 1 December 1994) (electronic distribution); 'US set to train Bosnian forces', *Sunday Telegraph* (13 November 1994) (electronic distribution).
2.  R. Dowden and J. Carlin, 'US secretly supplying arms to Bosnia,' *The Independent on Sunday*, (25 February 1995) (electronic distribution); C. Eagar, 'Shiny new guns appear in Bosnia's Twilight Zone', *Observer*, (12 March 1995) (electronic distribution).
3.  R. Fox, 'Iran and Sudan sending weapons to Bosnian Army', *Daily Telegraph* (16 November 1994) (electronic distribution).
4.  The former Swedish foreign minister replaced Lord Owen as the European Union co-chairman of the Steering Committee of the Peace Conference on Yugoslavia in June 1995.
5.  The US ambassador to Croatia, as well as the Croatian authorities, denied that this was a case of ethnic cleansing. Neither, of course, could tell what this exodus was.
6.  M. Heinrich, 'UN Officials Seek Inquiry into Krajina Killings', *Reuter*, Zagreb (18 August 1995); 'UN Reports Summary Executions, Possible Mass Graves in Krajina,' *Agence France Presse*, Zagreb (18 August 1995) (electronic distribution).
7.  'Ex-US Generals Help Croatia', *Associated Press*, (8 August 1994); J. Freedland, 'Clinton seeks mop-up diplomacy', *Guardian* (9 August 1995); 'Croatia takes effective control of what's left in Bosnia,' *San Francisco Chronicle* (11 August 1995). Robert Fox, 'Fresh war clouds threaten ceasefire', *Sunday Telegraph* (15 October 1995). (All electronic distribution.)
8.  As with almost all previous large-scale massacres of civilians in Sarajevo attributed to Serb artillery, the allegation that this massacre was caused

by a Serb mortar round was hotly contested. In contrast to the previous allegations, this time the UN official inquiry squarely blamed the Serb forces for the attack. However, Russian, Canadian, US and British officers on the ground voiced serious doubts concerning this allegation too. For a review of their arguments see David Binder 'Bosnia's Bombers', *The Nation*, 2 October 1995.

9. 'Operation Deliberate Force', NATO document, 6 November 1995, NATO WWW home page. The accuracy of these data cannot be independently verified.
10. *The Economist*, 9 September 1995, p. 53.
11. Ibid., 30 September 1995, p. 60.
12. President Milošević had accepted the Contact group's 51:49 division of the republic and was thus ready to cede 'the excess' of Bosnian Serb territory.
13. R. Cohen, 'Taming the Bullies of Bosnia', *New York Times Magazine*, 17 December 1995 p. 21 (electronic distribution).
14. Although he is the president of only one of its two federal units, Serbia, Milošević's authority to represent the whole of the Federal Republic of Yugoslavia was apparently never questioned.
15. Elections for the presidency and for the parliment were scheduled to take place at the latest in September 1996, under the supervision of the Organisation for Security and Cooperation in Europe.
16. In Dayton Milošević and Tudjman agreed in principle on the transfer of Eastern Slavonia, still under Serb control, to Croatia, after a transitional period of one to two years. The UN Security Council later authorised the creation of a special UN transitional administration and peacekeeping force (protected by NATO airpower) for this area.
17. J. J. Mearsheimer S. Van Evera 'When Peace Means War: The Partition that Dare Not Speak its Name', *New Republic*, vol. 213, 25 and (18 December 1995) (electronic distribution).
18. With the exception of Alija Izetbegović whose party received 37.4 per cent of the vote in the 1990 elections (see Chapter 8).
19. On the Larry King Live show, 21 November 1995, CNN Transcript #1597 (electronic distribution).
20. In his article 'The Bitter Taste of Peace' (*Turkish Daily News*, 14 September 1995, Bosnews digest 400, 17 September 1995, p. 5) Izetbegović wrote that 'the process of a peaceful reintegration of part of Bosnia currently under Chetnik control could begin. This is a painstaking task for the next two generations'. After listing the damage that the war did to Bosnia and the disadvantages of continuing war at this stage, he concluded 'if necessary, we will wage war, but then we must be sure that there was no other choice'.
21. In January 1996 Izetbegović publicly criticised Sarajevo television for broadcasting the New Year celebrations featuring Santa Claus; the latter, in his opinion, was 'foreign to our people.' 'Neprimjerena euforija: Izetbegovićevo pismo urednicima Radija i TV BiH,' *BHPRESS*, 2 January 1996 (electronic distribution).
22. D. Peranić, 'Dr Haris Silajdžić: Davno sam završio sa Strankom demokratske akcije,' *Naša Borba*, no. 352-3, 27–28 January 1996.

23. According to some US intelligence reports, a Bosnian Muslim attack is the most likely scenario after the US withdrawal from Bosnia–Hercegovina. B. Gertz, 'US report forecasts more strife in Bosnia,' *Washington Times*, 31 January 1996 (electronic distribution).

24. Deputy Secretary of State Strobe Talbott, 'US Leadership and the Balkan Challenge,' 9 November 1995, Office of the Spokesman, US Department of State, (electronic distribution).

25. In 1995 various potential Republican contenders in the US presidential race repeatedly accused president Clinton of a lack of leadership in his policy towards Bosnia–Hercegovina and called for US military aid for the Bosnian Muslims. The successful negotiation of the end of the war in Bosnia-Hercegovina thus removed a highly controversial issue from the US presidential race agenda.

# Index

Kosovo, 71, 118, 9
  the battle of, 8–9, 89, 102
  history of ethnic and political
    violence, 17–8, 81
  demographic increase in Albanian
    population, 75, 80
  the Albanian uprising of 1944, 50,
    81
  Albanian demonstrations after
    1967, 66–7, 81, 201–3
  the Albanian riots of 1981, 79, 81,
    85, 86
  and its Serb and Montenegrin
    inhabitants, 83–4
Krajina, the region of, 10, 50, 68,
    111–12, 125, 126–7, 130, 139, 141,
    143, 153, 154, 169, 176, 177, 180,
    181
Kučan, Milan, 105, 107–9

League of Communists–Movement
    for Yugoslavia (founded in
    1990), 130
League of Communists of
    Yugoslavia, *see* Communist
    party of Yugoslavia

Macedonians, 17, 26, 39–40, 46, 49, 86,
    116–17, 130, 148, 151
Maček, Vladko, 29, 31–2, 38
Marković, Ante, 77–8, 99–101, 114, 117,
    124, 131, 140, 209, 211
Marković, Mirjana (the wife of
    Slobodan Milošević), 130
Marković, Svetozar, 14, 19
massacres of civilians in
    Yugoslavia
  in Bosnia–Hercegovina under the
    Ottoman rule, 15, 43
  during World War I, 26
  during World War II, 35, 36, 42–5,
    93, 144
  during civil wars from 1991
    on, 145–6, 159, 173, 178–80
Mazowiecki, Tadeusz, 172–3
media
  in the Yugoslav conflict, 125, 150
  in the war in Slovenia, 135
  in the war in Croatia, 143–6

in the war in Bosnia–Hercegovina,
    159, 162, 170–2
Memorandum of Sovereignty of
    Bosnia–Hercegovina (1991), 116,
    148, 155, 206
Memorandum of the Serbian
    Academy of Sciences and
    Arts, 89, 91, 103, 204–5
Mihailović, Dragoljub-Draža, 35, 36–
    9, 41–2
Milošević, Slobodan, 71–2, 86, 111,
    114, 119, 122, 124, 126, 129
  biography, 203–5
  speech near Priština in 1987, 83–4,
    102
  mass mobilisation of Serbs, 84,
    89–90, 102–4, 118
  and the Yugoslav federal army,
    130–1
  and Serbs outside Serbia, 106, 127,
    130, 156, 162–3, 164, 176, 182, 183,
    187
Mock, Alois, 136
Montenegrins, 7, 15, 27, 36, 39, 46, 47,
    49, 81, 83, 85, 88, 101, 119, 130, 141,
    201
Muslim-Croat Federation, *see*
    Federation of Bosnia and
    Herzegovina
Muslim National Organisation, 18
Muslim party, *see* SDA
Muslims, *see* Bosnian Muslims

National Council of Slovenes, Croats
    and Serbs (1918), 3, 21–3, 198
national ideologies among South
    Slavs
  and historical myths, 5–9, 85, 98
  and religion, 6–7, 14
  under communist rule, 60–3,
    85–86
  the conflict of, 10, 9, 16, 44–5, 72–3,
    97–8, 189–90, 192
national self-determination, the right
    of, 3, 13, 21, 46, 61, 72–3, 93, 94,
    98, 123, 128, 149, 150
nationalism, 7, 41, 85–6, 128, 189
  Bosnian Muslim or Bosniac, 14, 18,
    94–97